COMMUNITY GROUPS
IN CONTEXT
Local activities
and actions

Edited by Angus McCabe and Jenny Phillimore

First published in Great Britain in 2018 by

Policy Press
University of Bristol
1-9 Old Park Hill
Bristol
BS2 8BB
UK
t: +44 (0)117 954 5940
pp-info@bristol.ac.uk
www.policypress.co.uk

North America office:
Policy Press
c/o The University of Chicago Press
1427 East 60th Street
Chicago, IL 60637, USA
t: +1 773 702 7700
f: +1 773-702-9756
sales@press.uchicago.edu
www.press.uchicago.edu

© Policy Press 2018

British Library Cataloguing in Publication Data
A catalogue record for this book is available from the British Library

Library of Congress Cataloging-in-Publication Data
A catalog record for this book has been requested

ISBN 978-1-4473-2778-3 paperback
ISBN 978-1-4473-2777-6 hardcover
ISBN 978-1-4473-2781-3 ePub
ISBN 978-1-4473-2782-0 Kindle
ISBN 978-1-4473-2779-0 ePDF

Cover design by Qube Design Associates, Bristol
Front cover image: istock
Printed and bound in Great Britain by CPI Group (UK) Ltd,
Croydon, CR0 4YY
Policy Press uses environmentally responsible print partners

Contents

List of tables and figures

Tables

Figures

Foreword

Voluntary action is embedded in the culture and communities of the UK. From helping neighbours and running play groups, to planting and nurturing local green spaces and helping our biggest national charities, voluntary work and voluntarism forms the web and weft of our society.

The Charity Commission records show that there are over 160,000 registered charities in the UK. But of course this is only part of the picture. Registered charities are dwarfed by the sheer volume of small informal groups whose members come together on a voluntary basis to carry out charitable activities day in and day out, every week of the year. Those informal groups are found in all communities and at all levels of society – they are certainly in every village and town, probably in every street and housing estate. They bring together old and young, men and women, those of every faith, colour and creed, in joint efforts to solve social problems and improve the lives of individuals, communities, themselves and others.

Despite being such an important part of our daily lives, these 'below the radar' groups were under-researched prior to the foundation of the Third Sector Research Centre (TSRC) in 2008. Over the ensuing years, the team has produced a set of research papers that help shine a light on the variety and richness of smaller community organisations.

The range and scope of these organisations is hinted at in an early paper from the TSRC, in which micro-organisations were painstakingly mapped, door to door: in just 11 English streets, an astonishing 58 micro-organisations were found to be alive and well, and the researchers concluded that this is likely to be a substantial underestimate of activity. In subsequent papers, TSRC looked both wide – for example, at the impact of austerity on below the radar groups – and deep, investigating less well understood corners of the voluntary sector such as those of the Gypsy, Roma and Traveller communities.

This book sets out a body of evidence about this vital aspect of our society and culture. It is a work to be welcomed by academics, community workers, sociologists, policymakers and all those with an interest in the wellbeing of communities in the UK today.

Sara Llewellin
Chief Executive
Barrow Cadbury Trust

Series editor's foreword

Third sector scholarship has often been criticised for a focus on highly-visible, quantifiable, and mappable elements of the organisational universe, such as the distribution of voluntary organisations, or levels of formal volunteering through those organisations. Yet over forty years ago scholars were warning of the regressive consequences of such approaches. Cartographic and scientific metaphors pervade the critiques of David Horton Smith and others, with their emphasis on lost continents, dark matter and so forth. It is crucial that a series such as this one does not have a focus solely on formalised and regulated third sector activities and Angus McCabe and Jenny Phillimore's edited collection on *Community groups in context* gives expression to that aspiration. It draws on extensive work in the Third Sector Research Centre both by the Centre's research staff and by its associates.

Although there are discussions of the challenges of definition and measurement in this field, the authors would agree that objective representation and cartographic exactitude are impossibilities in this area. Panoptical attempts at quantification have been attempted on numerous occasions, with variable results, and often for cathartic rather than academic reasons. It is to be hoped that serious funders don't continue to pour resources into such exercises – at least if they believe that the aim is to arrive at an authoritative estimate of the scale of community-led, grassroots activity. They won't find it – or, more accurately, they won't find any agreed estimate. They will certainly find, however, a kaleidoscope of initiative which raises many important questions about the nature of the third sector.

This book will appeal to those engaged in or having a stake in grassroots community activities (for example funders, academics, policymakers, practitioners and activists) for four key reasons.

Firstly, it offers unique insights into the **identity** of grassroots community organisations: what it is that makes them distinctive, enables them to provide a voice that is authentic and recognised as legitimate?

Secondly, a classic theoretical rationale for third sector activity is the identification and meeting of social needs – whether these be those of minority groups who lack leverage through the democratic process, or emerging issues as yet unacknowledged through formal welfare structures. Without descending into an instrumentalist, policy-oriented search, in which below-radar groups are trawled for signs of emerging social enterprises, as in the recent efforts of some thinktanks, this book offers important studies of **innovation**, through investigating how grassroots groups respond to the needs of small but distinctive communities.

Thirdly, there are concerns about **independence**, as with almost all parts of the third sector: how do groups which began life urgently articulating the needs of excluded groups without fear or favour maintain that position and retain the rootedness in community which gives them strength?

Finally, there is **inspiration**: the accounts given here are not rose-tinted narratives of heroic individuals who succeed against great odds. Instead they show how below-radar groups develop alternative, progressive visions, and articulate their case even in unpromising, austere times.

Concluding with quotations from Samuel Beckett may evoke negativity, but it also highlights the seemingly inexhaustible capacity of organisations not just to "try again, fail again [and] fail better" but also their determination, even when they may feel that progress is impossible, to "go on".

John Mohan
Director
Third Sector Research Centre

Acknowledgements

The editors wish to acknowledge the contribution of all the authors included in this publication as well as all those academics, activists and practitioners who have contributed to, and guided the work of, the Below the Radar work stream at the Third Sector Research Centre, University of Birmingham.

In particular, the editors acknowledge the continuing commitment and support of the Barrow Cadbury Trust, which made the research into small-scale community groups and activities possible.

Notes on contributors

Rosie Anderson is a Teaching Fellow in Social Policy at the University of Edinburgh. She completed her doctoral thesis, 'Reason and emotion in policy making: an ethnographic study', in 2015. Prior to returning to academia, she worked in journalism and as a policy manager in the third sector, specialising in communities policy and small to medium voluntary groups. She first became involved in the TSRC as a member of its practitioner advisory group, then latterly as an Associate Fellow.

Sarah Cemlyn is a Fellow in the School for Policy Studies, Bristol University, formerly a senior lecturer in social work and social policy. She has worked alongside Gypsy and Traveller communities for over 30 years as a community advice worker, education liaison worker and researcher focusing on equality, human rights and anti-discriminatory practice. Projects include a national study of social work affecting these communities, a review of inequalities across multiple domains for the Equality and Human Rights Commission, a UK country study for the European Parliament, and involvement in other local, national and international studies. She co-edited *Hearing the voices of Gypsy, Roma and Traveller communities* with Andrew Ryder and Thomas Acton.

Niall Crowley is an independent expert on equality and diversity issues. He is convenor of the Claiming Our Future network in Ireland and chairperson of the Equality and Rights Alliance. Prior to this, he worked for ten years as Chief Executive Officer of the Equality Authority in Ireland, the statutory body with a mandate to promote equality and combat discrimination on nine grounds. Before that he worked for 12 years with Pavee Point, a community organisation promoting Traveller rights. He is author of *An ambition for equality* (Irish Academic Press, 2006) and *Empty promise: Bringing the equality authority to heel* (A&A Farmar, 2008).

Lucy Mayblin is currently an Assistant Professor in the Sociology Department, University of Warwick. Previously she was an Economic and Social Research Council (ESRC) Future Research Leaders Fellow at the University of Sheffield. She has degrees in human geography, European studies, social research methods and sociology. Lucy has worked as a research associate at the Centre for Economic and Social Research at Sheffield Hallam University, the Centre for Urban and Regional Studies at the University of Birmingham, and for the

Interdisciplinary Centre for the Social Sciences at the University of Sheffield. Lucy is co-convenor of the British Sociological Association's Study Group on Diaspora, Migration and Transnationalism. Her research interests include: asylum, immigration, human rights, postcolonialism, cultural political economy and practices of policymaking.

Angus McCabe is a Senior Research Fellow at the Third Sector Research Centre, University of Birmingham. He has a background in community development work both in inner city and settings on peripheral estates. His research interests include resident-led change, social action and community-based education. He is currently leading on the Below the Radar work stream, which is researching the experiences of small community-based groups and activities, supported by the Barrow Cadbury Trust. Angus is a board member of the *International Community Development Journal* and an Associate of the Federation for Community Development Learning.

Jane Milling is Associate Professor of Drama at the University of Exeter. Her current research is around participation, community and creativity in contemporary culture, and the place and role of amateur theatre in our cultural ecology. She has written on *Modern British playwriting* (Methuen, 2012) and *Devising performance: A critical history* (2nd edn) (Palgrave, 2015). She also writes on popular and political performance in the 18th century.

Jenny Phillimore is Director of the Institute for Reseach into Superdiversity at the University of Birmingham and Professor of Migration and Superdiversity. She has researched widely in the fields of migration and superdiversity. Over the past decade, she has managed teams of researchers focusing on access to health, education, employment, training and housing integration, with a particular focus on integration and organisational change in the UK and EU. Jenny is a Fellow of the Royal Society for the Encouragement of Arts, Manufactures and Commerce, and of the Academy of the Social Sciences. She has advised local, regional, national and European government. She currently leads the ESRC/Norface-funded UPWEB project (The Welfare Bricolage Project), which is developing a new concept of welfare bricolage to explore how residents in superdiverse areas address health concerns.

Teresa Piacentini is a sociologist at the University of Glasgow. An experienced researcher, interpreting practitioner and activist, she has spent most of her professional and academic career working and researching with asylum seekers, refugees and migrants in Scotland. Her research interests lie in the broad field of migration studies, specifically focusing on migrants' experiences of 'settlement', integration and belonging. She is particularly interested in everyday bordering practices and the creation and development of spaces of resistance to bordering within asylum seeker, refugee and migrant populations.

Hilary Ramsden is an artivist and lecturer at the University of South Wales in physical and visual theatre, street arts, rebel clown and walking. Her practice is guided by an overarching thematic concern of the investigation of play and humour within performance and how this can be used in learning and knowledge creation. She is currently involved in the Wye Valley River Festival 2016, with partners Desperate Men Street Theatre and Wye Valley Area of Outstanding Natural Beauty. She was a member of lesbian-feminist Siren Theatre Company, founder and co-artistic director of Walk & Squawk Performance Project and a co-founder of the Clandestine Insurgent Rebel Clown Army.

Andrew Ryder has a long history of work with and for Gypsy, Roma and Traveller communities. Between 1990 and 2001, he worked as a teacher in state schools and with the British Council and taught Gypsy/Roma children in the UK, Hungary and Portugal. From 2002 until 2006, he was the policy officer for the Gypsy and Traveller Law Reform Coalition (GTLRC 2002–2006), an umbrella group that lobbied for more Traveller sites and greater social inclusion. The GTLRC was awarded the Liberty Human Rights Award in 2004. Andrew also acted as researcher to the All Party Parliamentary Group for Traveller Law Reform from 2002 to 2007 and continues to provide support and advice. Between 2006 and 2009, he was the National Policy Officer for the Irish Traveller Movement in Britain. Andrew is currently an Associate Professor at the Corvinus University of Budapest and an Associate Fellow at the Third Sector Research Centre, University of Birmingham.

Robin Simpson has been Chief Executive of Voluntary Arts (VA) since September 2005. VA provides a universal voice for approximately 63,000 voluntary arts groups across the UK and Ireland, involving more than 10 million participants in creative cultural activities. VA provides information and advice services, undertakes lobbying and advocacy work, and delivers, and supports the delivery of, projects to develop participation in creative cultural activities.

Andri Soteri-Proctor is an artist and works within her local community. Prior to this, she was a researcher on a variety of projects concerning the voluntary and community sector. For her PhD she examined the sector's engagement with government employment initiatives (under the Labour government). She later joined the Third Sector Research Centre at the University of Birmingham where she worked on the adaptation of different methods to develop tools that would help identify small and informal social groups and activities that do not always appear in official records. The aim was to contribute towards a fuller understanding on the voluntary and community sector landscape. This work was inspired by the methodological challenges arising from work on women's voluntary sector activities and organisations, which she carried out in the 1990s at the University of East London.

Phil Ware is an Associate Fellow of Third Sector Research Centre, working on research linked to the Below the Radar programme. His background is in community development and play, working in and with the community and voluntary sector in Birmingham and Dudley. Phil's interests include the impact that community groups, and black and minority ethnic (BME) groups in particular, can have both in relation to the internal environments of the sector, and to external policymakers and funders. His most recent work looks at the voice and influence of BME community groups in relation to this, and includes research undertaken with groups in the West Midlands, the North West and the South West, together with strategic organisations regionally and nationally. *'Very small, very quiet, a whisper.' Black and minority ethnic groups: Voice and influence* was published by TSRC in Briefing Paper and Working Paper formats in 2013. *'Black people don't drink tea.' The experience of rural black and minority third sector organisations* was published, again by TSRC, in 2015.

Why get below the radar?
The importance of understanding
community groups and activities

Angus McCabe and Jenny Phillimore

There is a growing body of literature on the voluntary, or third, sector (Milbourne, 2013). Equally, there is a long tradition of research into communities, stretching back in the UK to the series of reports produced by the Community Development Projects in the UK in the early to mid-1970s (Craig et al, 2008).

However, the former tends focus on formal voluntary organisations: those constituted and regulated by the Charity Commission or the Regulator of Community Interest Companies or third sector organisations involved in the delivery of public services (Rees and Mullins, 2016). Even in studies on smaller groups in the sector, the focus tends to be on organisations with incomes of between £25,000 and £1 million – namely smaller charities (Crees et al, 2015; Hunter et al, 2016) – rather than community groups without paid staff, with little, or no, income and not involved in the delivery of public services.

In the case of the latter, much of the community development literature has a theoretical focus (Somerville, 2011) or relates to professional interventions with communities (Taylor, 2015). In short, relatively little attention has been paid to informal, or semi-formal, community groups and activities. This situation is neatly summarised by Toepler (2003) as follows:

> Perhaps one of the few remaining big mysteries in non-profit sector research is the question of what we are missing by excluding those organisations from empirical investigations that are not easily captured in standard data sources. (p 236)

This assertion remains largely true 15 years after it was written.

Yet, as the following chapters in this book argue, it is important to understand the role of the informal in what is now termed civil society.

First, although the statistics are difficult to verify, community-based or below the radar groups are the largest part of the sector. Across time, the National Council for Voluntary Organisations' almanacs and profiles of the sector (Jas et al, 2002; Kane et al, 2015) estimate the number of such groups at between 600,000 and 900,000. This compares with just over 165,000 registered charities as of March 2016. Again, much of the literature on the impact of austerity measures and funding cuts in the UK has focused on this cohort of organisations to the detriment of understanding the effects on small-scale community activity (Davidson and Packham, 2012). Second, this is the space in which, perhaps, a majority of the population experiences voluntary action – while, again, the literature tends to focus on formalised volunteering (Ellis Paine 2013). Finally, successive governments have placed increasing emphasis, or pressure, on small community groups to deliver on a wide range of policy agendas: from neighbourhood regeneration through to community safety, the promotion of health and wellbeing and the prevention of violent extremism, to name but a few.

In the absence of detailed research on small, informal community groups and activities, only a partial picture, or understanding, of voluntary action is available. This may skew understandings of the nature of civil society and the willingness, or capacity, of informal groupings to respond to those wider political agendas. It is this gap in knowledge that the current book attempts to address. It is only a start. Much remains to be done.

What *Community groups in context: Local activities and actions* aims to offer is a picture of the richness and complexity of informal and semi-formal community activity. The term 'community' itself has been, and remains, contested (Hoggett, 1997). The policy focus on community, either as 'a problem' or 'a solution', waxes and wanes (Taylor, 2012). The idea of 'community groups' is equally contested. They 'fail' to grow – or, to use the political jargon, 'scale up'. This has been seen as evidence of poor management – rather than a desire to stay small and locally focused (Ishkanian and Szreter, 2012). They can be exclusive, if not oppressive, in defending entrenched interests to the detriment of others within communities. Alternatively, they can be a celebration, a confirmation, of the importance of associational life (Gilchrist, 2009) or a vital resource supporting vulnerable individuals with limited recourse to state welfare.

Further, the position of community activity within a distinct entity called the third sector is subject to debate. Is there a continuum between large, multimillion-pound charities and small-scale community activity or is the concept of 'a sector' false (Alcock, 2010)? Alternatively, is community action qualitatively different either in focus or modes of working from formal organisation (Gilchrist, 2016)?

This book attempts to capture the complexities and contested nature of informal community groups and debates on community action.

In **Part One,** Angus McCabe and Jenny Phillimore, by way of a more detailed introduction, offer definitions of the terms used, lay out the size and scope of small-scale below the radar community activity and Andri Soteri-Proctor identifies the methodological challenges of research at a community level.

Part Two opens up the debate on whether community groups are 'distinctive' (Angus McCabe and Jenny Phillimore), the changing policy environment within which such groups operate in the UK and Ireland (Angus McCabe, Niall Crowley) and how they are managing, or surviving, austerity (Angus McCabe and Jenny Phillimore).

Part Three places the focus on identifying the diversity of below the radar community activity and then examines aspects of community activity that are relatively under-researched in the mainstream third sector literature – the work of Gypsy, Traveller and Roma groupings (Andrew Ryder and Sarah Cemlyn) and the role of grassroots arts organisations (Hilary Ramsden, Jane Milling and Robin Simpson), black and minority ethnic groups (Lucy Mayblin) and the idea of 'beyond refugeeness' for long-established refugee and migrant groups (Teresa Piacentini). The authors also begin to open up the discussion on the nature of 'the sector' addressed in Part Four.

Part Four explores three emerging themes in voluntary sector literature. Phil Ware identifies issues of **voice and influence** for black and minority ethnic groups, particularly in rural settings. Angus McCabe and Jenny Phillimore examine activist **learning** for community engagement and organising. Finally, Rosie Anderson examines the role of **emotion** in community activists' engagement with policymaking processes.

The Conclusion then summarises key themes from the current book, identifies priorities for future research at a community level and reflects on possible futures for grassroots community action.

References

Alcock, P. (2010) 'A strategic unity: defining the third sector', *Voluntary Sector Review*, vol 1, no 1, pp. 5-24

Craig, G., Popple, K. and Shaw, M. (eds) (2008) *Community development in theory and practice: An international reader*, Nottingham: Spokesman.

Crees, J., Davies, N., Jochum, V. and Jane, D. (2015) *Navigating change: An analysis of financial trends for small and medium sized charities*, London: NCVO.

Davidson, E. and Packham, C. (2012) *Surviving, thriving or dying: Resilience in small community groups in the North West of England*, Manchester: Manchester Metropolitan University.

Ellis Paine, A., Moro, D. and McKay, S. (2013) 'Does volunteering improve employability? Insights from the British Household Panel Survey and beyond', *Voluntary Sector Review*, vol 4, no 3 pp 355-76.

Gilchrist, A. (2009) *The well-connected community: A networking approach to community development*, Bristol: Policy Press.

Gilchrist, A. (2016) *Blending, braiding and balancing: Combining formal and informal modes for social action*, Working Paper 136, Birmingham: Third Sector Research Centre.

Hoggett, P. (1997) *Contested communities: Experiences, struggles, policies*, Bristol: Policy Press.

Hunter, J. and Cox, E. with Round, A. (2016) *Too small to fail: How small And medium-sized charities are adapting to change and challenges*, Manchester: IPPR North.

Ishkanian, A. and Szreter, S. (2012) *The Big Society debate: A new agenda for social welfare?*, Cheltenham: Edward Elgar.

Jas, P., Wilding, K., Wainwright, S., Passey, A. and Hems, L. (2002) *UK voluntary sector almanac 2002*, London: NCVO.

Kane, D., Jochum, V. Dobbs, J., Pikoula, M., James, D., Crees, J., Ockenden, N. and Lloyd, G. (2015) *UK civil society almanac 2015*, London: NCVO.

Milbourne, L. (2013) *Voluntary sector in transition: Hard times or new opportunities?*, Bristol: Policy Press.

Rees, J. and Mullins, D. (2016) *The third sector delivering public services: Developments, innovations and challenges*, Bristol: Policy Press.

Somerville, P. (2011) *Understanding community*, Bristol: Policy Press.

Taylor, J. (2015) *Working with communities*, Melbourne: Oxford University Press.

Taylor, M. (2012) 'The changing fortunes of community', *Voluntary Sector Review*, vol 3, no 1, pp 15-34.

Toepler, S. (2003) 'Grassroots associations versus larger nonprofits: New evidence from a community case study in arts and culture, *Nonprofit and Voluntary Sector Quarterly*, vol 32, no 2, pp 236-51.

PART ONE

Scoping and mapping community actions and activities

ONE

Below the radar? Community groups and activities in context

Angus McCabe and Jenny Phillimore

Chapter aims

This chapter addresses:

• definitions of 'below the radar' community groups and activities;
• the size and scope of informal and semi-formal community activity;
• the contested nature of concepts of below the radar community groups and activities.

Background

Interest in small-scale, below the radar community groups and activities has grown in recent times and cuts across a wide range of policy concerns: from engaging black and minority ethnic (BME) community organisations in community cohesion agendas and combating violent extremism, through to commissioning public services at the local level, supporting grassroots community economic development in excluded neighbourhoods and involving community-based organisations in modernising local governance, community safety, asset management, health and wellbeing.

Under New Labour administrations, it was possible to identify two key strands to policy relating to small-scale community groups: first, the expectation that such groups, along with the wider voluntary sector, would take on a greater responsibility for the delivery of public services (Home Office, 2004) or the management of previously public sector assets (Quirk, 2007); and second, an assumption that they had a role in promoting active citizenship, addressing 'democratic deficit' and (re)engaging citizens in democratic processes (Mayo et al, 2013).

These developments coincided with a series of investments in small organisations or, indeed, individuals to develop their capacity to engage in policy and service delivery, including, for example, the Active Learning for Active Citizenship programme, Community Empowerment Networks and, subsequently, Regional Empowerment Partnerships. In this context:

> A healthy community sector is critical for the sustainability of local communities. It is not an end in itself. It helps deliver social capital, social cohesion and democratic participation. Better public investment in the [voluntary and community] sector will result in a better quality of life for local people and local communities, partly through their own direct activities and partly through their interaction with public services. (CLG, 2007, p 1)

Under the UK coalition and subsequent Conservative governments, this interest was sustained in the short-lived Big Society initiative and, subsequently, the Localism Act of 2011 – albeit with both demonstrating a changed language (from community engagement to social action, for example) and offering substantially less resource. Further, the emphasis shifted: citizens, and groups of citizens, were to be managers of, and volunteers in, what had been public services (such as libraries) rather than influencing the configuration of those services.

Beyond official government policy, there has also been a growing interest in community-, or resident-led, change. This has ranged from the adoption of asset-based community development approaches in the promotion of health and wellbeing (Glasgow Centre for Population Health, undated), the Joseph Rowntree Foundation's programme of light-touch support for community groups involved in neighbourhood regeneration (Taylor et al, 2007) and the Big Local programme of resident-led change in England (NCVO et al, 2015).

The wider policy context in which below the radar groups operate is explored in more detail in Chapters Five and Six.

Defining 'below the radar'

> The phrase under the radar is ungainly, but is the best available terminology for those organisations which are not included in the main national registers. The term is often associated with small community organisations which are not large enough to register with the Charity Commission

or Companies House and are perhaps associated more closely with community building and participation than with service delivery. However, many very small organisations do register and so suggestions that the under the radar segment of the sector is synonymous with smaller charities can be misleading. (OTS, 2008, p 2)

The phrase below, or under, the radar (BTR) is often used to describe small, community-based organisations and activities in the UK. There are a number of ways of conceptualising the term. Strictly interpreted, it refers to groups that do not have a recognised legal status and are not, therefore, on the Charity Commission or other regulatory registers. Indeed, the innovation charity Nesta (Marcus and Tidey, 2015, p 10) takes an even wider view in its definition that 'below the radar is taken to mean [any] network of unrecorded social activity'.

Consideration of legal status has dominated understandings of under or below the radar (BTR) in the literature. For example MacGillivray and colleagues (2001) use the term BTR to refer to those groups or activities that are 'unregulated' or 'semi-formal' and, therefore, do not appear in official databases. While it could be argued that this legal or regulatory approach is appropriate for some parts of the sector, many very small operations do register in some way, so that they are able to access funds from grant-making trusts (Zetter et al, 2005; Phillimore et al, 2009).

The over-reliance on legalistic and financial definitions of below the radar has been acknowledged (OTS, 2008). Accordingly, some commentators argue that very small registered organisations and activities may operate under a financial, rather than regulatory, radar. There is no consensus about the threshold of income that leaves activities under the financial radar. The National Council for Voluntary Organisations (NCVO) describes charities with incomes of less than £10,000 per annum as 'micro-charities' (NCVO, 2009). Further, in a study of resilience in charities using an analysis of the Scottish Charity Register, McCrae and Nowak (2010) found that 80% of organisations on the register had incomes of less than £25,000 per annum and that the majority of these were 'micro-groups' with annual turnovers of less than £2,000.

Thompson (2008), researching BTR third sector groups working with children and families, identified two funding thresholds: organisations with funding less than £250,000, which are small, relative to the big children's charities; and 'smaller' under the radar organisations with income of less than £50,000 per year.

Alternatively, CEFET[1] (2007) used an annual income of £35,000 to define 'grassroots or street-level' organisations when researching EU-supported social inclusion projects. This level of finance was, it argued, unlikely to support more than one worker, meaning that these small groups were likely to be managed from within excluded communities. Such levels of funding were likely to leave groups with limited capacity to work beyond their immediate area, or secure longer-term 'sustainable' income streams.

MacGillivray and colleagues (2001) do not identify any maximum annual income levels associated with being under the radar, preferring instead to stress the lack of dependable funding of any significance. This, however, ignores organisations that may hold substantial capital assets, for example tenants or village halls, but limited annual revenues. Others may have annual turnovers of over £50,000, or even £250,000, generated through trading activity such as community centres with bars or room hire facilities, but employ no full-time or professional staff. The majority of such groups are likely to fall under a support definition of under the radar, with incomes of less than £10,000 per annum that are largely self-generated (Community Matters and LGA, 2006). Similarly, although the existence of a distinctive BME third sector is contested (see Chapters Nine and Thirteen), research in this area demonstrates that it is dominated by small organisations and semi-formalised activities. A combination of low incomes and irregular funding therefore placed most migrant and refugee community organisations (MRCOs) below the radar whether registered or not (Zetter et al, 2005; Phillimore et al, 2009).

Closely related to the issue of finance, other commentators have noted the absence of capital resources in small-scale community groups (NCVO, 2009). Micro-activities or organisations often have no regular premises or full-time or permanent staff, use of volunteers' homes or donated spaces (MacGillivray et al, 2001) – a situation that is particularly mirrored in small MRCOs (Zetter et al, 2005; Phillimore et al, 2009).

Other forms of radar below which small community groups fall include:

- a support, funding or capacity-building radar, where activities do not receive any kind of resource from the state or network organisations such as Local Development Agencies;
- a policy radar, where organisations or activists are not engaged in any kind of policy agenda either because they have not been recognised or credited with any role or have elected to remain outside this particular radar;

- a technological radar, where community groups have no website or social media presence (Harris and McCabe, 2016);
- an influence radar, where, despite a desire to influence policy or provision, organisations are unable to raise awareness about their concerns.

Once definitions of below the radar groups move beyond purely legalistic terms of reference, the boundaries become 'fuzzy'. What is being researched, or discussed in the policy literature, are 'micro-charities', small-scale cooperatives and social enterprises as well as unregulated groups. Such a 'loose and baggy' approach may therefore raise questions over the usefulness of the term in understanding small-scale civil society actions, although it is an issue that also plagues research into the voluntary sector as a whole (Kendall and Knapp, 2005).

In terms of systemic analysis of community actions, the lack of a clear definition may be problematic. It is, however, possible to offer a counter-argument. The majority of literature on the third sector focuses on formal voluntary organisations and charities. What this omits is the informal and its importance. For example, while attention has been paid to the growth of foodbanks (Loopstra et al, 2015) and time banking (Gregory, 2015), substantially less is known about informal community exchange and barter systems (McCabe et al, 2013). Attention to formality, therefore, offers only a partial picture of civil society actions.

The scale of below the radar activity

Little is known about the exact extent of small-scale voluntary, community or below the radar activity. Discussing the rural voluntary sector, Blackburn and colleagues (2003) note the absence of a detailed knowledge about, and therefore the need to map the extent, scale and nature of, micro-voluntary organisations and community groups in rural areas. Looking at infrastructure development needs in Greater Manchester, where mapping has taken place, Martikke and Tramonti (2005) note that there is still no authoritative list of services and question whether there can be such a list, given the diversity of the sector. A lack of understanding of the extent and workings of civil society organisations, particularly within smaller/more recently arrived communities, is a recurrent theme, particularly in the literature on civil society within recently arrived communities (CLG, 2009).

This lack of knowledge about the nature and extent of small-scale community activity is not just a UK phenomenon. In the US, Holland

and Ritvo (2008) argue that the majority of third sector organisations are not on the Internal Revenue Service records and are not legally constituted. Toepler (2003) suggests that over 70% of US voluntary and community organisation (VCOs) are very small organisations, of which only 30% are registered.

This situation is neatly summarised by Toepler (2003), who concludes that:

> Perhaps one of the few remaining big mysteries in non-profit sector research is the question of what we are missing by excluding those organisations from empirical investigations that are not easily captured in standard data sources. (p 236)

In terms of measuring, or quantifying, the third sector, there are 161,300 registered charities in the UK (Kane et al, 2015), with a further 10,000 community interest companies (ORCIC, 2015) and 6,796 cooperatives (Co-operatives UK, 2015). Beyond this there are estimates of 6,700 (based on data held by Companies House) for the number of non-profit enterprises with social goals, and of between 3,490 and 5,091 for the number of exempted charities (NCVO, 2009). In total, therefore, there are just over 200,000 third sector organisations that are known to regulatory bodies. An additional 127,000 sports and recreational groups might also be considered as part of the mainstream sector (Sport England, 2002).

Once the wider term of civil society is applied, the third sector becomes far more difficult to quantify in robust statistical terms. MacGillivray and colleagues (2001) argue there are more than 900,000 micro-organisations in the UK. The New Economics Foundation suggests that there are between 600,000 and 900,000 (cited in NCVO, 2009/Kane et al, 2015) and NCVO consistently estimates that there are some 870,000 'civil society' organisations. However, over at least the past decade, the various NCVO almanacs note that the quality of data on informal community organisations is poor. Further, profiles of community action do not, as yet, include or quantify virtual/online actions associated with new social movements (Della Porta and Diani, 1999; Harris and McCabe, 2016).

Depending on which estimate is accepted, these figures suggest that small community organisations are some three to five times greater in number than the 'mainstream', registered and regulated, voluntary sector. Yet, as noted, comparatively little is known about the definition, scale, or functioning of this part of the sector, despite the assumptions that small-scale community groups and activities can address a wide range of policy concerns and agendas.

The nature of below the radar activity

Academic research into the third sector is a relatively recent phenomenon in the UK and beyond. Archambault (1997) describes the voluntary sector in France as 'terra incognito', while American authors (Minkler, 2005; Holland and Ritvo, 2008) have commented on the lack of systematic and longitudinal research into voluntary, let alone community, organisations. The first major studies on scope, definitions and typology emerged in the early to mid-1990s (Kendall and Knapp, 1996; Salamon and Anheier, 1997). International and comparative literature is also in its relative infancy (Barbetta, 1997) and research into below the radar community activities is even less developed. Most publications focus on the formal service delivery part of the sector, and the larger agencies with capacity to formally provide services (Kendall, 2003; Milbourne, 2013). Research on below the radar groups is most likely to appear in the community development literature (Ledwith, 2005; Craig et al, 2008) and to focus on contested concepts of community and models of working with communities, rather than community organisations themselves (Banks et al, 2003; Gilchrist, 2009). Substantive research into below the radar activity is underdeveloped and relies heavily on anecdote and received wisdom rather than, necessarily, rigorous evidence.

For example, proponents of asset-based community development have sought to highlight the social and economic value of small-scale community activities (O'Leary et al, 2011). In austere times there has been a particular focus within the formal voluntary sector on demonstrating their added value, largely in financial terms through approaches such as social return on investment and social auditing (Kay, 2011). These techniques have largely been applied to individual charities delivering public services in an effort to demonstrate cost effectiveness related to tendering for services and the cost savings that that effectiveness affords the state. As Mohan and Clifford (2016, p 80) note, unincorporated associations are 'less likely to report public service delivery as a key element of their activities' and have therefore not adopted or (as Ramsden and colleagues argue in Chapter Eight) actively resisted such techniques. Quantifying, empirically, the collective added (or possibly negative) value of community groups and activities is, therefore, currently, impossible and relies on intuition rather than evidence.

Despite the paucity of quantified data, surveys of small-scale community activity undertaken to date (RAWM, undated; Soteri-Proctor, 2011; Robinson and Chapman, 2013) suggest an extremely diverse 'sector'. The focus may range from self-help around particular healthcare and support needs through to short-life community campaigns on, for example, environmental improvements. Activities are wide-ranging:

- from arts and sports groups through to informal finance arrangements (for example, the Pardoner and Committee schemes within BME communities; Soteri-Proctor, 2011);
- from the sharing of food and clothing (McCabe et al, 2013) through to informal advice services;
- from the organisation of regular community events through to 'walking buses' on routes to and from schools;
- from housing 'care and repair' through to 'shared care schemes' with older people;
- form service user movements in mental health and learning disability through to house mosques and churches;
- from local history groups through to those involved in culturally specific celebrations of religious or other festivals and significant events in countries of origin;
- from groups campaigning for change through to those committed to maintaining the status quo or actively resisting change.

The above list is by no means exhaustive. What is not captured, even in the more detailed, local, surveys, is what might be describes as 'home-based civil society': the reading or craft groups that meet in members' houses rather than any public venue (see Chapter Two of this volume). Further, these initiatives, more often than not, exist outside (or actively resist) attempts to formalise the informal through schemes such as time banks or the creation of local alternative currencies (for example in Brixton and Bristol).

What merges is a rich tapestry of activity that 'may ... either be marginal (from the economic perspective) or crucially important (from the voluntarism or social capital perspective)' (Toepler, 2003, p 238).

A below the radar sector?

In the US, Toepler (2003), studying 'grassroots organisations', notes that traditional foundational theories of the non-profit sector have taken the twin failures of markets and governments as their starting point

(Kalifon, 1991). Thus, it may be argued that third sector organisations exist as alternative providers of goods and services and bring added value in their capacity to innovate and reach particularly marginalised groups (Boateng, 2002). Alternatively, others argue that very small VCOs may make very little contribution in this sphere where they are driven more by notions of solidarity, mutuality and voluntary altruism than the provision of professionalised services (Barnes et al, 2006).

Indeed, reflecting on the diverse below the radar activities listed earlier (and the estimated number of unincorporated associations), there remains a series of shared, if not unifying, characteristics: an often implicit belief in the importance of associational life (Gilchrist, 2009), degrees of informality and being driven by volunteers and activists rather than paid professionals.

Yet, returning to the literature, what emerges (see, for example, Chapters Eight and Nine) is a series of reports and research papers not on 'a sector' but a series of sub-sectors. There are, for example, literatures that are specific to BME groups; faith-based organisations; tenants' and residents' groups; and voluntary arts groups.

BME groups

The literature argues that BME groups are generally concerned with two main types of activity: filling gaps in public services where the mainstream has failed to meet needs, and cultural solidarity or identity (Sivanandan, 1982; Carey-Wood, 1997). Chouhan and Lusane (2004) found that BME VCOs often provided a range of specialist services for young people, older people and disabled people, including advice, health services (mental and physical) and welfare and income support. Others have noted that such groups also play a role in community advocacy, campaigns for increased rights, anti-discrimination and access to mainstream services (McLeod et al, 2001). These studies focus on the whole BME sector rather than simply BTR activity. Smaller BME groups focus less on service provision and more on identity politics, social and cultural support (McCabe et al, 2013).

Faith-based organisations

Little research was undertaken on the role and function of religious/ faith-based social action (FBOs) until the late 1990s (Cnaan and Milofsky, 1997). FBOs are characterised by their small scale and reliance on volunteers, with much activity happening in often unconsecrated and therefore 'unregistered' places of worship. Since the events of 9/11 in the US and 7/7 in London, there has been a growth in research into FBOs, though again this focuses on two dimensions – their role in the prevention of violent extremism (Allen, 2010) or addressing austerity and 'plugging the gaps' in welfare systems (Dinham, 2012; McCabe et al, 2016).

Tenants' and residents' groups

Many of the definitions of neighbourhood and residents groups incorporate BTR activity. Downs (1981, cited in Cnaan and Milovsky, 1997) identifies two types of neighbourhood-based organisations, both with the primary aim of improving the quality of life of residents. The first incorporates any group (voluntary, public or for profit) operating within a neighbourhood and serving the interests of residents. Many of these will be on the radar of housing providers and social landlords. The second includes neighbourhood representative organisations. These are local, completely voluntary, managed by local residents and seek to represent all residents. Many of them could be argued to operate BTR financially, if not in terms of campaigning profiles at the hyper-local level.

Voluntary arts groups

Dodd and colleagues (2008) estimate that there are around 49,140 voluntary and amateur arts groups in England. Of these, it is unclear how many are below the radar. Churchill and colleagues (2006) see the voluntary arts as a movement in which people take part voluntarily for enjoyment, community development, self-improvement and social networking. Activities are largely self-financed, run by dedicated volunteers who are passionate about one particular art form, and take the form of societies, clubs and classes. Little is known in research terms about the role of formal cultural and arts-based organisations, let alone BTR activities in this field. Indeed, Benns and Fox (2004) further sub-divide voluntary and community groups into art forms and activities, craft, literature, performing arts, visual arts and cross-form, finding that performing arts represented over two thirds of all groups in their study area of Dorset and Somerset.

Then, there is an even smaller, specific, literature on rural community groups (Grieve et al, 2007) and community-based sports associations (Sport England, 2002), which reflects the segmentation of research in this field.

Common challenges

While the existing literature tends to sub-divide small-scale community groups into particular spheres of activity (such as housing), identity groups (for example, BME organisations) or settings (urban or rural), there is considerable agreement on the challenges facing such groups across their spheres of interest. Common themes include access to finance, policy and influence, and volunteers.

Access to finance

There is a long-established literature, both academic as well as local surveys, on the difficulties of accessing finance, particularly for small community-based organisations – whether formally constituted or not. This stretches back to Rochester and colleagues (2000), Kendall (2003) and Thompson (2008). Since 2008, with the global financial crisis and the coalition administration's introduction of austerity measures, there has been a growing body of research into the impacts of cuts on the sector as a whole (Crees et al, 2015; Hunter et al, 2016). Smaller groups that are particularly below the radar may face a number of additional disadvantages in the current climate. First, while there is an emphasis on increasing the role of such groups in service delivery, it has been argued that pre-qualifying questionnaires and the criteria outlined in invitations to tender, around annual turnover, fully audited accounts and so on, actually exclude them from the commissioning or procurement process (BVSC, 2009) and that the system favours larger, long-established voluntaries (Kenny et al, 2015). Second, such small groups may either be ignorant of statutory funding opportunities (Blackburn et al, 2003) or fail to understand often complex eligibility criteria (Garry et al, 2006). Third, writing about refugee and migrant organisation, Lukes and colleagues (2009) make a point that may be more generally applicable to below the radar groups:

> The current trend in funding arrangements is increasingly pushing MRCOs towards structuring along standard mainstream principles to increase their chances of securing commissioned service delivery. This seems to create a dilemma for MRCOs since it is the case that, the more a MRCO becomes structured along mainstream standards the higher the likelihood that it erodes its nature and value as a grass-roots community initiative. (p 1)

Much of the above research, however, applies to small voluntary organisations historically in receipt of some form of state funding – whether grants or the now defunct Area Based Initiatives monies. The experiences of unfunded community groups is qualitatively different. It may not be cuts to funding per se that threaten such groups but, for example, the loss of no- or low-cost access to meeting places and increased difficulties in recruiting volunteers or accessing pro-bono advice (McCabe, 2010). It is this multiplier effect that threatens such groups rather than the loss of any single funding source.

Policy and influence

A number of commentators have noted the lack of representation of informal activities and organisations in policy arenas and the difficulties they have influencing policy. Thompson's (2008) research on small VCOs working in the children and young people's sector noted the difficulties groups had trying to gain influence. For example, one of the informants stated:

> 'Small voluntary organisations are not always invited to consultation sessions and only hear about them in a roundabout way – again these tend to be held during the week – even after school is very difficult for us.' (p 19)

Lack of influence, despite localism and the Big Society initiative, remains a central issue. While successive governments have stressed the importance of community engagement in policy formation and delivery – and more recently on the concept of co-production (Stephens et al, 2008) –below the radar groups are frequently excluded (deliberately or unconsciously) from expressing interests or exerting influence (Ishkanian and Szreter 2012; see also Chapter Thirteen of this volume).

Volunteers

The Big Society, localism and the transfer of public services is predicated on the assumption that volunteers, active citizens, are an infinite resource (Stott, 2011). Yet, looking at longitudinal and social class data, Mohan (2012) proposes that, over time, the 'pool' of voluntary activists is relatively stable and goes on to argue that those in poor communities are least likely to volunteer. While this may be contested (depending on the definition of volunteering adopted), recent evidence indicates that small community groups are struggling to recruit and retain activists in the face of increasing levels of demand for, and the complexity of presenting needs faced by, their services (McCabe et al, 2016).

Conclusion: some contested issues

This chapter has argued that the term below the radar has been used in rather unprecise ways to describe small-scale community activity. The realities are much more nuanced and complex. Indeed, just as the concept of community is contested (Hoggett, 1997) so is the idea of below the radar and the role of small-scale community groups and activities (Somerville, 2011).

Community, and therefore, community groups, is not simply a shorthand for 'good' – a harking back to a supposed golden era of 'voluntary-ism' (Green, 1993). Such groups can be exclusive and discriminatory as well as inclusive and liberating for participants. They can respond, at the local level, to the demands of a vocal minority at the cost of addressing the needs of the less powerful (Cooper, 2008).

Further, the term below the radar has the potential to be patronising. It is a top-down categorisation, adopted, on occasion, by researchers and policymakers, rather than a term used by community groups themselves. It has been described as a deficit model of community action (McCabe and Phillimore, 2009); such groups fail to grow and 'scale up' because they are poorly managed – rather than wishing to retain a highly local focus and rejecting expansion in favour of replication.

Much of the contestation about below the radar activity is located within a wider debate on the current and future position of the third sector as a whole. Debate has focused on the role of the voluntary sector in the delivery of public services (Rees and Mullins, 2016) or on more theoretical, and politicised discussions on the sector's identity and independence (Milbourne and May, 2014; NCIA, 2015), with, for example, Meade (2009, p 124; see also Chapter Four of this volume) arguing 'that state-funded NGOs are colonising the few political and discursive spaces that might otherwise accommodate more "organic" social movements'. Others (including the coalition administration of 2010-15) suggest that state interventions 'squeeze out' voluntary action (Dominelli, 2006) or, alternatively, that 'community groups transform the private troubles of support groups into public issues for policy remediation'. (Labonte, 2005, p 89).

Whatever the limitations of the phrase below the radar as a description of small-scale community groups, it is increasingly important to acknowledge, and develop a more nuanced understanding of, informal community actions and activities that have been marginal in the debates discussed here and under-represented in the mainstream literature on the third sector. Otherwise small-scale community groups will remain, in the words of the Community Sector Coalition (CSC, undated) 'unseen, unequal, untapped'.

Key learning

- The term 'below the radar' is contested. For some it is a useful shorthand description for small scale civil society actions. For others it is a pejorative term, implying that community groups lack the skills and knowledge, rather than the desire, to grow.
- There are various definitions of 'below the radar' community groups. Strictly, the term refers to those not appearing on Charity Commission data sets or the registers of other regulatory bodies. Some commentators, however, include 'micro-charities': those organisations that appear on the lists of the regulators, but have insecure income of under £25,000–£35,000 per annum.
- Small community groups may have a high profile within their own neighbourhood or community of interest, but exist below various 'radars'. They may not appear on local voluntary sector or local authority directories, are unknown to funders and policymakers or have no online presence.
- 'Below the radar' community groups and activities form the largest part of the third sector, but are the least researched and therefore, perhaps, the least understood part of that sector. Research in this field has tended to focus on larger, formal and funded voluntary organisations delivering public services.

Reflective exercises

- Is the term below the radar useful in describing, or understanding, small-scale community groups and actions?
- What is the role of below the radar activity in austere times: campaigning and lobbying for change, mitigating the impacts of poverty and inequality though delivering services or sustaining social relationships?
- In the research literature, below the radar groups tend to be sub-divided into a series of sub-categories: sports groups, craft associations, faith-based organisations, refugee and migrant community groups and so on. Such sub-divisions suggest that such groups have more differences than things they have in common. To what extent do you agree?

Notes

[1] The European Social Fund Technical Assistance organisation for the East Midlands from 1991 to 2013.

References

Allen, C. (2010) *Islamophobia*, Farnham: Ashgate.

Archambault, E. (1997) *The nonprofit sector in France*, Manchester: Manchester University Press.

Banks, S., Butcher, H., Henderson, P. and Robertson, J. (2003) *Managing community practice: Principles, policies and programmes*, Bristol: Policy Press.

Barbetta, P. (1997) *The nonprofit sector in Italy*, Manchester: Manchester University Press.

Benns, K. and Fox, R. (2004) *Valuing voluntary arts: The state of the sector in Dorset and Somerset*, London: Voluntary Arts England.

Barnes, M., Newman, J. and Sullivan, H. (2006) Discursive arenas: deliberation and the constitution of identity in public participation at a local level', *Social Movement Studies*, vol 5, no 3, pp 193-207.

Blackburn, S. Skerratt, S., Warren, M. and Errington, A. (2003) *Rural communities and the voluntary sector: A review of the literature*, Plymouth: University of Plymouth.

Boateng, P. (2002) *The role of the voluntary and community sector in service delivery: A cross cutting review*, London: HM Treasury.

BVSC (Birmingham Voluntary Service Council) (2009) *Commissioning and the third sector*, Birmingham: BVSC.

Carey-Wood, J. (1997) *Meeting refugees' needs in Britain: The role of refugee-specific initiatives*, London: Home Office.

CEFET (2007) *The key to inclusion: A report on the state and potential of empowerment approaches to inclusion work in the English regions*, Nottingham: CEFET.

Chouhan, K. and Lusane, C. (2004) *Black voluntary and community sector funding: Its impact on civic engagement and capacity building*, York: Joseph Rowntree Foundation.

Churchill, G., Brennan, M. and Diamond, A. (2006) '"Inform, Include, Inspire"– the voluntary and amateur arts in the East Midlands', online report available at: www.voluntaryarts.org/inform/Inform_Include_Inspire_CDROM_draft/report_24.html (accessed 13 March 2016).

CLG (Communities and Local Government) (2007) *Report from the Local Community Sector Task Force*, London: CLG.

CLG (2009) *Summary report: Understanding Muslim ethnic communities*, London: CLG.

Cnaan, R. and Milofsky, C. (1997) 'Small religious nonprofits: a neglected topic', *Nonprofit and Voluntary Sector Quarterly*, vol 26, S3–S13.

Community Matters and LGA (Local Government Association) (2006) *Community buildings – maximising assets*, London: LGA.

Cooper, C. (2008) *Community, conflict and the state; Rethinking notions of 'safety', 'cohesion' and 'wellbeing'*, Basingstoke: Palgrave Macmillan.

Cooperatives UK (2015) *The cooperative economy 2015*, Manchester: Cooperatives UK.

Craig, G., Popple, K. and Shaw, M. (eds) (2008) *Community development in theory and practice: An international reader*, Nottingham: Spokesman.

Crees, J., Davies, N., Jochum, V. and Jane, D. (2015) *Navigating change: An analysis of financial trends for small and medium sized charities*, London: NCVO.

CSC (Community Sector Coalition) (undated) *Unseen, unequal, untapped, unleashed: The potential for community action at the grass roots*, London: CSC.

Della Porta, D. and Diani, M. (1999) *Social movements: An introduction*, Oxford: Blackwell Publishing.

Dinham, A. (2012) *Faith and social capital after the debt crisis*, Basingstoke: Palgrave Macmillan.

Dodd, F. Graves, A. and Taws, K. (2008) *Our creative talent: The voluntary and amateur arts in England*, London: DCMS.

Dominelli, L. (2006) *Women and community action*, Bristol: Policy Press.

Garry, K., McCabe, A. and Goodwin, P. (2006) *Opening the door: An evaluation of the Heart of Birmingham Teaching Primary Care Trust Health and Regeneration Grants Programme*, Birmingham: Digbeth Trust.

Gilchrist, A. (2009) *The well-connected community: A networking approach to community development*, Bristol: Policy Press.

Glasgow Centre for Population Health (undated) *Asset based approaches for health improvement: Redressing the balance*, Glasgow: Glasgow Centre for Population Health.

Green, D. (1993) *Reinventing civil society: The rediscovery of welfare without politics*, London: Institute of Economic Affairs.

Gregory, L. (2015) *Trading time: Can exchange lead to social change?*, Bristol: Policy Press.

Grieve, J. Jochum, V. Pratten, B. Steel, C. (2007) *Faith in the Community: the contribution of faith-based organisations to rural voluntary action*, Commission for Rural Communities with NCVO, London.

Harris, K. and McCabe, A. (2016) *Community action and social media*, Birmingham: Third Sector Research Centre.

Hoggett, P. (1997) *Contested communities: Experiences, struggles, policies*, Bristol: Policy Press.

Holland, T.P. and Ritvo, R.A. (2008) *Nonprofit organisations: Principles and practices*, New York, NY: Columbia University Press.

Home Office (2004) *Think smart … think voluntary sector! Good practice guidance on procurement of services from the voluntary and community sector*, London: Active Communities Unit, Home Office.

Hunter, J. and Cox, E. with Round. A. (2016) *Too small to fail: How small and medium-sized charities are adapting to change and challenges*, Manchester: IPPR North.

Ishkanian, A. and Szreter, S. (2012) *The Big Society debate: A new agenda for social welfare?*, Cheltenham: Edward Elgar.

Kalifon, S.Z. (1991) 'Self-help groups providing services: conflict and change', *Nonprofit and Voluntary Sector Quarterly*, vol 20, no 2, pp 191-205.

Kane, D., Jochum, V., Dobbs, J., Pikoula, M., James, D., Crees, J., Ockenden, N. and Lloyd, G. (2015) *UK civil society almanac 2015*, London: NCVO.

Kay, A. (2011) *Prove! Improve! Account! The new guide to social accounting and audit*, Wolverhampton: Social Audit Network.

Kendall, J. (2003) *The voluntary sector: Comparative perspectives in the UK*, London: Routledge.

Kendall, J. and Knapp, M. (1996) *The voluntary sector in the UK*, Manchester: Manchester University Press.

Kendall, J. and Knapp, M. (2005) 'A loose and baggy monster: boundaries, definitions and typologies', in J. Davis Smith, C. Rochester and R. Heldley (eds) *An introduction to the voluntary sector*, London: Routledge.

Kenny, S., Taylor, M., Onyx, J. and Mayo, M. (2015) *Challenging the third sector: Global perspectives for active citizenship*, Bristol: Policy Press.

Labonte, R. (2005) 'Community, community development and the forming of authentic partnerships', in M. Minkler (ed) (2005) *Community organising and community building for health*, New Brunswick: Rutgers University Press.

Ledwith, M. (2005) *Community development: A critical approach*, Bristol: Policy Press.

Loopstra, R., Reeves, A., Taylor-Robinson, D., Barr, B., McKee, M. and Stuckler, D. (2015) 'Austerity, sanctions, and the rise of food banks in the UK', *British Medical Journal* (Clinical research edn), 350, h1775.

Lukes, S., Jones, V. and San Juan, Y. (2009) *The potential of migrant and refugee community organisations to influence policy*, York: Joseph Rowntree Foundation.

MacGillivray, A. Conaty, P. and Wadhams, C. (2001) *Low flying heroes. Micro social enterprise below the radar screen*, London: New Economics Foundation.

Marcus, G. and Tidey, J. (2015) *Community mirror: A data driven method for 'below the radar' research*, London: Nesta.

Martikke, S. and Tramonti, S. (2005) *Spinning the spider's web*, Manchester: Greater Manchester Centre for Voluntary Organisation.

Mayo, M., Mendiwelso-Bendek, Z. and Packham, C. (2013) *Community research for community development*, Basingstoke: Palgrave Macmillan.

McCabe, A. (2010) *Below the radar in a Big Society? Reflections on community engagement, empowerment and social action in a changing policy context*, Birmingham: Third Sector Research Centre.

McCabe, A. and Phillimore, J. (2009) *Exploring below the radar: Issues of themes and focus*, Birmingham: Third Sector Research Centre.

McCabe, A., Buckingham, H. and Miller, S. with Musabiyimana, M. (2016) *Faith in social action: Exploring faith groups' responses to local needs*, Birmingham: Third Sector Research Centre.

McCabe, A., Gilchrist, A., Harris, K., Afridi, A. and Kyprianou, P. (2013) *Making the links: Poverty, ethnicity and social networks*, York: Joseph Rowntree Foundation.

McCrae, A. and Nowak, I. (2010) *Office of the Scottish Charity Regulator: A short study of resilience in Scottish Charities*, Glasgow: Axiom Consultancy.

McLeod, M., Owen, D. and Khamis, C. (2001) *The role and future development of black and minority ethnic organisations*, York, Joseph Rowntree Foundation

Meade, R. (2009) 'Classic texts: Jo Freeman. *The tyranny of structurelessness* (c. 1972)', *Community Development Journal*, vol 44, no 1, pp 123-7.

Milbourne, L. (2013) *Voluntary sector in transition: Hard times or new opportunities?*, Bristol: Policy Press.

Milbourne, L. and May, U. (2014) *The state of the voluntary sector: Does size matter?*, Paper 1, London: NCIA.

Minkler, M. (ed) (2005) *Community organising and community building for health*, New Brunswick, Rutgers University Press.

Mohan, J. (2012) 'Geographical foundations of the Big Society', *Environment and Planning A*, vol 44, no 5), pp 1121-9.

Mohan, J. and Clifford, D. (2016) 'Which third sector organisations are involved in the delivery of public services? Evidence from charity accounts and from survey data', in J. Rees, J. and D. Mullins (eds) *The third sector delivering public services: Developments, innovations and challenges*, Bristol: Policy Press.

NCIA (National Coalition for Independent Action) (2015) *Fight or fright: Voluntary services in 2015. A summary and discussion of the inquiry findings*, London: NCIA.

NCVO (National Council for Voluntary Organisations) (2009) *UK civil society almanac 2009*, London: NCVO.

NCVO, Institute for Volunteering Research and Office for Public Management (2015) *Big local: The early years evaluation report*, London: Local Trust.

O'Leary, T., Burkett, I. and Braithwaite, K. (2011) *Appreciating assets*, Dunfermline: International Association for Community Development.

ORCIC (Office of the Regulator of Community Interest Companies) (2015) *Annual report of the Regulator of Community Interest Companies 2014-15*, London: ORCIC.

OTS (Office of the Third Sector) (2008) *Draft guidance: National survey of Third Sector Organisations 'Under the Radar' Pilot*, London: OTS.

Phillimore, J., Goodson, L., Hennessy, D. and Ergun, E. (2009) *Empowering Birmingham's migrant and refugee community organisations: Making a difference*, York: Joseph Rowntree Foundation.

Quirk, B. (2007) *Making assets work: The Quirk review*, London: Communities and Local Government.

RAWM (Regional Action West Midlands) (undated) *Under the radar: A study of voluntary and community organisations not on the business or charities register*, Birmingham: RAWM.

Rees, J. and Mullins, D. (2016) *The third sector delivering public services: Developments, innovations and challenges*, Bristol: Policy Press.

Robinson, F. and Chapman, T. (2013) *The reality check: Final report from the second phase of the Third Sector Trends Study*, Newcastle: Northern Rock Foundation.

Rochester, C., Hutchinson, R. and Harris, J. (2000) *Small agencies project report*, London: Centre for Voluntary Organisation, London School of Economics.

Salamon, L.M. and Anheier, H.K. (1997) *Defining the nonprofit sector: A cross-national analysis*, Manchester: Manchester University Press.

Sivanandan, A. (1982) *A different hunger: Writings on black resistance*, London: Institute of Race Relations.

Somerville, P. (2011) *Understanding community*, Bristol: Policy Press.

Soteri-Proctor, A. (2011) *Little big societies: Micro-mapping of organisations operating below the radar*, Birmingham: Third Sector Research Centre.

Sport England (2002) *Participation in sport in England 2002*, London: Sport England.

Stephens, L., Ryan-Collins, J. and Boyle, D. (2008) *Co-production: A manifesto for growing the core economy*, London: New Economics Foundation.

Stott, M. (ed) (2011) *The Big Society challenge*, Cardiff: Keystone Development Trust.

Taylor, M., Wilson, M., Pardue, D. and Wilde, P. (2007) *Changing neighbourhoods: The impact of 'light touch' support in 20 communities*, York: Joseph Rowntree Foundation.

Thompson, J. (2008) *Under the radar. A survey of small voluntary and community sector organisations working with children, young people and families*, London: NCVCCO.

Toepler, S. (2003) 'Grassroots associations versus larger nonprofits: new evidence from a community case study in arts and culture', *Nonprofit and Voluntary Sector Quarterly*, vol 32, no 2, pp 236-51.

Zetter, R., Griffiths, D. and Sigona, N. (2005) 'Social capital or social exclusion? The impact of asylum-seeker dispersal on UK ethnic minority organisations', *Community Development Journal*, vol 40, no 2, pp 169-81.

TWO

Getting below the radar: micro-mapping 'hidden' community activity

Andri Soteri-Proctor

Chapter aims

This chapter aims to:

- identify techniques for mapping small-scale and semi-formal 'below the radar' community groups and activities;
- explore the challenges of getting below the radar;
- place these activities within the wider context of civil society, the voluntary sector and policy initiative.

Introduction

As noted in Chapter One, below the radar has been used as a shorthand term for small voluntary organisations, community groups, semi-formal and informal activities in the third sector (Phillimore et al, 2010), more traditionally known as the 'community sector'.

The majority of statistical analyses on the third sector are drawn from administrative records collected for other purposes, such as the Charity Commission register of recognised charities in England and Wales or the register of Companies Limited by Guarantee in Companies House (Backus and Clifford, 2010; Clark et al, 2010). While knowledge from these sources contributes towards understanding an important part of the sector, it is only a part (Clark et al, 2010; Phillimore et al, 2010). With claims that most organisations in the sector do not appear on official lists, combined with assertions about their 'distinctiveness', there has been interest in capturing those 'uncounted groups' that do not appear in national data sets and local directories. Examples include a pilot study commissioned by the Cabinet Office (Ipsos MORI Social Research Institute, 2010), research for the Third Sector Trends Study commissioned by the Northern Rock Foundation (Mohan et al, 2011) and Marcus and Tidey's (2015) pilot data-driven approach to identifying below the radar groups.

Whichever research approach is taken, there still remain challenges in capturing and understanding the differences between what constitutes 'above' and 'below' the radar groups. To illustrate, in the case of work that adopts an approach of exploring a perceived 'absence' of voluntary activity (so-called 'charity deserts' – Lindsey, 2012), Mohan (2011) notes 'formidable' challenges in matching information between local listings and administrative records both in terms of the quality of local listings and the different definitional boundaries used for what is included. Further, he notes that this has contributed to varied estimated ratios on the size of what is on or below the radar: '… in terms of entities with at least some recognisable degree of organisation, the numbers of third sector organisations might vary by a factor of as many as nine' (Mohan, 2011, p 4).

Despite shifting use of terminology (see Chapter Four), government interest in this part of the third sector is, if still under-researched, far from new. There have been various policies across different administrations that are relevant to below the radar activity. These include black and minority ethnic (BME) community organisations' engagement with community cohesion agendas (Harris and Young, 2009), grassroots economic development in excluded neighbourhoods, and the involvement of community-based organisations in modernising local governance, community safety and health planning and policy (McCabe, 2010; Phillimore et al, 2010). Alongside these could be included investment in developing the capacity of small organisations to engage with policy formation and service delivery, including Community Empowerment Networks and Regional Empowerment Partnerships (McCabe et al, 2010).

Under the coalition administration, at least a rhetorical, interest in community activities reached a high watermark with the Big Society agenda and the development of community rights in the Localism Act (2011). While that interest has waned at a national policy level, for practitioners, it has re-emerged at a more local level alongside asset-based community development models, particularly in the field of public health (Glasgow Centre for Population Health, undated; CLES and NEF, 2013). Here, support for below the radar community activities (from knitting groups to reading circles) has become a mechanism for promoting health and wellbeing and building community resilience in hard times (Norman, 2012).

Yet, below the radar community activity remains the least well researched and, perhaps, the least understood part of the voluntary sector. This chapter draws on the Third Sector Research Centre's (TSRC) micro-mapping, or street-level mapping, project. It aims to further empirical understanding of small, informal and semi-formal groups and activities through a series of key research questions, including:

- What do below the radar groups, activities and organisations look like? What is their role and function and how do they operate?
- Is it possible to more accurately quantify such groups and their contribution to civil society?
- What are the motivations of those involved in below the radar groups and activities?
- What is the lifecycle of small-scale community group organisations?
- What is the impact of more informal community action and organising?
- What is the relationship between informal groups and the formal third sector?

Mapping the below-radar third sector

To date, most voluntary and community mapping exercises have relied on secondary data (Mohan et al, 2011). This has involved starting with regulatory authority (for example Charity Commission) datasets and supplementing these with information held in local directories. However, it is the very small informal groups that are least likely to be captured in regulatory or local listings – a view echoed by other scholars who have undertaken systematic analyses on different types of listing (see, for example, work in the US by Grønbjerg and Clerkin, 2005).

Attempting to move beyond official and semi-official sources, TSRC developed an innovative methodology to complement this work for the piloted Street-Level Mapping Project (SLMP). This involved going out on to the streets to actually see what lies beneath these formal, regulated, third sector radars. The methodology was adapted from the Local Voluntary Activity Surveys (LOVAS), which was carried out in 1994 and 1997 and aimed to map and subsequently survey the entirety of 'volunteering' in a number of localities (Marshall, 1997; Marshall et al, 1997).

The definition of below the radar community groups was more than two people coming together on a regular (rather than one-off) basis to do activities in and around (public and third sector) space for not-for-profit purpose. Even with this, however, there are conceptual biases that are further exacerbated by place-based fieldwork in which some types of below the radar groups are still likely to be excluded. These include, for instance, groups that do not have a fixed base, such as mobile groups and virtual networks, and those that operate from private dwellings, public houses and cafes – types that are documented elsewhere (see, for example, Craig et al, 2010). Furthermore, this does not include those 'very active citizens' who in and of themselves are recognised by some authors as considerable resources to their local communities – referred to in some literature as 'great keepers together' (Seabrook, 1984) but are not necessarily attached to any specific organisation – formal or informal.

Building on the earlier LOVAS research, the purpose of SLMP was to find all (or, more strictly, as much as possible) organisational activity that was taking place in small local areas. The specific commitment was to go beyond existing records and listings of third sector groups to seek out activity that might not be listed, indeed might not have an address or even a name. In other words, those activities that tend to go 'uncounted' and perhaps be described as a 'hidden' population of voluntary action. The research, from the initial data trawls of regulatory databases and local directories through to the completion of the street-level work, took one year on a part-time basis, using the support of volunteers with existing local knowledge and networks.

The areas selected for the street-level mapping, in the West Midlands and North West of England, were chosen for their differing demographics. While both score highly on indices of deprivation, High Street is a superdiverse inner-city locality, while Mill Town is predominantly a white working-class area. Both the areas involved were anonymised to comply with the requirements of ethical approval for the research. The areas studied may be summed up as follows.

High Street

High Street is a residential area consisting of six streets, one of which includes a high street with restaurants and supermarkets selling a diverse range of foods, and a mix of faith-based buildings and public buildings, including a jobcentre and library. Within a few miles of a busy city centre, High Street is situated in a highly populated ward with more than 25,000 residents. The ward has a high BME population (82%)

compared with the city's average (30%). It has a long history of migrant settlement, with an established Asian and Black-Caribbean community and a recent increase in migrant and asylum-seeking groups. At the time of the fieldwork in 2009-10, 54% of the population at ward level was economically active, which was lower than the city's average of 61%.

Figure 2.1: Map of High Street

Mill Town

Reflecting on experiences from the High Street pilot, a different approach was used to construct the route in Mill Town to allow more detailed investigative time. This involved developing contacts and meeting staff from regional and local infrastructure agencies as well as local authority neighbourhood liaison officers. Using information from these meetings, an area was selected with contrasting features in terms of the ethnic demographic – that is predominantly white British – though there was anecdotal evidence of a growing refugee, asylum and migrant population settling in the area. The route was then constructed by identifying five focal points for voluntary and community organisations, based on a walking interview with the Chief Executive of the local infrastructure agency. This was followed up with street searches and included, where possible, talking to people working in and around the five focal points of (shared) 'space'.

The selection of sites offered the potential for a range of insights into the breadth of groups operating in what seemingly constitute different types of urban area. Further, in research terms, this selection offered an opportunity to question findings arising from other research in this field that focuses on formal charities. This includes, for example, the following assertion:

> Charities in the affluent area are more numerous, run by volunteers, and meet a broad range of social, community and cultural needs of the community. Charities in the deprived area are less numerous, meet urgent needs related to deprivation, and are more likely to be larger charities run by professionals with statutory funding. (Lindsey, 2013, p 95)

Fewer charities in deprived areas may not, necessarily, be equated with less activity to 'meet urgent needs related to deprivation'.

It could be argued, therefore, that the neighbourhoods selected were, in some way, atypical of any broader picture of levels of voluntary action. However, the methods adopted in the micro-mapping have subsequently been replicated in very different (named) wards in Birmingham and in one rural community (Whitehead, 2012). Butarova and colleagues (2013), Atanga and colleagues (2013) and Creta and King (2014) researched both inner-city neighbourhoods and peripheral estate, some with diverse communities, others that were predominantly white working class (but again with similar levels of deprivation), with very similar results in terms of the volume and diversity of informal community action.

Digging down below the radar

The process of 'digging down' below the radar consisted of four levels of activity. The first three involved identifying:

- regulated and registered organisations at the postcode level using the Charity Commission and related databases;
- organisations appearing in local authority and voluntary sector directories, again at the postcode level;
- groups that had an online presence (for example, appearing in online commercial directories) but did not appear in 'official' directories of voluntary organisations.

The fourth level of activity, undertaken at street level, consisted of three parts:

- solo walks – walking through streets looking at noticeboards and adverts in, for example, shop windows, outside buildings and elsewhere;
- visits to buildings and open spaces that people might gather in – for example, community centres, faith-based buildings, leisure centres and libraries. In High Street visits were also made to shops on the high street (attempts to speak with people in shops were, however, dropped for the second pilot as this proved too time-consuming). Visits involved scouring noticeboards, and picking up leaflets and adverts for groups. In two cases, both involving community centres, researchers were given access to diaries and appointment calendars to collect information on groups who used rooms to meet at the centre; and
- conversations and interviews with people who were identified as having knowledge about activities going on in and around buildings and the local area.

What was not attempted, largely for resource reasons, was a fifth level of research activity, namely, the collection of social media activity data (such as postings on Facebook and Twitter) in the areas investigated: an approach that has since been refined by Nesta (Marcus and Tidey, 2015).

Researchers used a form to collect basic information on leads and other potential below the radar groups. That said, even using a simple four-page form in any systematic way presented challenges – often this was because while individuals reported having knowledge of groups, they did not tend to have complete information or even a full name for the person(s) leading activities.

What does it look like beneath the 'official' radar?

One of the most important findings from our street-level mapping study is the scale and range of informal activity that is going on beneath the radar of registered organisations. From the substantial amounts of information collated in just two small locations that amount to 11 English streets, we found at least 58 varieties of self-organised activity that did not appear on regulatory lists.

We arrived at this figure through a process of elimination from information on more than 215 entities in local directories by excluding, for example, groups that did not operate within the street-walking routes; projects and activities provided by registered charities and other public and private sector organisations such as businesses, leisure centres and libraries; and activities organised by individuals primarily to generate their own income, such as judo and language classes.

Moreover, we suspect that this figure (of 58) is a conservative estimate of below-radar groups and activities in these two locations: with more time and more resources to follow up incomplete leads, it is highly likely we would have found a greater number of activities (for example, reading groups and informal exchange systems).

The niche, the specific, and the very local?

These 58 below-radar groups covered a diverse range of services and activities, some of which were for those who shared a particular topic of interest and others for a 'target community'. These included those from a particular ethnic background, faith or country of origin, as well as elderly people, youth groups and disabled people and combinations of these, such as an Asian elders. Using available data from these groups, six 'types' of below-radar group were identified. While these categorisations are somewhat arbitrary and simplistic, they have been devised primarily for descriptive and analytical purposes rather than to suggest that groups are one-dimensional. Indeed, in reality, findings show substantial overlap between several of them (see pen portrait 1).

Pen portrait 1: local action group in Mill Town

Meeting place: no fixed abode, though members are known to frequent a centre for elderly Pakistani men

This is a group of people who have taken responsibility for improving the local environment by planting flowers in communal areas.

The local authority approached them to ask if they would continue with their work and offered them (the potential) of a small pot of money on the condition that they become a constituted group. They were unsure whether they wanted to do this.

The six categories identified are explained below. Those groups that did not fit into any of these six categories were classed as 'other groups'.

Arts and music

In this category, art and music appeared to be the central focus of activity. Four groups were categorised under this type: a jazz group, a writers' group, a dance group and an art group.

Multicultural and multiple faith and ethnic identities and activities

This category included activities targeted at people from several (usually more than two) faiths, ethnicities and countries. Seven groups were identified as belonging to this category – several of these involved recent UK arrivals, although some included a mix of established ethnic communities and new arrivals. Examples include a 'multinational football team', initially set up as part of a community cohesion project by a registered charity to bring together young isolated (refugee) men; a young men's pool club for (isolated) refugee and asylum seekers; and a patchwork quilting group for refugee and asylum-seeking women.

'Niche'/specialist interests

This category included groups of people who came together to share very specific, niche interests. There were three groups in this category: a dowser group, a group interested in (old-style) film making and film watching, and another interested in transmitters and radios.

Self-help/mutual support

This category included groups of people who supported each other, usually through identified shared experiences and mutual monetary support. Eight groups were classified and included a group for single mums; a seasonal lone-parent group that met weekly over the summer at a church hall (see pen portrait 2); parents whose children had died as a result of gun crime; women's aid support; and a support group for people who were hard of hearing.

Pen portrait 2: a seasonal group – 'the summer lone-parent group' in High Street

Meeting place: church

This group was identified from a postcard advert on a noticeboard in a leisure centre located in a park. The advert was pitched at lone parents, offering them a chance to meet with others to reduce feelings of isolation and an opportunity for their children to learn through play. The advertised venue was a local church hall with weekly meetings over a six-week period (during school summer holidays). Participants were asked for a weekly £1 contribution to cover the cost of tea and biscuits.

Three groups were identified as supporting each other primarily for mutual monetary purposes, all of which were reported to stem back to practices and needs of migrant Pakistani communities settling in the local area during the 1950s. Two of these three groups were 'death committees' (see pen portrait 3) and the third a 'friends saving club'. There was substantial overlap between these and other groups in the 'multicultural and multiple faith and ethnic identities and activities' and 'single-identity cultural, faith and ethnic activities' categories.

Pen portrait 3: death committee in Mill Town

Meeting place: no fixed abode, although members frequent a centre for elderly Pakistani men

The death committee was set up in the 1950s for members of the Pakistani community: by making a regular contribution to a shared pot, this was initially set up to help cover the cost of sending a member's body back 'home' after their death. Over time, with fewer overseas burials, the cost now tends to cover funerals in the UK.

This was reported to be one of two such committees that operate across the local authority and was identified from an interview with the centre manager of a voluntary organisation. The committee does not have a fixed abode and, instead, those who run the scheme visit places where their members tend to meet to collect money, including a local centre for elderly Pakistani men and two local mosques.

Single-identity cultural, faith and ethnic activities

This category includes groups that offer support for people from a particular ethnic or faith group or country of origin (for those from established communities or recent arrivals to the UK (see pen portrait 4). Fifteen groups were identified as falling into this type, 11 in High Street and four in Mill Town. They covered a wide range of activities and interests for a diverse group of users from different countries and ethnicities. Cumulatively, the 11 groups in High Street covered people from 10 different countries, including Angola, Lithuania, Russia and Sudan. While several of these offered opportunities to learn English and classes for children to learn their parents' 'mother tongue', the majority also organised cultural and social activities, such as cooking lessons and sewing, as opportunities to come together. Some included 'bridge-building' activities between communities, while others had target populations with multiple identities, such as young people from a particular faith, and women from a particular ethnic group.

Pen portrait 4: Women's Friendship Club

Meeting place: community resource centre in High Street

This group was identified from a room-booking diary at a community resource centre that offered communal offices and meeting rooms to refugee and migrant organisations in High Street. The club was primarily geared towards offering social activities to women from a specified part of Eastern Europe, with the additional dimension of encouraging friendship with 'British' women.

This group arguably fell within the multiple identity group; nevertheless, the main focus of the group was geared towards women from a particular country.

Social club-based activities

This category included what some might consider 'hobby' groups. There were eight groups, some of which overlapped with other types. Interestingly, all bar one group were advertised for elderly people. They included a Bridge club, line dancing, machine knitting, sewing classes and 'senior sports', while others offered more general activities for elderly people. The eighth group was a social club for young disabled people.

Other groups:

There were four groups that did not sit well in any of these six types: a community farm for abused animals, a local action group that looked after communal areas by, for example, planting flower beds (pen portrait 1) and a group of friends and family who put together savings on a regular basis to send money to orphans and widows from a nominated village in Pakistan.

A summary of the six categories of below-radar activity is outlined in Table 2.1. Note, however, that the four 'other' groups are not included. A further nine groups are not included in the table because there was insufficient information to classify them.

In short, the groups identified on High Street and in Mill Town could be characterised as involving 'serious leisure' (Stubbins, 2001), mutual support and meeting basic needs (Lindsey, 2012) – or combinations of all three.

Table 2.1: Types of below-radar groups and activities

Type	Brief description	Examples	Number (High Street)	Number (Mill Town)	Total
Art and music	Art and music appear to be the focal point	Jazz; arts; writing; folk-dance	1	3	4
Multicultural and multiple faith and ethnic identities and activities	Groups focusing on bringing together people from different countries, faith and ethnicities; mainly for recent arrivals to the UK, but there are groups for more established settlers and a mix of these	Football group and pool group for isolated young men recently arrived in the UK; user-cum-volunteer self-support on various issues such as housing and employment	2	5	7
Niche and specialist interest	People who come together to share a very specific, niche interest	Dowser group; those with an interest in radio transmissions	0	3	3
Self-help/mutual support	Groups that support each other because of shared experiences or for monetary support	Death committees; friends saving club; lone-parent meeting club; women's aid group (not part of the national network); deaf group; parents of children who have died from gun crime	3	5	8
Single-identity cultural, faith and ethnic activities	These groups focus on people who are from a particular ethnic or faith group, or country of origin, and offer a diverse range of activities, including learning English and developing friendships and spiritual wellbeing	Befriending group to establish friendships with Russian and British people; learning English; cultural and social activities to improve English and reduce isolation, including sewing and cooking together; volunteer-run language classes (parents' mother tongue); spiritual groups	11	4	15
Social club-based activities	Social activities for groups; in this study these were mainly targeted at elderly people, those in their 'third age'	Bridge club; line dancing	0	8	8
Total			17	28	45

Common themes below the radar

Even within such small localities, the diversity of groups below the radar is clearly evident – with variations between and within the six 'types' outlined in Table 2.1. Yet, for all that diversity, certain common themes emerge from the street-level sample of 58 groups.

First, these groups are, by and large, embedded in their communities, operating within a specific socio-cultural context at the local level (see also Creta and King's 2014 study of Sparkbrook in Birmingham). Many of them reflect the interests and needs of those within their local area, for example, the informal language class that arose from cuts to local provision of classes in English for Speakers of Other Languages (ESOL), as one member explained:

> "… it was just through meeting other women in the other organisations over a cup of coffee … we just thought it wasn't very fair, we didn't find it logical that the very people needing this provision couldn't tap into it because of financial issues. And it sort of developed on from there as a sort of coffee morning group where we invited women to come along and just talk and in that way they could improve their English because they were from different countries, different backgrounds. Just by talking they could make friends, they could improve their English language skills … and it developed from there."

Further, activities reflected the characteristics of their localities. Groups in High Street tended to fall into the two categories multicultural identity and single cultural identity, and captured more than 10 different ethnicities, faith and countries, reflecting an area that is 'super diverse' (Phillimore, 2014). In contrast, there seemed to be more variation in Mill Town, including groups with niche interests and those providing activities for elderly people, as well as multicultural and single-cultural identity groups. This variation is likely to reflect the local community, which comprises white British and established Pakistani populations as well as recent migrants, and the different approach we undertook to pilot the second area using voluntary and community spaces as focal points.

Second, the findings call into question the common idea that small, below the radar, groups and activities tend to be short-lived and transitory (Twelvetrees, 2008). Different amounts of information were gathered on each of the groups. However, from available findings, evidence demonstrates a wide range in groups' years of operation. Some, for example, had been active for less than a year at the time of fieldwork. In contrast, there were others that had been in operation for several decades, such as the aforementioned death committee (see pen portrait 3). In another case, one group reported that it could trace its history as far back as the 1930s.

Third, while the groups researched were self-organised, they were not 'islands' (Gilchrist, 2009). Many of them were connected to and drew on other groups' resources for their activities and work. This included use of space in, for example, a church or voluntary organisation's premises, which then facilitated connections between different groups. This, in turn, enabled them to draw on the knowledge and expertise of others (both activists and paid workers) in the buildings in which they met (Gilchrist, 2009; see also Chapter Twelve in this volume).

Fourth, even very small below the radar groups needed some financial resource to survive and thrive. Most of the groups involved in the street-level mapping were adept at generating resources by **'tapping in'** to their own users. For example, a writing group asked participants for a £3 weekly donation to cover the cost of room hire, while users of the seasonal lone-parent group (see pen portrait 4) contributed £1 weekly. Some were also successful in **'tapping out'** beyond their users to obtain and blend resources for their work and activities from others. This included accessing small grants, acquiring gifts of equipment and materials, participating in entrepreneurial activities such as making and selling jewellery and accessing pro-bono advice.

A further dimension was **'giving out'**, highlighting that while many below-radar groups existed to support their own users, there were several cases of very small local groups giving out resources (money and time) to wider communities. All three of these examples of generating and distributing resources demonstrate that below the radar groups, in this study at least, do not operate as islands.

Finally, in many respects, self-organised activities in this study can be seen as the activities of individual '*bricoleurs*'. This is a term commonly used in the social entrepreneur literature and has been adapted from the work of Lévi-Strauss (1967) to refer to individuals who are able to draw on and acquire a mix of resources to get on with what they are doing, making ends meet by blending whatever they can for their own purpose(s) (Di Dominico et al, 2010). More recently, the concept of *bricolage* has been applied to the management of public services in austere times (Bugge and Bloch, 2016) and to addressing health concerns in diverse areas (Phillimore, 2016).

A number of examples of successful bricolage were found through the street-level mapping. The women's group offering informal ESOL pulled together small-scale resources from a range of sources to 'keep going'. The animal rescue group managed to access pro-bono legal advice and veterinary services while raising funds through events run by other below the radar groups in Mill Town.

Two types of *bricoleur* emerged at the local level: first, individual *bricoleurs*, who, in this study, obtained and blended a mix of resources to support and sustain their *own* group; and second, community *bricoleurs*, who operated beyond the boundaries of any one group and instead pulled together resources for *several* groups and individuals. In terms of small-scale below the radar activities, *bricolage* skills have become increasingly important as a tactic for surviving austerity: putting together the previously disconnected to build community and community services (Lowndes and Roberts, 2013).

Final reflections on street-level micro-mapping

In austere times, street-level micro-mapping might seem a diversionary activity: fiddling (or bean counting) while Rome burns. Although studying local action at the micro-level may make it difficult to draw generalised findings (applicable to civil society across the UK and in very different contexts), the research does highlight a number of important issues.

First, as noted in Chapter One, current figures for the number of unincorporated community groups in England is, and has been consistently, based on best-guess estimates (Kane et al, 2015). At the micro-level, the current research suggests that those estimates have some degree of accuracy. Informal, unincorporated, associational activity, in each locality, outweighed formal charitable organisation 'by a factor of as many as nine' (Mohan, 2011, p 4) – or more in the case of High Street. These findings have been replicated in subsequent micro-mapping exercises that have adopted a similar methodology (Atanga et al, 2013; Butarova et al, 2013; Creta and King, 2014). While there may be a value in further exploring the potential of community-based social media as a (potentially cost-effective) tool for micro-mapping, scaling up the approach to arrive at more robust data on small-scale civil society would, however, neither be feasible nor, perhaps, even desirable.

Second, there is the policy context in which public agencies, if not central government, are increasingly interested in the capacity of informal below the radar community groups to deliver on public service agendas, in particular health and wellbeing (Glasgow Centre for Population Health, undated). However, as argued in Chapters Four and Six, this is, at best, an ill thought-out idea based on misconceptions of the role and purpose of community-based activities by making assumptions that such activities can be co-opted for political and policy ends (NCIA, 2015).

In this context, then, there are two important lessons to consider from the research findings. The groups identified throughout the research were reliant on low- or no-cost spaces to meet: the very spaces that (as argued in Chapter Six) are being closed down. The heavy reliance on such dwindling resources reflects the current gap between those promoting grassroots activities in policy agendas (Foot and Hopkins, 2010) and the practical realities on the ground. Grassroots community activity is, and cannot be, a substitute or replacement for collective welfare systems (Alcock, 2016).

Finally, there is an 'academic' interest. The findings call into question some of the dominant discourse in the literature on volunteering and social capital (Field, 2003), namely that levels of social action and capital are lower in 'poor' communities. They also challenge the concept of 'charity deserts' (Lindsey, 2012). In the postcode area for the High Street research, there were only 19 registered charities, but just over 150 community groups in city-wide directories, and, in total, 336 groups were found through the subsequent web-search and street-mapping exercises. While it is impossible to generalise from the sample size, these findings are reinforced by Whitehead's research (2012) in a rural community in south-east England. Here 100 groups appeared in local directories, but through a process of snowballing, a further 100 below the radar groups were found. Gleeson and Bloemraad (2010) and Williams (2011) argue that studies that draw on more formal aspects of the voluntary sector and more formally recognised voluntary activity to operationalise social capital consequently result in incomplete evidence and potentially misleading conclusions on the distribution of social capital (Mohan et al, 2010; Mohan, 2011).

In short, the level of formality in voluntary organisations should never be mistaken for the volume of activity in any community. The greater numbers of volunteer-led charities in affluent areas (Lindsey, 2012) should not be taken as a proxy indicator for the absence of community action in deprived neighbourhoods. The communities and community groups involved in the street-level micro-mapping had an abundance of social capital. What they lacked, and struggled for, was financial capital – perhaps that is one of the ingredients necessary to convert below the radar action into formal voluntary work.

Key learning

- Micro-mapping is a useful research tool for identifying very small scale, informal community groups and activities that exist beyond any formal databases.
- Micro-mapping is a means of capturing the range of activities at a community level. This applies particularly to super-diverse areas where groups based on culture, ethnicity, interest or identity may be invisible beyond their own immediate community.
- Micro-mapping, as a research methodology, is labour intensive and therefore costly. Replicating this approach may therefore be problematic on a larger city, regional or national level.
- The approach has been adopted as a means of supporting asset based community development models of service provision and the transfer of public services to community groups. Such groups, however, may lack the desire, and certainly the resources, to deliver public services on the scale required in austere times. This is, in any instance, not their primary purpose.
- The number of formal voluntary organisations in any neighbourhood should not be taken as a proxy for, or indicator of, actual levels of community activity.

Reflective exercises

- Why is street-level micro-mapping of below the radar activity at a community level time- and resource-intensive?
- There is growing public service interest in below the radar community activity based on the assumption that such groups can deliver public policy goals such as increased community cohesion and the promotion of health and wellbeing. What, in austere times, might be the uses, or abuses, of micro-mapping below the radar activities in the delivery of public services?
- From your experience, and in the light of the concept of 'charity deserts', reflect on the statement that 'the level of formality in voluntary organisations should never be mistaken for the volume of activity in any community'.

References

Alcock, P. (2016) *Why we need welfare: Collective action for the common good*, Bristol: Policy Press.

Atanga, T., Hunt, R., Kanu, V., Pearce, A., Robinson, D., Stoleru, P. and Watkin, A. (2013) *Third Sector Mapping Pilot: Pilot mapping in three wards*, Birmingham: Birmingham City Council

Backus, P. and Clifford, D. (2010) *Trends in the concentration of income among charities*, Birmingham: Third Sector Research Centre.

Bugge, M. and Bloch, W. (2016) 'Between bricolage and breakthroughs – framing the many faces of public sector innovation', *Public Money and Management*, vol 36, no 4, pp 281-8.

Butarova, M., Chamberlain, J., Cerasella, I,. Bloise Thompson, S. and Tipping, J. (2013) *Mapping third sector 'under the radar' organisations in Birmingham*, Birmingham: Birmingham City Council.

Clark, J., Kane, D., Wilding, K. and Wilton, J. (2010) *UK civil society almanac 2010*, London: National Council for Voluntary Organisations.

CLES (Centre for Local Economic Strategies) and New Economics Foundation (2013) *Big Lottery fund national wellbeing evaluation*, London: BIG Lottery.

Clifford, D., Geyne Rajme, F. and Mohan, J. (2010) *How dependent is the third sector on public funding? Evidence from the National Survey of Third Sector Organisations*, Birmingham: Third Sector Research Centre.

Craig, G. with Adamson, S., Ali, N. and Demsash, F. (2010) *Mapping rapidly changing minority ethnic populations: A case study of York*, York: Joseph Rowntree Foundation.

Creta, S. and King, M. (2014) *Third Sector Mapping Project: Pilot mapping in Sparkbrook*, Birmingham: Birmingham City Council.

Di Dominico, M.L., Haugh, H. and Tracey, P. (2010) 'Social bricolage: theorizing social value creation in social enterprises', *Entrepreneurship Theory and Practice*, vol 34, no 4, pp 681-703.

Field, J. (2003) *Social capital*, London: Routledge.

Foot, J. and Hopkins, T. (2010) *A glass half-full: How an asset approach can improve community health and well-being*, London: Improvement and Development Agency.

Gilchrist, A. (2009) *The well-connected community: A networking approach to community Development* (2nd edn), Bristol: Policy Press.

Glasgow Centre for Population Health (undated) *Asset based approaches for health improvement: Redressing the balance*, Glasgow: Glasgow Centre for Population Health.

Gleeson, S. and Bloemraad, I. (2010) *Where are all the immigrant organisations? Reassessing the scope of civil society for immigrant communities*, Working Paper Series (02-16-2010), Berkeley, CA: Institute for Research on Labour and Employment, University of California.

Grønbjerg, K.A. and Clerkin, R.M. (2005) 'Examining the landscape of Indiana's nonprofit sector: does what you know depend on where you look?', *Nonprofit and Voluntary Sector Quarterly*, vol 34, no 2, pp 232-59.

Harris, M. and Young, P. (2009) 'Developing community and social cohesion through grassroots bridge-building: an exploration', *Policy & Politics*, vol 37, no 4, pp 517-34.

Ipsos MORI Social Research Institute (2010) *Local surveys of unregistered TSOs: Ipsos MORI summary report*, London: Ipsos MORI Social Research Institute.

Kane, D., Jochum, V., Dobbs, J., Pikoula, M., James, D., Crees, J., Ockenden, N. and Lloyd, G. (2015) *UK civil society almanac 2015*, London: NCVO.

Lévi-Strauss, C. (1967) *The savage mind*, Chicago, IL: University of Chicago Press.

Lindsey, R. (2013) 'Exploring local hotspots and deserts: Investigating the local distribution of charitable resources', *Voluntary Sector Review*, vol 4, no 1, pp 95-116.

Lowndes, V. and Roberts, M. (2013) *Why institutions matter: The new institutionalism in political science*, Basingstoke: Palgrave Macmillan.

Marcus, G. and Tidey, J. (2015) *Community mirror: A data-driven method for 'below the radar' research*, London: Nesta.

Marshall, T.F. (1997) *Local Voluntary Activity Surveys (LOVAS): Research manual*, LOVAS Paper 1, London: Research & Statistics Directorate, Home Office.

Marshall, T.F., Woodburn, S. and Miller, J. (1997) *Comparing the areas: LOVAS sweep 1. Variations in size of sector, volunteering, staff and incomes*, LOVAS Paper 3, London: Research & Statistics Directorate, Home Office.

McCabe, A. (2010) *Below the radar in a Big Society? Reflections on community engagement, empowerment and social action in a changing policy context*, Birmingham: Third Sector Research Centre.

McCabe, A., Phillimore, J. and Mayblin, L. (2010) '*Below the radar' activities and organisations in the third sector: A summary review of the literature*, TSRC Working Paper 29, Birmingham: Third Sector Research Centre.

Mohan, J. (2011) *Mapping the Big Society: Perspectives from the Third Sector Research Centre*, Birmingham: Third Sector Research Centre.

Mohan, J., Barnard, S., Branson J., and Kane, D. (2011) *Entering the lists: What can be learned from local listings of third sector organisations?*, Newcastle upon Tyne: Northern Rock Foundation.

Mohan, J., Kane, D., Branson, J. and Owles, F. (2010) *Beyond 'flat-earth' maps of the third sector: Report to the Northern Rock Foundation*, Newcastle upon Tyne: Northern Rock Foundation.

NCIA (National Coalition for Independent Action) (2015) *Fight or fright: Voluntary services in 2015. A summary and discussion of the inquiry findings*, London: NCIA.

Norman, W. (2012) *Adapting to change: The role of community resilience*, London: Young Foundation.

Phillimore, J. and McCabe, A. with Soteri-Proctor, A. and Taylor, R. (2010) U*nderstanding the distinctiveness of small scale, third sector activity: The role of local knowledge and networks in shaping below the radar actions*, Birmingham: Third Sector Research Centre.

Phillimore, J. (2014) 'Diversity and social welfare', in W. Vertovec (ed) *Routledge international handbook of diversity studies*, London: Routledge.

Phillimore, J. (2016) Migrant maternity in an era of superdiversity: new migrants' access to, and experience of, antenatal care in the West Midlands, UK', *Social Science & Medicine*, vol 148, pp 152-9.

Seabrook, J. (1984) *The idea of neighbourhood: What local politics should be about*, London: Pluto Press.

Stubbins, R. (2001) 'Serious leisure', *Society*, vol 38, no 4, pp 53-7.

Twelvetrees, A' (2008) *Community work* (4th edn), Basingstoke: Palgrave Macmillan.

Whitehead, P. (2012) 'A study which aims to identify if there are "below the radar" ("BTR") groups or activities in Cranleigh Parish, Surrey, and to assess how their presence may relate to the ability of the community to deliver "Big Society" objectives', Unpublished BA dissertation, University of Gloucestershire.

Williams, C.C. (2011) 'Geographical variations in the nature of community engagement: a total social organisation of labour approach', *Community Development Journal*, vol 46, no 2, pp 213-28.

PART TWO

Community groups and activities in context

THREE

Are we different? Claims for distinctiveness in voluntary and community action

Angus McCabe and Jenny Phillimore

Chapter aims

Drawing on 126 interviews with community activists, this chapter critically examines:

- how and why community groups come into existence and are sustained;
- whether claims for the distinctiveness of community groups and activities are justified;
- the function of social networks in community action.

Background

The literature on the voluntary and community sector is littered with claims of its distinctiveness – if not uniqueness. Unlike the private sector, voluntaries are not motivated by profit. Whereas the statutory sector is bureaucratic, and allegedly slow to act, voluntary organisations are fleet of foot, adaptable and responsive. The sector is, at least in principle, value driven (Corry, 2011), guided by concepts of cooperation and solidarity (Warren, 2001) and working for community cohesion and strengthening local networks of care (Edwards, 2008).

Debate on the distinctiveness of the sector, has, however, shifted in the past decade, as has the language used to describe the sector: from the generic 'voluntary organisations' to the idea of a voluntary, then third, sector and on to a more amorphous concept of civil society. At the same time, the idea that the sector exists as a cohesive whole has been called into question:

> Internal diversity has been incorporated into the presentation of a sector constructed with a breadth and profile to stand alongside, and even to challenge, the public and private sectors.... [However] different agendas mean that the notion of a third sector is inevitably a contested one, and may lead some to challenge the relevance of the concept itself. (Alcock, 2010, pp 1, 4)

Billis (2010) goes further and argues that (at least some) voluntary and community organisations have moved towards more hybrid modes of operation: espousing the values of voluntarism while becoming more bureaucratic or business-like. Further, following the 2008 global financial crisis and the subsequent recession, austerity measures and cuts to public funding in the UK, there are those who argue that the core values that may have been used to define the sector's distinctiveness have been eroded and that there are now (at least) two different sectors, divided between the haves (large charities) and the have-nots (community groups). An argument has been made that larger charities have to some extent been co-opted by the state – with an accompanying loss of the autonomy, independence, pluralism and 'ungoverned spaces' that are important to citizens:

> Voluntary services exist to do the things that Government cannot, will not, or should not do; to complement, not substitute for public services and entitlements: to innovate, reach excluded groups, aid access to mainstream services, offer services which have to be independent (such as advice and advocacy) and act as commentator and critic of public services and State action. Once a voluntary group becomes a servant of the State this unique role is compromised. (NCIA, 2015, p 1)

The classic definitions of the voluntary sector remain in place – informality, independence, non-profit distribution and voluntarism (Salamon and Anheier, 1997). However, perhaps, as Kenny and colleagues (2015) argue, it is time for voluntary and community organisations to question their role and function, and the 'easy' claims made by the sector for itself: of solidarity and a commitment to equalities and social justice. What 'the sector' looks like, or perhaps more importantly 'feels' like, is, therefore, increasingly contested and controversial (see Chapter Five). Certainly it is a sector 'in transition' (Milbourne, 2013). Much of the research looking at motivations has focused on the 'formal' or large-scale sector. It is conceivable that below the radar (BTR) organisations, with their at best tentative connections to the state, will fare differently from larger organisations and be able to retain their independence and autonomy.

This chapter focuses on the experiences of BTR voluntary organisation and in particular on the 'look' and 'feel' of the BTR part of the sector. It does so from a longitudinal perspective: drawing on an initial scoping focus group involving 25 policymakers, academics and practitioners followed by 126 interviews undertaken between 2010 and 2015 with community activists, representatives from 'micro-organisations' (registered but with incomes of less that £10,000 a year) and community anchor and network groups as well as policymakers. The range of participants is summarised in Table 3.1. After each wave of research, preliminary findings were reviewed by a BTR reference group of activists, practitioners, academics and policymakers.

Table 3.1: Profile of respondent groups/organisations

Year	National: policymakers and network organisations	Regional: government offices and network organisations	Local network organisations (CVS/RCC)*	Funders (grant-making trusts)	Community activists/ members of volunteer-led organisations	Total
2010	12	6	7	2	22	49
2012	10	4	5	2	20	41
2015	8	4	3	2	19	36
Total	30	14	13	6	61	126

Note: * Councils of Voluntary Service and Rural Community Councils
Source: Phillimore and McCabe (2010; 2015), McCabe and Phillimore (2012).

While resource limitations precluded fully national coverage, interviews were conducted across four England regions – the West Midlands (36), London and the South East (35) the North West (30) and the South West (25) – to ensure a geographical spread of experiences and views.

Through analysis of this data, we explore shifts in attitudes and beliefs over a seven-year period about ideas that BTR organisations are a unified and distinctive part of the voluntary sector.

Coming into existence

Perhaps a starting point for examining claims that community groups have distinctive characteristics in terms of voluntary action is to identify why they come into existence. After all, there is no requirement for them to be established in law or statute (NCIA, 2015).

A key theme in terms of the motivations that spur the establishment of a BTR group is the importance of emotion – a subject that, as Rosie Anderson points out (Chapter Thirteen) is sorely neglected in the literature in this field. For some community activists that starting point is raw anger: 'this is wrong', 'this should not be happening to me/my community'. Anger may be generated by planning permission for large capital projects (witness the campaigns against the high-speed rail link between Birmingham and London or against the expansion of Heathrow). Such emotional starting points may (as Conn, 2011 has argued) contribute to misunderstandings between statutory agencies, policy makers and activists – with a perceived 'gulf' between the former as rational decision makers and the latter as engaged at a primarily emotional level. Alternatively, anger as a motivator may turn into vigilante action (for example, the firebombing of the homes of suspected paedophiles) or to protect entrenched, privileged, power structure and oppress others (Cooper, 2008).

Our interviews with individuals who had established community groups revealed that feelings of loss or absence were also an important factor motivating action. For activists from black and minority ethnic (BME) groups, such feelings emerged when gaps in services were identified because of the state's perceived failure to meet the needs of marginalised groups. Similarly representatives from migrant and refugee community organisations (MRCOs) involved throughout the research talked about actions occurring to provide mutual aid to new arrivals who were unable to locate that support elsewhere. For several rural groups, the motivation for action was to develop a community shop following the closure of the local privately run store. Such action proliferated where there were no alternatives – when, in the words of one women's group leader, "you have no money, no food or you just have to do something" – particularly in areas that had a history of making things happen and a culture of risk taking "where there is a 'crucible' – places with long history of welcoming and bringing people together – around existing institutions that are accepting of risk taking – place to be welcome and not expecting formality, easy going, see what develops, tolerance of low level risks" (women's group activist).

There were, however, dangers in taking risks, even where these were well intentioned. Having been concerned about increased waiting times for welfare benefits advice experienced by local people, a residents' association provided an advice role – without any training or accessing the appropriate insurance. It became aware that it had, in a number of cases, misadvised local tenants.

A common enemy, whether that was desperation or poverty, or campaigning for a living wage or against corporate developers, was also seen as a key motivator for activity. Shared anger could be powerful in mobilising communities (Lupton, 2003; Richardson, 2008). Emotion, as a motivator, was frequently linked to other factors. There may be cultural expectations that individuals must take action and a risk of 'huge cultural penalties' for refusing someone in need. Those interviewed from MRCOs repeatedly talked of the importance of 'looking after your own', 'putting something back', helping people who were going through a similar situation by offering support to "friends I didn't know ... you have to open your door to those in need" (Refugee group interview). For others, belief systems came into play. There was an expectation within and across faith communities of providing practical, financial or emotional support for others, especially where the importance of helping those less fortunate than oneself was core to religious texts (Furbey et al, 2006; McCabe et al, 2016a) and therefore considered a duty.

Individual characteristics, or traits, also played a role in 'getting things going'. Activists were often described as passionate, charismatic, self-motivated and skilled. A respondent who had helped establish a rural community group argued that having a 'gobby activist' as part of the group was important, although such individuals can alienate the wider community and potentially restrict the numbers wanting to get involved in actions or activities. There was also agreement that community action was often gendered (Dominelli, 2006): women were most likely to start a small-scale activity, "although the higher up the hierarchy you go it's men" (faith organisation expert).

What, however, bound these motivations together after the initial driver for action was the social aspects of action: "people are group animals and naturally want to come together" (community activist). Indeed, a common theme, across different stakeholders, was the crucial importance of BTR groups and activities in 'bringing isolated people and communities together', 'connecting people' and 'overcoming isolation'. In short, such groups were seen by respondents as 'social glue' rather than, as has been argued elsewhere, being divisive, particularly around issue of race, minority communities and migration (Henderson and Kaur, 1999; Ryder et al, 2014).

Keeping it going?

'Sustainability' became a buzzword for communities and community activities in the 2000s, both in policy terms and in the academic literature (Raco, 2007). However, sustaining anger and emotional engagement over long periods is difficult. After the emotional motivations for establishment, other motivators are necessary to enable groups to sustain action and it is to these we now turn.

Not all BTR groups just keep going. Sometimes people come together for a campaign that may be short-lived or alternatively last years, but then disperse, either because the campaign was successful or it failed in its desired outcome – the end of the group can be an indicator of success as well as failure. Life cycles of actions varied according to need. Some groups, particularly in the arts, thrived for many years, without any perceived need for change. Others arose in response to need and became very active, followed by a period of being dormant – until a new issue or need arose. Alternatively, some groups outlived their perceived usefulness to the community and were seen as serving a set of vested interests (Meade, 2009). Many of the individuals interviewed spoke of their groups depending heavily on just a few individuals. These activists could, and did, burn out. The issue the group was seeking to address may not have disappeared, but actions stopped and only re-emerged when new individuals were activated.

Common cause, over time, was important in sustaining focus and action. But in the long term it was perhaps the social nature of community groups that kept people engaged. Such sociality is an aspect of community life that has often been underplayed in policy and research terms (Taylor, 2012). Community groups are often considered to be 'amateurish' because they focus on process and interaction and are informal in nature (Gilchrist, 2016) rather than being task orientated. Yet focusing on sociality can underplay the multi-layered functions of even apparently single purpose groups:

> "I'm thinking of another sports club we looked at. I guess their main activity was providing boxing activities and things like that but they provided general social activities for people – sort of an opportunity to get-together, running all sorts of events, activities to clean up and tidy the venue. I guess they had the sort of common purpose – they were about providing that main activity but all the other activities that contributed to that were incredibly diverse, which then meant that people could come along and dip in however they chose and saw fit really because they do provide quite a broad social function within society at local level." (Chief officer, development agency)

The notion of offering some kind of pay-back to those who participate, either in terms of recognition within one's community or through emotional and social support rather than financial reward, was said to keep people, and the actions they initiate, going after the initial drive for establishment. Respondents noted that many people left the groups they were involved in because, after years of commitment, others forgot to thank them or, because the pay-back sought (perceived status, being seen as a community leader, a 'pillar' of the community) was not forthcoming.

Are community groups distinctive?

> "I describe the totality of the voluntary sector as an iceberg ... it's just trying to get across the idea that most of the community organisations are below the water as in an iceberg and that has profound implications on how that sector is seen and understood and in terms of relationships of power as well, you can have quite a skewed picture – because the bit below the water is not recognised in terms of voice, in terms of policy or even research proposals." (Community activist, residents' association)

As noted in Chapter One, the majority of the voluntary, or third, sector is unregistered, in the form of what are described as BTR groups. Throughout the seven years of BTR research undertaken by the authors, the overwhelming argument by respondents from network organisations and grassroots activists themselves has been that BTR actions are distinctive for a variety of reasons.

A key proposition was that unlike in formal actions where roles were clearly defined, there were blurred boundaries between the personal and civic lives of actors and activists – "It's completely their life ... they never clock off" (development agency interview) – while formal organisations were professionalised and there were clearer boundaries between work and other activities. 'Never clocking off' carries with it risks, not only of burn-out, but also, where those activists hold passionate but opposing views, of conflict (McCabe et al, 2016b).

BTR activists were said to take risks that 'professional' organisations would not consider. They were apparently not tied to any specific ways of working associated with having contracts to deliver and instead were free to lobby as they see fit. They were driven by political, social, cultural or faith values rather than financial reward. Respondents working at the policy level, while acknowledging the innate conservatism of some groups, argued that these drivers enabled actions driven from the grassroots to be innovative.

Respondents from local, regional and national umbrella/network organisations argued that the level of small-scale community actions was frequently underestimated and unrecognised either by policymakers or more formal institutions and charities:

> "What we know about these groups in terms of formal lists actually bears no resemblance to the levels of activity within groups. There tends to be the groups everyone knows about and then invisible groups. It's those invisible groups that [names area] were perhaps the most active in their community – but were unknown beyond it." (Network organisation representative)

Or, as another activist noted: "never mistake the level of formality with the actual level of activity".

BTR groups were argued to be embedded within their communities, either as communities of identity/interest or geography. They were said to be well networked and able to reach people in need by working in a highly localised way with specialised local or community of interest knowledge: "Small organisations are the closest to community – they can alert policymakers to issues before they become problem 'you know issue is coming'" (policy-level interview). Such organisations were seen as possessing experiential knowledge, being led by communities for communities, with sufficient trust and respect to be able to address the most sensitive of issues, including child abuse and domestic violence, in ways that would not have been open to the public sector or formal voluntary sector. They did not stigmatise participants because of they were poor or disabled, because all those involved in running actions "are in the same boat, in the case of refugees, literally" (faith-based organisation interview). The danger of such a hyper-local (or intra-group) focus was, however, that some community groups were sometimes unable to locate neighbourhood-level issues within the bigger policy picture or form alliances with others facing similar challenges (McCabe et al, 2016b). Such constraints, however, were as much a matter of access to resources to network and build alliances as a perceived lack of vision and understanding.

Respondents argued that BTR groups were more fluid, flexible and informal than the mainstream sector. Without a formal structure and constitution, they could quickly adapt to needs as they emerged: "They are uninhibited by bureaucracy, able to act immediately without the need for formalised meetings – as a result the rules are different [and] not mediated by money exchange" (women's group respondent). Representatives from national network organisations also perceived lack of formal structures, often viewed by government as a deficit that needed to be remedied, as a potential strength, while adding a note of caution: "If you are below the radar and there is no-one on the outside looking in how do you know what you are doing is okay? Where are the 'checks and balances' in small, fairly informal, groups?" (network organisation respondent). This lack of 'checks and balances' was recognised by research participants, particularly in groups where 'self-elected' leaders had emerged, without a wider mandate from their community. Time, rather than elective processes or expertise, could become the (hidden) basis for holding power and influence within informal groups.

However, such informality was seen as one of the features making small-scale community groups different from regulated organisations. Formal organisations had rules and tightly defined hierarchies, while their concept of a 'volunteer' differed from that of BTR voluntary organisations:

> "Volunteer management within these groups is very informal, very active, responds to what people want, little chats – it doesn't have the levels of bureaucracy that a lot of formal volunteering seems to have and people felt quite strongly when we talked to them that if a formal volunteer management system was imposed upon these sorts of groups it would kill those groups." (Voluntary Sector Council employee respondent)

Indeed, many of those activists interviewed did not, or would not, define themselves as volunteers – they were simply 'doing something' in their community.

Without a formal structure and constitution, BTR groups could adapt to needs as they emerged:

> "They are uninhibited by bureaucracy, able to act immediately without the need for formalised meetings – as a result the rules are different [and] not mediated by money exchange." (Women's group respondent)

Other respondents, representatives from national network organisations, noted the lack of formal structures as a potential strength, while adding a note of caution:

> "If you are below the radar and there is no-one on the outside looking in how do you know what you are doing is okay? Where are the 'checks and balances' in small, fairly informal, groups?"

A further argument for the distinctiveness of BTR activity concerned the way it dealt with needs holistically. Women's, BME and new community organisations were considered by those active in such groups to offer support and solutions to complex needs in a totally different manner from state institutions. They often provided help that was highly personalised and responsive to immediate needs rather than eligibility criteria: "They create genuine personal connections on a level that is appropriate. A person-to-person connection that big agencies just cannot do" (rural group respondent). Ironically, in austere times, the time-consuming nature of person-to-person connectivity might limit the capacity of such groups to address the sheer scale of problems confronting communities.

Small-scale community activities were said to 'breed' a culture of self-reliance and mutual support. They relied heavily on volunteers and were cost effective because they paid no salaries. Groups were often self-funded and accessed resources (not only in affluent areas) from within their communities. Such resources offered additional flexibilities:

> "You are not dictated to by anyone external; you can do what you want to do within the resources that you have. You are more likely to meet needs in an effective way. You are free to say what you want, independent and not tied to any funding, funder or project delivery targets." (Women's group respondent)

Their goals varied, including taking on assets, such as the community shop, building a community centre/village hall or managing a facility (for example, older people's day care) linked to a faith building. For example, a Sudanese group combined limited personal resources to cover the costs of a flight home for a community member who was struggling to survive in the UK. In another instance, a small Pakistani group interviewed raised £20,000 from within their own community to build a school in Pakistan. However, while respondents talked about innovation and risk in terms of activities and services, those community groups interviewed that had taken on physical assets (the village hall and community shop) were risk averse in financial terms. Capital had been raised for these projects through grants and fundraising rather than through loans – even 'soft' loans from, for example, community development finance initiatives.

The limitations of distinctiveness

Many arguments were made by respondents regarding the distinctiveness and associated efficacy of BTR groups. Participants were reflective and sometimes self-critical or indicated that they were aware of the limitations of BTR actions. Some critiqued the concept of 'below the radar' and its use to describe small-scale community actions. For other research participants, the term had value. Below the radar as an idea was said to relate to how it 'felt' to be engaged in informal voluntary activities: "[The term] does say something that is a truth. There's a whole mess of vibrant life going on that's not recognised." For others, however, the phrase was "unhelpful as it presented a deficit model" that implied that community activity remained below the radar because groups lacked the capacity to grow and develop. Other interviewees found the term disempowering, because it, for them, implied failure on the part of activities or groups and was using the 'wrong lens' (to use a research term) to understand small-scale community activity, as "they are not below the radar but the heart and soul of the sector" (development agency respondent) and "may be invisible to some, but are highly visible where it matters, in their own communities" (community activist).

While, then, the term itself was contested (Phillimore et al, 2009), there was agreement around the challenges facing, and limitations of, BTR activities. Access to resources was a key issue. Without finance, however generated (either through grants or monies raised from within the community), many small groups were acutely aware that they lacked the capacity to respond to increasing needs within their community (McCabe et al, 2016a). Further, while much of the recent literature has focused on the impact of financial cuts (Milbourne, 2013; NCIA, 2015), access to other resources that may themselves be in short supply were crucial to small groups.

Many groups were dependent on some kind of social space, often tapping into physical resources like a school, faith building, library or local authority community centre to run their activities. Whereas, at the start of the research in 2008, this was a relatively easy process, by 2012 groups were reporting increasing difficulties in finding spaces to meet that were affordable (no or low cost) as such spaces had closed or had begun charging commercial rental rates as an income-generating strategy for their own survival.

People also used networking skills or 'social capital', rather than external 'financial capital' (loans or contracts) to access the knowledge or resources they needed to make something happen. Interviewees stressed the importance of resources beyond the purely financial:

> "In terms of people and resources, I think there's an awful lot of barter, there's an awful lot of gift exchange goes on. I think the goodwill of friends and family and community accounts for an awful lot in keeping these places (community centres/village halls) running in practice. I mean I don't think their balance sheets represent, you know, the true value of what gets put into them, what gets generated by them." (Voluntary Sector Council employee interview)

Yet again, reflecting on recent experiences recorded in interviews in 2015, BTR groups consistently reported difficulties in recruiting and retaining activists and volunteers. In austere times, people were increasingly living in uncertain circumstances, with insecure jobs and low pay, which meant taking on several jobs to survive. In this environment, despite the will to participate, people lacked the resources – either financially and/or in terms of time – to do so.

The potential, or real, limitations of BTR activity went beyond financial issues. The rhetoric of distinctiveness included the idea that community groups had horizontal, highly participatory and democratic decision-making processes. However, they could be driven by autocratic individuals. While community groups are sometimes portrayed as inclusive, some were in fact highly exclusive – along the lines of race or gender exclusion. Then there was an issue concerning participation:

> "Who participates? Well there is an issue of inclusivity. [Arts] groups can appear to be exclusive because they come together around a shared interest – so obviously they become groups of like-minded people.... There is an issue of insularity in lots of small groups. This may not be deliberate but they can create accidental barriers which exclude others." (Voluntary arts group respondent)

Participation was linked by research participants to ideas of accountability. To some the simple fact that people voted with their feet – "If people do not knock at your door you are not good enough" (MRCO respondent) – was sufficient accountability. Further, formal constituted structures did not necessarily evidence accountability, as leaders often put friends or family on 'the committee'. Uneven power relations, as noted, often related to the amount of time dedicated to an issue rather than formal status, meant that some individuals pursued their agenda regardless of the needs of their communities or formal decision-making processes. Accountability very much depended on the quality and vision of leadership and the ability of those leaders to work collectively and 'keep people on board'. Below the radar groups could be genuinely member led and, without a formal constitution, were only answerable to themselves rather than a wider community constituency.

Finally, issues of power and influence were raised by respondents. The 'involvement of communities' and local groups in decision making was seen by most interviewees as largely tokenistic:

> "When small groups are asked to have an input to policy it never gets beyond consultation. It is not a two-way process ... there is a lack of education around the policy process and understanding that process ... also a reliance on external people gathering community views – rather than the community itself. And the balance of power in policy processes makes it very difficult for communities to influence professional services." (Community activist)

Sometimes lack of accountability meant that groups failed to adapt to meet the needs of those they were meant to serve. Power struggles and associated fracturing led some groups to lose their way and to cease providing for their communities. At a personal level, there was the risk of small numbers of people becoming 'overcommitted or overstretched' in their community activities. Development agency representatives talked of the 'stresses and strains' of being involved at a community level in regeneration initiatives; community activists spoke of 'the real risks to health, mental health and relationships': "People can destroy their own lives by taking on responsibility for their community. Especially in communities that face a high level of chaos".

Lack of emotional support and opportunities for 'time out' for activists was seen as a neglected element of both research- and community-orientated policy (from neighbourhood renewal through to localism) and is explored in more depth by Rosie Anderson in Chapter Thirteen.

A hardening of attitudes?

Looking back to 2008 and the early phase of Third Sector Research Centre BTR research, a majority of community groups involved saw themselves as part of an admittedly 'loose and baggy' sector (Kendall and Knapp, 1996). There was, however, a perceived continuum between small community groups and large charities that related to values rather than financial resources or modes of operating:

> The value and uniqueness of the sector is rooted in its own values ... which include, at their best, enabling those furthest from power to have a voice; understanding the needs of, and reaching those missed by, mainstream services. (*The Guardian* Q and A live discussion, cited in McCabe, 2013, p 39)

After 2010, a pattern emerged across the BTR interviews of 'them' and 'us': the formal voluntary sector versus the community sector:

> "What the sector is about is social justice, that is what it is about, but actually I think a lot of the sector has forgotten that in a meaningful way; I think everyone can sign up to it in a superficial way in terms of values and mission statements and shiny documents ... but I'm not sure that a lot of the professionalised voluntary sector is about a direct engagement with people that changes their lives and accords to principles of social justice, I think it's about getting some money that provides some services that may or may not impact on people's lives in a hopefully social just way – it's a lot more distanced." (Community activist)

Some respondents thought that larger voluntaries and, in particular, charities had 'lost their way', both in terms of their connectedness with communities or service users and their values:

> "All organisations start with a passion – big organisations often lose sight of values – it's easier to hold out for your values when unfunded – you do what you want to do. So there is a lack of [having to] compromise." (BME group representative)

Allied to this feeling of a divided, bilateral, 'sector', was a sense of resentment around the roles small community groups were now expected to play by policymakers (such as taking on increasing responsibility for assets and services) combined with pressures bubbling up from local residents for them to meet needs. For example, the development and proliferation of community-based foodbanks were seen by some as evidence of a distinctive sector – able to respond quickly to emerging needs. Others questioned why there were foodbanks in the world's fifth richest economy (McCabe et al, 2016a)? For all the political rhetoric, communities and community groups felt they were being abandoned.

> "The real issue is that politicians, agencies, talk about communities and community services. But the agencies, the politicians are not in there working at the community level. It's the far right in England, Sinn Fein and the paramilitaries in Northern Ireland. It's them who are taking over the community agenda – because they are in there." (Community activist)

Community action was often seen as a '*postcode lottery*', and groups had been forced into had a 'focus on firefighting rather than change'. The state was perceived as favouring community-based action as a solution to lack of resources and as a '*cheaper option*' in tackling social problems: "*We have lost our way as a society and are looking at (community) organisations as salvation*" (BME group respondent). An interviewee in a rural area commented that community groups were increasingly "*filling the gaps left when statutory services withdraw from (rural) areas*". However, relying on small groups to improve local relations was "*a band-aid for haemorrhages*" (faith group respondent) that could only be solved through strategic action.

Some BTR activities and organisations did aspire to grow. Respondents felt that groups such as the Trussell Trust and the Strangers into Citizens Campaign to regularise undocumented migrants, as well as responses to domestic violence, had emerged from micro-level grassroots activity. However, most of the community-based organisations in the research, even when facing increasing demand for their services, had resisted the pressure to grow (or 'scale up'; Coutu, 2014) and become formalised. Some groups were thought to be successful because they were small. Respondents felt growth would distance them from the communities that they represented to the point that they would lose the unique qualities that went with being led by local people for local people.

Examples include a small tenant management organisation that has resisted housing department pressure to take on the management of a neighbouring estate, and the community shop that has refused to take over other shops in neighbouring villages. Such groups were more interested in replicating their model through sharing their ideas and expertise with others than in growth.

Others involved in the research had, over time, 'retreated' from tackling 'the big issues' and were feeling overwhelmed. For example, one tenants' group, concerned by the closure of local youth services, attempted, in 2010, to build alliances with anti-cuts and youth groups in their city. Within two years' this drive had waned and a decision was taken to focus on 'core business' alone: housing maintenance and repairs.

Conclusion

Over the past decade, therefore, a picture of the third sector has emerged which highlights shades of difference between informal community action and the formal voluntary sector. Again, characterising such differences (as research participants did) as a simple voluntary organisations versus community groups is an oversimplification in an increasingly fragmented 'sector'. For example, social enterprises sought to distance themselves from charities and the concept of charity itself, while arts and sports groups (see Chapter Eight) argued that they constituted discrete, or distinct, sub-sectors of voluntary action.

Further, relying on collective memory to trace perceived change in voluntary and community action can be problematic. For many commentators, the 2010 election marked a watershed for the third sector with the introduction of cuts and austerity measures (Ishkanian and Szreter, 2012; Milbourne, 2013). As far back as 2007, the Charity Commission issued a wake-up call to the sector and public authorities, noting the stripping out in the sector of smaller organisations with funding of less that £100,000. Equally, predicting the future would be difficult. Reflecting back to 1945 and the introduction of the welfare state, there were those, such as Richard Crossman, who predicted the demise of charity. This did not, and has not, happened. Similarly, post-2010 austerity measures have not witnessed (as some predicted) a collapse, or at least substantial reduction, in levels of voluntary action (Abbas and Lachman, 2012). That is not to say that below the radar groups and the third sector as a whole (Rochester, 2013) are avoiding profound changes:

"I don't want to predict what the future, say in five years, will look like for voluntary never mind community groups. There may be a leaner but more efficient and effective sector, a more entrepreneurial and business like sector – or just a leaner one. What we will see played out in some form is a profound change in the relationships between people, government and the sector." (Development agency representative)

One of those profound changes in the sector as a whole is the fragmentation of its strategic unity (Alcock, 2010) – if that ever really existed.

Key learning

- Various claims have been made for small scale community groups. They possess unique levels of local knowledge, are flexible and responsive in ways that more formal organisations (and statutory agencies) cannot be, and have the capacity to surface and respond to unmet needs.
- However, research into how community groups form, develop and sustain themselves is limited. Policy rhetoric around 'community' may not therefore, be matched by the realities of community life and action.
- Community groups may not always be 'good' per se. Community action may not always be inclusive. It has the capacity to exclude people, marginalise already vulnerable groups and, on occasion, community action 'tops over' into oppressive actions and vigilantism.
- Community groups are diverse in their characteristics. This has led some commentators to question the idea of a distinctive community sector. Rather, there appear to be a series of sub-sectors focused on particular interests or activities (for example the arts, sports, housing etc). There are, however, a number of shared characteristics in terms of motivations, degrees of informality and accessing resources.

Reflective exercises

- Consider the statement that 'Before 2010 there was a voluntary *and* community sector. Now there is a voluntary *versus* community sector.' To what extent do you agree with this?
- Consider the argument that 'It's a really well-established committee that has well-established ways of working because the key individuals have been involved for a long time. It is very difficult to come in as a new person and challenge some of those ways of working.' Can community groups outlive their purpose and usefulness?
- Reflect on the proposition that community groups are inclusive and democratic or, alternatively, autocratic and exclusive. Why are such dichotomies not particularly useful when thinking about community groups?

References

Abbas, M.-S. and Lachman, R. (2012) *The Big Society: The Big Divide*, Bradford: JUST West Yorkshire.

Alcock P. (2010) *A strategic unity: Defining the third sector*, Briefing Paper 24, Birmingham: Third Sector Research Centre.

Billis, D. (2010) *Hybrid organizations and the third sector: Challenges for practice, theory and policy*, Basingstoke: Palgrave Macmillan.

Charity Commission (2007) *Stand and deliver: The future for charities providing public services*, London: Charity Commission.

Conn, E. (2011) *Community engagement and the social eco-system dance*, Birmingham: Third Sector Research Centre.

Cooper, C. (2008) *Community, conflict and the state: Rethinking notions of 'safety', 'cohesion' and 'wellbeing'*, Basingstoke: Palgrave Macmillan.

Corry, O. (2011) 'Defining and theorising the third sector', in R. Taylor (ed) *Third sector research*, New York, NY: Springer.

Coutu, S. (2014) *The scale-up report on economic growth*, London: techUK.

Dominelli, L. (2006) *Women and community action*, Bristol: Policy Press.

Edwards, M. (2008) *Why business won't save the world*, London: Demos.

Furbey, R., Dinham, A., Farnell, R., Finneron, D. and Wilkinson, G. with Howarth, C., Hussain, D. and Palmer, S. (2006) *Faith as social capital: Connecting or dividing?*, Bristol and York: Policy Press and Joseph Rowntree Foundation.

Gilchrist, A. (2016) *Blending, braiding and balancing: Combining formal and informal modes for social action*, Birmingham: Third Centre Research Centre.

Henderson, P. and Kaur, R. (eds) (1999) *Rural racism in the UK: Examples of community-based responses*, London: Community Development Foundation.

Ishkanian, A. and Szreter, S. (2012) *The Big Society debate: A new agenda for social welfare?*, Cheltenham: Edward Elgar.

Kendall, J. and Knapp, M. (1996) *The voluntary sector in the UK*, Manchester: Manchester University Press.

Kenny, S., Taylor, M., Onyx, J. and Mayo, M. (2015) *Challenging the third sector: Global perspectives for active citizenship*, Bristol: Policy Press.

Lupton, R. (2003) *Poverty Street: The dynamics of neighbourhood decline and renewal*, Bristol, Policy Press.

McCabe, A. (2013) 'Is the third sector so special? What's it worth?', in Third Sector Research Centre *Unity in diversity: What is the future of the third secto*r?, Birmingham: Third Sector Research Centre.

McCabe, A. and Phillimore, J. (2012) *All change? Surviving 'below the radar': Community groups and activities in a Big Society*, Birmingham: Third Sector Research Centre.

McCabe, A., Buckingham, H. and Miller, S. with Musabyimana, M. (2016a) *Belief in social action: Exploring faith groups' responses to local needs*, Birmingham: Third Sector Research Centre.

McCabe, A., Wilson, M., Macmillan, R., Morgans, P. and Edwards, M. (2016b) *Our bigger story: The first chapter. Big Local First interim evaluation summary report*, London: Local Trust.

Meade, R. (2009) 'Classic texts: Jo Freeman. *The tyranny of structurelessness* (c. 1972)', *Community Development Journal*, vol 44, no 1, pp 123-7.

Milbourne, L. (2013) *Voluntary sector in transition: Hard times or more opportunities?*, Bristol: Policy Press.

NCIA (National Coalition for Independent Action) (2015) *Fight or fright: Voluntary services in 2015.*

A summary and discussion of the inquiry findings, London: NCIA.

Phillimore, J. and McCabe, A. (2010) *Understanding the distinctiveness of small scale third sector activity*, Birmingham: Third Sector Research Centre.

Phillimore, J. and McCabe, A, (2015) *Luck, passion, networks and skills: Recipe for action below the radar*, Birmingham, Third Sector Research Centre.

Phillimore, J., McCabe, A. and Soteri-Proctor, A. (2009) 'Under the radar? Researching unregistered and informal third sector activity', Paper presented at NCVO/VSSN conference, Warwick, 18 September.

Raco, M. (2007) *Building sustainable communities: Social policy and labour mobility in post-war Britain*, Bristol: Policy Press.

Richardson, L. (2008) *DIY community action: Neighbourhood problems and community self-help*, Bristol: Policy Press.

Rochester, C. (2013) *Rediscovering voluntary action: The beat of a different drum*, Basingstoke: Palgrave Macmillan.

Ryder, A., Cemlyn, S. and Acton, T. (2014) *Hearing the voices of Gypsy, Roma and Traveller communities: Inclusive community development*, Bristol: Policy Press.

Salamon, L. and Anheier, H. (1997) *Defining the non-profit sector: A cross-national analysis*, Manchester: Manchester University Press.

Taylor, M. (2012) 'The changing fortunes of community', *Voluntary Sector Review*, vol 3, no 1, pp 15-34.

Warren, M. (2001) *Democracy and association*, Princetown, NJ: Princetown University Press.

FOUR

Community as policy: reflections on community engagement, empowerment and social action in a changing policy context

Angus McCabe

Chapter aims

Drawing on policy and related academic literature, this chapter aims to provide an overview of:

• the changing meanings of community and the power of community in policy discourse;
• the expectations placed on communities and community groups to deliver on a range of policy agendas;
• the capacity, and willingness, of community groups to engage with government agendas.

As such it broadens the debate beyond specific responses to austerity (Chapters Five and Six) to place the idea of below the radar activity both at the centre and the periphery of policy thinking over the past decade.

Background

In a Cabinet Office press release (5 August 2010) not long after the election of the UK's coalition government, the communities secretary, Eric Pickles, announced 'Today we are turning Government upside down' by returning decision making to the local, 'nano', level. At the same time, the minister for the Cabinet Office argued that 'Big Society' was to be a radical departure from the previous government's policies in that it was 'a real cultural shift' and an end to 'big Government, just tweaking things at the centre of power'.

Beyond government, there was, after the 2010 election, recognition by academics and commentators that:

> Bottom-up and community-led activities which so often bubble along under the radar are receiving new public recognition. This is in part because we are on the threshold of political change and deep economic restraint … [but also] taps into a powerful tradition of mutualism, co-operatives and the social economy – a tradition which straddles different ideological standpoints. (Oppenheim et al, 2010, p 2)

The coalition, in the early days, presented Big Society as an opportunity to reframe the relationship between government and communities. The term 'third sector', which, under New Labour, assumed a cohesive and coherent entity, gave way to the more fluid terminology of civil society. Community engagement all but disappeared from policy discourse in favour of an apparently more dynamic 'social action'. Regeneration, as personified by the plethora of Area Based Initiatives post-1997, and criticised as a series of top-down, target-driven directives that frequently failed to empower communities (Lupson, 2003), were to be replaced by community-led, or community-driven, change: 'creating more responsible and active communities where people play a part on making society a better place' (Maude and Hurd, 2010).

While concerns were expressed about the introduction of austerity measures and associated cuts to budgets, for some, policy, under the badge of Big Society, offered a platform to transform the power and role of communities and community groups in policy formation and reshaping of the relationship between those groups, the established voluntary sector and government (Chanan and Miller, 2010; Coote, 2010a; Rowson et al, 2010).

At one level, however, it is possible to overplay 2010 as a sea change in political thinking about community. After all, in the early years of New Labour administrations, community was promoted, not as 'a problem' but as part of the solution: promoting regeneration (SEU, 2001), tackling area inequalities from the bottom up, developing community enterprise (again a theme across administrations) in areas where the market had failed (Cabinet Office, 2006; HM Government, 2011) and sustaining a communitarian vision of social justice. Later, after the 2001 riots in northern cities and, particularly, the attacks on 9/11 in

New York and 7/7 in London, community (or some communities) seemed to again (for later administrations) become part of the problem. In came the Respect agenda and Prevent, the prevention of violent extremism legislation. Regeneration programmes had, largely, 'failed' to transform the communities they had targeted, despite substantial investment (DCLG, 2010a).

Further, while the policy language changed in 2010, there were striking similarities in policy concerning community both before and after the 2010 election. Participatory budget setting remained, as did the emphasis on the role of social enterprise. The National Citizen Service bore more than a passing resemblance to youth volunteering proposals in *Building Britain's future* (HM Government, 2009). The echoes of double devolution and 'communities in control' (DCLG, 2008) in the Localism Act and the asset transfer agenda (DCLG, 2007) remained, though in an extended form in terms of the concept of community rights (McCabe, 2010). Both Labour and Conservative 2010 election manifestos emphasised the need for voluntary organisations to diversify their funding base to be less dependent on government. At the time of the 2010 election, Labour was also committed to unspecified budget reductions.

Underlying these apparent continuities, however, there was a subtle, but important, change in the use of the very term community in political and practice discourses. The idea of community empowerment was replaced, certainly in the academic literature, by the concept of co-production as a collective, rather than individualised, mode of operating and building social capital (Bovaird et al, 2015). Similarly, there has been a shift from communities as 'change agents' to an emphasis on building community resilience (rather than the individual resilience promoted in earlier children's service literature – DeV Peters et al, 2005) to withstand (or at least adapt to) shocks, adversity and austerity (Bacon et al, 2010; Norman, 2012).

Again these shifts reflect the contested nature of 'community' (Somerville, 2011) and its changing fortune in various policy arenas which has long been recognised in academic discourse (Taylor, 2012).

From community engagement to social action?

In June 2010, the Department for Communities and Local Government (DCLG) and Third Sector Partnership Board Task and Finish Group on Deprived Neighbourhoods (2010a) produced a discussion paper and recommendations on the role of the voluntary and community sector in deprived neighbourhoods. This made explicit reference to 'below' or 'under' the radar community groups, with the following recommendations, as outlined in the accompanying executive summary (DCLG and Third Sector Partnership Board Task and Finish Group on Deprived Neighbourhoods, 2010b, p 4):

> Developing the Big Society will be enhanced by:

> 4) Development work on 'below the radar organisations' which ensures greater visibility, connection and working with civil society organisations traditionally missed by local partnerships and programmes.

> 5) A re-appraisal of existing VCS (Voluntary and Community Sector) policy to ensure greater relevance and inclusion of largely unfunded groups including wider civil society organisations.

These papers go on to argue for the 'transformative role' of the voluntary and community sector in deprived neighbourhoods, which 'is virtually without limit' (DCLG and Third Sector Partnership Board Task and Finish Group on Deprived Neighbourhoods, 2010b, p 6). Such an interpretation of the role of the sector was, as noted, for some, a welcome recognition of the importance of small, community-based, groups and activities, which, in the words of the Community Sector Coalition (undated), had been unseen, unequal, untapped. However, while the adoption of the term 'below the radar' by government (and in earlier Office of the Third Sector publications: OTS, 2008) suggests a co-option to achieve policy objectives, the term has subsequently disappeared from policy documents and agendas.

While Big Society, as a policy 'strapline' was short lived, some of the core principles remained in the 2011 Localism Act. For the first time, the concept of community rights was enshrined in legislation: the rights to challenge, manage and buy existing services or assets. Again, this was broadly welcomed in parts of the sector (for example, by national community sector organisations such as Community Matters and Locality) albeit with rather muted technical criticisms that the timescales involved in exercising these rights were not feasible for smaller organisations, particularly in deprived neighbourhoods, in the face of potential private sector competition (Smith, 2013).

The early years of the coalition government, then, represented a high-water mark in terms of political rhetoric around the concept of community and the role of community groups. Yet such rhetoric begged, at least, three questions:

- What was meant by 'social action' in recent political discourse?
- Did community groups have the capacity, or willingness, to engage in a 'transformative' role?
- What have been the experiences of community groups themselves in relation to policy shifts over time?

First, when the term social action is used, what does it actually mean? Its roots, in the literature, lie in the radical traditions of Freire (1970) and Alinsky (1971): citizens taking direct action to challenge injustice or hold the powerful to account. Indeed, one of the first moves of the coalition government was to fund the Locality-managed Community Organisers programme – with its roots in the American Industrial Areas Foundation and War on Poverty – as a more radical alternative to, more consensual, UK-based models of community development (Craig et al, 2011).

As early as 2011, however, it became apparent that social action meant volunteering rather than anything more direct or radical. The Tottenham disturbances occurred following a peaceful demonstration about the shooting dead by the police of Mark Duggan, a young black man, on 7 August 2011. While the disturbances were roundly condemned, the post-riot community clean-ups were praised as an example of what voluntary effort, social action, could achieve (Dillon and Fanning, 2013). Alinsky, as Taylor (2011) has pointed out, would probably be 'spinning in his grave' at the co-option of social action by a political establishment.

Yet it is possible to overemphasise the changing terminology between New Labour administrations and the coalition. As Mayo and colleagues (2013) noted, the former's investment in active citizenship and learning for democratic participation (Active Learning for Active Citizenship) was relatively short-lived and replaced by the Together We Can programme with its emphasis on more traditional models of volunteering.

Second, do community groups have the capacity, or willingness, to engage in 'transformation' on government terms? The early agendas of the coalition government – first in the Big Society debate (Ishkanian and Szreter, 2012) and subsequently in the implementation of the 2011 Localism Act – had an implicit assumption that voluntary action is an infinite resource. Yet, in terms of levels of participation, there was a 'glass half empty, glass half full' debate, depending on different perspectives. For example, from one viewpoint, 'Half the public do not actually want to be involved in decision-making in their local area. Even more – 55% – do not wish to be involved in decision-making in the country as a whole' (Ministry of Justice and Hansard Society, 2009, p 36). Indeed, the Conservative Party manifesto *Big Society not Big Government* (2010), while aspiring to increase community action, notes that 'volunteering levels have remained static since 2001 and only 3% of the population participate in civic society'.

In contrast, the Ipsos MORI (2009) survey of third sector organisations found that voluntary and community organisations did want to engage in the delivery of public services and that the key determinant in positive relationships between the sector and local/central government was the extent to which they could influence both local and national policy decisions. A willingness to engage and influence is, however, very different from the capacity to take on the management of services previously provided by the state.

There has been substantial debate about the perceived decline in civil society or social capital (Putnam, 2000). Yet, in its 2010 survey of volunteering, the Department for Communities and Local Government (DCLG, 2010b) found that:

> In 2008-09, 26 per cent of people in England participated in formal volunteering at least once a month. This represents a fall since 2005 when 29 per cent of people participated, although there was no statistically significant change relative to 2007-08 (27%). Thirty-five per cent of people in England participated in informal volunteering at least once a month, a fall since 2005 when the figure was 37 per cent. Again, there was no change relative to 2007-08 (35%).

If these statistics are interpreted negatively (that is, 79% of the population do not volunteer), there is a view that civil society is, if not in crisis, certainly static or in gradual decline. However, the data only applies to 'formal volunteering' rather than the wealth of informal community activities that take place below the radar and in black and minority ethnic communities (Phillimore et al, 2010). Further, these figures look particularly robust when compared with data on public participation in the democratic process:

> Eleven per cent of adults can be classified as 'political activists', according to the [National Audit Office] definition, i.e. in the last two or three years they have

done at least three political activities from a list of eight....
Over half the public (51%) report not having done any of
these activities, an increase of three points since last year.
Compared to 37% who had made charitable donations.
(Ministry of Justice and Hansard Society, 2009, p 3)

In short, former Prime Minister David Cameron has said that the
Conservative Party manifesto was 'an invitation to join the government
of Britain'.[1] The current data on volunteering activity leads us to
question whether there are enough people willing to do so. As Mohan
(2015) argues, however, successive governments do not intervene to
promote voluntary action, so rates of volunteering have, historically,
remained consistent over time and exist without direct government
interventions.

Finally, there are concerns about how community groups have
experienced both policy shifts in expectations around their role and
the ways that ongoing austerity measures shape opportunity and
experiences.

From Big Society, through localism, to policy neglect

The previous chapter explored how below the radar community groups
and activities were affected by austerity measures and their strategies for
survival. But has their role in, and response to, policy implementation
changed since that, high, albeit rhetorical, water mark of Big Society
and localism?

What emerges is a 'double retreat' from policy that emphasises
the transformative power of community groups in recent years and,
particularly, since the 2015 election. On the one hand that retreat has
been by government. The government strategy for building a stronger
civil society (HM Government, 2010b) makes explicit reference to
voluntary and community groups, as does the Office of the Third
Sector (OTS, 2010). By 2011, the strategy for social investment (HM
Government, 2011) talks almost exclusively about social enterprise.
Indeed, Alcock (2010) notes that government pronouncements exclude
community or community organisations, a trend that has continued
into the Conservative administration. Rather, ministers talk about
voluntary organisations and social enterprises. For example, interviewed
in *Third Sector* magazine (January 2015), Rob Wilson, the minister
for civil society stated that: 'We need to find a much more active and
responsive system ... we have to help build much more capacity in the

[voluntary] sector to be able to deliver what Government is going to need in the future.'

Gone is the weight of expectation (HM Government, 2010b) that community groups can deliver not only 'more for less' but also:

- the restoration of faith in political systems;
- more cohesive communities; and
- greater equality and 'fairness'.

This decline in apparent policy interest within government coincided with a heated and prolonged debate within the voluntary sector about its role and core values. For some, the concept of distinctive sectoral values became subsumed into presenting the sector in terms of purely economic terms: cost-benefit analysis, social return on investment and the savings that government can generate though contracting with voluntary organisations (TSRC, 2013). For others, at least part of the sector (see also Chapter Five for an Irish perspective on this debate) 'sold out' post-2010:

> We see large national charities continue to develop as private sector look-a-like [sub] contractors driven to increase their market share in a privatised Welfare State. Many middle sized local voluntary services will decline and vanish, with the loss of expertise and accumulated practice experience, or revert to their historical roots of small volunteer-based community groups, operating outside market regimes. (NCIA, 2015, p 16)

In this scenario, 'alternatives to the market and radical action will mostly be found in informal groups and networks operating on the basis of mutual aid, reciprocity, activism and conviviality' (NCIA, 2015, p 16).

Much of that heated debate has been within the sector rather than located within a wider, more reflective, discussion on civil society, generating heat rather than light. Further, questions may be raised around NCIA's vision of radical action being located in informal, below the radar, groups, as research by the Third Sector Research Centre (TSRC) in this area suggests there has been a retreat by community groups themselves from 'taking on the big issues'.

The hopes that early austerity measures would be a passing phase have faded to a point of disillusion. The anticipated contribution to democratic renewal also begs the question of whether citizens and communities have sufficient trust in traditional political systems to engage in those formal democratic processes. Indeed much of the political emphasis in the 'trust debate' has been horizontal and related to cohesion and trust within and between communities. Less attention has been paid in formal policy, debates and in the academic literature on the voluntary sector (Cooper, 2008; Kenny et al, 2015) to parallel issues of 'vertical' trust – between citizens, their government and elected members. This raises a further question about the nature of democracy that communities can, or are willing to, engage with and whether, when representative or deliberative democracy is perceived to fail to meet needs, direct action and a more participatory democracy may take on a new legitimacy.

Taking on 'the big issues': power and community groups in austere times

Linked to a decreasing policy interest in community groups and communities are, quite specific, issues on voice and influence (addressed further in Chapter Eleven).

Under New Labour, the community 'sector' had a seat at the policy table through Departmental Strategic Partnership arrangements. While it is difficult to attribute influential outcomes to this period in terms of policy and legislation, community remained, at least, on the agenda. Strategic Partnerships have now gone, as have the regional government structures in which community groups were represented in some way. Regional Development Agencies and Government Offices for the Regions were early casualties of austerity measures and have been replaced by largely private sector driven Local Economic Partnerships, which have far less interest in community action. Further, those national bodies 'representing' community sector interests have all but disappeared – with the closures of the Community Development Exchange (2102) and the Urban Forum (2014) through to the loss of the Community Development Foundation and Community Matters in 2016.

The ending of these national infrastructure and support programmes and organisations is, however, a largely mechanistic issue of governance. Perhaps more profound forces are at play around questions of whether citizens and communities want to join the government, or at least the management of current state services, or whether they are best served by taking action outwith government. These concerns relate directly to the growing literature on the co-production of public services (Bovaird et al, 2015). Academics cite long-established models of co-production between citizens and public services such as volunteer firefighters and the relationship between the ambulance service and rural community first responders. However, co-production implies equity in the relationship between 'the producers'.

Not only is there limited empirical evidence on the cost-effectiveness or efficacy of co-production (Bovaird et al, 2015), but where there are examples of communities taking on the delivery of previously public services (for example, play and youth work) they have done so as a measure of last resort, often as a response to pressures from within their own community, and without support, financial or otherwise, from statutory agencies (McCabe et al, 2016). Indeed, some have begun to argue that, rather than being transformative, co-production cannot be a panacea or solution to the challenges facing local authorities (Durose et al, 2013).

Government (both national and local) has actually been successful in galvanising community action, generally when it has angered people. In the past decade, examples have included the campaigns against the fox-hunting ban and the high speed rail link (HS2) between Birmingham and London, the anti-Iraq war demonstrations, anti-globalisation actions at the G8 and G20 Summits and most recently, anti-fracking campaigns and communities lobbying local and central government on the Syrian refugee crisis. Research at the TSRC shows how anger is one of the key motivators for driving communities to take action (Phillimore and McCabe, 2015). Incidents have, so far, been related to isolated, single-cause, campaigns rather than constituting the 'mass civic action' that Lord Wei referred to in a speech to the Institute for Government (6 July 2010).

At the local level there continues to be numerous examples of communities taking action on environmental issues and again, anger is a key motivator. Yet this is often an under-recognised aspect of community motivations to participate. Systems for community engagement over the past decade have stressed the value of 'participation' or perhaps more accurately 'consultation', but underplayed both the creative and potentially destructive aspects of these strategies in terms of generating tensions between the state and communities and, indeed, between communities. Rather, emphasis has been placed on models of consensus building that could be alternatively interpreted as mechanisms for conflict avoidance.

In terms of understanding community participation either in the double devolution of New Labour or the coalition's Big Society, there are two further political issues that bear some consideration.

First, there is, and has been, a lack of systematic analysis of power relationships between communities, the state and the corporate sector. This may seem a strange statement, given that the themes of trust in politics and power run through *Building Britain's future* (HM Government, 2009) to statements on Big Society. David Cameron, for example, in a speech on 'fixing broken politics' on 26 May 2010, has argued that citizens and communities:

> 'See a world that is built to benefit powerful elites, and they feel a terrible but impotent anger. So we rage at our political system because we feel it is self-serving, not serving us. Pounded by forces outside their control, people feel increasingly powerless ... deprived of opportunities to shape the world around them, and at the mercy of powerful elites that preside over them.'

Then, there are statements such as: 'Only when people are given more power ... can we achieve fairness and opportunity for all' (Cabinet Office, 2010). Yet, at the same time, equalities have slipped off the government's agenda (Jackson and Clark, 2012; Silver, 2012), with growing inequalities and disillusionment with 'powerful elites' continuing to grow (Henderson and Vercseg, 2010; Sayer, 2015).

The emphasis, then, is on devolving power to the neighbourhood or 'nano-level'. Yet as David Cameron's speech implies, power, real power, is rarely given away but has to be seized (Gramsci, 1929). Setting aside this ideological argument, the reality is that while communities can effect change, there are structural and global factors (from mass unemployment to the power of multinational corporations and global warming) that cannot be easily solved at a nation-state level, let alone in neighbourhood specific Area Based Initiatives (Lupson, 2003) or at a 'nano' community level (Emejulu, 2015).

The idea of power at the neighbourhood or nano-level raises questions about the role of the state itself. The notion implies that, by devolving power to communities and creating a 'small state', vertical trust between formal politics and citizens will somehow be restored. However, this assumption avoids, or perhaps does not fully address, the question of what the role of the state within, or in relationship to, civil society is, can or should be – and even less attention has been paid to the role of the private sector. Freedom House (2005) expressed concern that 'small states' are often actually failing states lacking the power to maintain law and order.

Then there are the arguments presented by Wilkinson and Pickett (2009) that governments have a central role in ensuring checks and balances within economic and social systems that reduce inequality and promote healthier, more prosperous yet equal societies. Further, writing in *The Guardian*, Anne Coote, Head of Social Policy at the New Economics Foundation, warned:

> We do need a state that is democratically controlled, and that enables everyone to play a part and acts as an effective mediator and protector of our shared interests. Democratic government is the only effective vehicle for ensuring that resources are fairly distributed, both across the population and between individuals and groups at local levels. (Coote, 2010b)

Beyond a debate on the role of governments in civil society, there is, and has been, an underlying assumption (which also underpinned much of New Labour's policies) that all community engagement, all social action is good. Community groups can be 'autonomous, empowered and dynamic' but may also be (seen from a different perspective) 'dissenting, resistant, dysfunctional and destructive'[2] or indeed oppressive, as, for example, can be seen by the co-option of community development by the Far Right.

The lack of acknowledgement of anger as a motivator for social action and the lack of a systemic analysis of power and the role of the state in civil society present real challenges to the idea of devolving power to communities. Yet there may be other, much more personal, barriers to making the aspirations of Big Society and localism a reality.

While there is a body of literature on what motivates formal volunteering (Davis Smith, 1998; Locke, 2008) the drivers for community engagement are not well understood at a policy level – nor is 'enough known about the skills and support citizens need [to be active]. This is particularly true for hard to reach groups which are currently least likely to be engaged' (Rogers and Robinson, 2004, p 7).

A sense of civic duty may be one factor in voluntary action. However, being active in a community is primarily social. Even in campaigning groups there is a strong driver to meet people, feel connected and have fun (Phillimore et al, 2010). This is not to minimise the value of community-based social activity. It is something wider and deeper than 'volunteering as serious leisure' (Rochester et al, 2009, p 13) and the organisation of sporting activities. It is about the basic social need of humans to interact. Clubs, societies, village fêtes and so on all make significant contributions to social cohesion as well as to combating isolation and promoting health and mental wellbeing. These are all government agendas (both now and in the recent past) but such outcomes are not why such groups exist; rather they are a by-product of their existence. Groups often are there to meet human needs (for associational life, or even for basic survival) not deliver on policy agendas. The lack of focus on explicit government goals can be seen either as a weakness in community-based activity or as a celebration of the independence of civil society and its active, or passive, resistance to being co-opted into delivering government agendas.

Conclusion

The Carnegie UK Trust Commission of Enquiry into the Future of Civil Society in the UK and Ireland commented:

> Civil society activity meets fundamental human wants and needs, and provides an expression for hopes and aspirations. It reaches parts of our lives and souls that are beyond the state and business. It takes much of what we care about most in our private lives and gives it shape and structure. Helping us amplify care, compassion and hope. (Carnegie UK Trust, 2010, p 3)

Below the radar community groups, despite a decline in policy interest, despite austerity, continue to meet those 'fundamental human wants'. However, as Oppenheim and colleagues (2010, p 4) warned, 'simply rolling back the state and expecting communities to leap into the driving seat will not be the answer'. Indeed, Bacon and colleagues (2010), writing for the Young Foundation, note that governments of whatever shade have not, and are not, best equipped to understand and support wellbeing in communities, and, with a tendency towards 'discreet silos of service' (Sampson and Weaver, 2010, p 1), are ill suited to meeting community needs either holistically or flexibly. This last point may well be an argument for the devolution of power and service delivery to communities where there can be a more detailed knowledge of community needs and holistic responses to those needs (Phillimore et al, 2010).

These responses are, however, increasingly at the micro-level. The exploration in early below the radar research of alliances formed in the face of cuts (between, for example, tenants and residents groups and young people concerned with cuts to youth services) have all but disappeared. There has, in some ways, been a retreat at the community level. If poverty and inequality cannot be addressed at a macro level, social relationships and community networks may mitigate against their worst effects locally (McCabe et al, 2013) but not, fundamentally, alter inequalities.

Over the past two decades, governments' interest in community and community groups has waxed and waned; communities have, variously, been part of the solution or part of the problem. Yet, within a shifting policy landscape, three issues remain: issues that impact on community groups and activities but also have a wider resonance.

First, it seems unlikely, for all the aspirations of devolution, service modernisation and localism, that community trust in politics will be restored with the rolling back of the welfare state to a residual role where consumers with resources have more access to quality choices while services for the poor become increasingly poor. Further, if, as has been argued, voluntary action is a finite resource (Mohan, 2015), community groups may well not be in a position to take up 'discarded' public services.

Second, policies that appear to lack a systemic analysis of power, and the role of the state in relation to civil society, cannot deliver equality or fairness. The views of Henry Tam (2010, p 121), reflecting on power, inequality and equality, remain timely:

> Resistance to progressive reforms, at the local, national and global levels, will undoubtedly persist. Short-term concessions from the powerful should not be mistaken for lasting achievements. Where arbitrary power can still be exercised by the rich over the poor, bosses over workers, parents over their children, men over women, wardens over inmates, superpowers over small countries, one ethnic group over another, the weaker groups will remain at the mercy of the strong, and routinely suffer as a result of their malice or misjudgement. So long as such iniquities exist, the struggle for inclusive communities will continue.

Finally, it is apparent that the initial austerity measures of 2008 and 2010 are no longer a short, sharp shock. 'Normal' service, certainly in terms of local government, 'traditional' modes of service delivery and funding, will not be resumed (Parker, 2015). Indeed, there are those that argue that austerity measures and a policy implement have been replaced by a long-term, neoliberal, ideology of 'the new thrift', where 'protest about inequalities and injustices [are] re-stitched to a narrative of rampant greed, irresponsible consumerism and moral decay' (Jensen, 2013, p 14) and the demonisation of the poor and marginalised (Jones, 2011).

What is being played out here is a fundamental shift in the relationship between communities, community groups and the state. The end game, however, is not in sight.

Key learning

- Over the last two decades there has been an increasing political and policy focus on communities and community groups. There has been, and is, an expectation that small scale civil society actors can address issues as diverse as community cohesion, safety, resilience, health and wellbeing.
- Community groups may address some of the above policy agendas – but that is not their primary reason for existence. They may respond to growing levels of community need but often lack the capacity or resources to do so on the scale required in some neighbourhoods.
- As needs increase, some community groups have retreated from 'the big issues' of poverty, inequality and social justice to emphasising support for members/self-help. Others have attempted to take on new service delivery roles to meet those needs – a role for which they may be ill-equipped in terms of skills and knowledge.
- What is being 'played out' in small scale civil society, is a fundamental shift in the relationship between citizens, communities and the state and a growing divide between 'the have's' and the 'have–nots' both within society at large and in the third sector itself.

Reflective exercises

- Reflect on why government and policymakers' interest in communities and community groups may 'wax and wane'.
- Consider the statement that communities and community groups have 'retreated' from the big issues over the past decade (poverty, inequality and so on) to focus on social relationships and community networks at the micro-level.
- Has the relationship between the state and small community/civil society organisations changed fundamentally? What is the evidence from your experience and why might this be?

Notes

[1] Cited in *The Economist*, 22 July 2010.

[2] Unpublished report on Connected Communities Workshop, 22 June 2010, University of Birmingham.

References

Alcock, P. (2010) 'A strategic unity: defining the third sector in the UK', *Voluntary Sector Review*, vol 1, no 1, pp 5-24.

Alinsky, S. (1971) *Rules for radicals: A pragmatic primer for realistic radicals*, New York, NY: Vintage Books.

Bacon, N., Brophy, M., Mguni, N., Mulgan, G. and Shandro, A. (2010) *The state of happiness: Can public policy shape people's wellbeing and resilience?*, London: Young Foundation.

Bovaird, T., Stoker, J., Jones, T., Loeffer, E. and Pinilla Roncancio, M. (2015) 'Activating collective co-production of public services: influencing citizens to participate in complex governance mechanisms in the UK', *International Review of Administrative Sciences*, vol 82, no 1, pp 47-68.

Cabinet Office (2006) *Social enterprise action plan: Scaling new heights*, London: Cabinet Office.

Cabinet Office (2010) *Building the Big Society*, London: Cabinet Office.

Carnegie UK Trust (2010) *Making good society: Summary of the final report of the Commission of Enquiry into the Future of Civil Society in the UK and Ireland*, Dunfermline: Carnegie UK Trust.

Chanan, G. and Miller, C. (2010) *The Big Society: How it could work. A positive idea at risk from caricature*, PACES.

Community Sector Coalition (undated) *Unseen, unequal, untapped, unleashed: The potential for community action at the grass roots*, London: CSC.

Conservative Party (2010) *Big Society not Big Government: Building a Big Society*, London: Conservative Party.

Cooper, C. (2008) *Community, conflict and the state: Rethinking notions of 'safety', 'cohesion' and 'wellbeing'*, Basingstoke: Palgrave Macmillan.

Coote, A. (2010a) *Ten big questions about the Big Society*, London: New Economics Foundation.

Coote, A. (2010b) 'Cameron's 'big society' will leave the poor and powerless behind', *The Guardian*, 20 July, available at: www.theguardian.com/commentisfree/2010/jul/19/big-society-cameron-equal-opportunity

Craig, G., Mayo, M., Popple, K., Shaw, M. and Taylor, M. (2011) *The community development reader: History, themes and issues*, Bristol: Policy Press.

Davis Smith, J. (1998) *1997 National Survey of Volunteering*, London: Home Office.

DCLG (Department for Communities and Local Government) (2007) *Making assets work: The Quirk review of community management and ownership of public assets*, London: DCLG.

DCLG (2008) *Communities in control: Real people, real power*, London: DCLG.

DCLG (2010a) *The New Deal for Communities experience: A final assessment. The New Deal for Communities evaluation: Final report – Volume 7*, London: DCLG.

DCLG (2010b) *2008-09 Citizenship survey: Volunteering and charitable giving topic report*, London: DCLG.

DCLG and Third Sector Partnership Board Task and Finish Group on Deprived Neighbourhoods (2010a) *The Big Society: The role of the voluntary and community sector in deprived neighbourhoods. Discussion paper*, London: DCLG.

DCLG and Third Sector Partnership Board Task and Finish Group on Deprived Neighbourhoods (2010b) *The Big Society: The role of the voluntary and community sector in deprived neighbourhoods. Executive summary*, London: DCLG.

DeV Peters, Leadbeater, B. and McMahon, J. (2005) *Resilience in children, families and communities: Linking context to policy and practice*, New York, NY: Kluwer Academic/Plenum Publications.

Dillon, D. and Fanning, B. (2013) 'The Tottenham riots: the Big Society and the recurring neglect of community participation', *Community Development Journal*, vol 48, no 4, pp 571-86.

Durose, C., Justice, J. and Skelcher, C. (2013) *Beyond the state: Mobilising and co-producing with communities – insights for policy and practice*, Birmingham: Institute of Local Government Studies.

Emejulu, A. (2015) *Community development as micropolitics: Comparing theories, policies and politics in America and Britain*, Bristol: Policy Press.

Freedom House (2005) *Freedom in the World*, Washington, DC: Freedom House.

Freire, P. (1970) *Pedagogy of the oppressed*, London: Penguin.

Gramsci, A. (1929) (edited by G. Hoare and G. Nowell-Smith, 1971) *Selections from the prison notebooks*, London: Lawrence and Wishart.

Henderson, P. and Vercseg, I. (2010) *Community development and civil society: Making connections in the European context*, Bristol: Policy Press.

HM Government (2009) *Building Britain's future*, London: HM Government.

HM Government (2010a) *The coalition: Our programme for government*, London: HM Government.

HM Government (2010b) *Building a stronger civil society: A strategy for voluntary and community groups, charities and social enterprises*, London: HM Government.

HM Government (2011) *Growing the social investment market: A vision and strategy*, London: HM Government.

Ipsos MORI (2009) *National Survey of Third Sector Organisations*, London: Cabinet Office/Office of the Third Sector

Ishkanian, A. and Szreter, S. (2012) *The Big Society debate: A new agenda for social welfare?*, Cheltenham: Edward Elgar.

Jackson, M. and Clarke, J. (2012) *Open for all? The changing nature of equality under Big Society and localism*, Manchester: Centre for Local Economic Strategies/Voluntary Sector North West.

Jensen, T. (2013) 'Riots, restraint and the new cultural politics of wanting', *Sociological Research Online*, 18 (4) 7, pp 1-20, available at: www.socresonline.org.uk/18/4/7.html

Jones, O. (2011) *Chavs: The demonization of the working class*, London: Verso.

Kenny, S., Taylor, M., Onyx, J. and Mayo, M. (2015) *Challenging the third sector: Global prospects for active citizenship*, Bristol: Policy Press.

Locke, M. (2008) *Who gives time now? Patterns of participation in volunteering*, London: Institute for Volunteering Research.

Lupson, R. (2003) *Poverty Street: The dynamics of neighbourhood change and renewal*, Bristol: Policy Press.

Maude, F. and Hurd, N. (2010) Cited in Government Press Release, 'Government puts Big Society at heart of public sector reform', HM Government 18 May 2010, available at: www.gov.uk/government/news/government-puts-big-society-at-heart-of-public-sector-reform

Mayo, M., Mendivelso-Bendeck, Z. and Packam, C. (2013) *Community research for community development*, Basingstoke: Palgrave Macmillan.

McCabe, A. (2010) *Below the radar in a Big Society? Reflections on community engagement, empowerment and social action in a changing policy context*, Birmingham: Third Sector Research Centre.

McCabe, A., Gilchrist, A., Harris, K., Afridi, A. and Kyprianou, P. (2013) *Making the links: Poverty, ethnicity and social networks*, York: Joseph Rowntree Foundation.

McCabe, A., Wilson, M., Macmillan, R. with Morgans, P. and Edwards, M. (2016) *Our bigger story: The first chapter big local first interim evaluation summary report*, London: Local Trust.

Ministry of Justice and Hansard Society (2009) *Audit of political engagement 6*, London: Ministry of Justice/Hansard Society.

Mohan, J. (2015) *Shifting the dials? Stability, change and cohort variations in voluntary action*, Birmingham: Third Sector Research Centre.

NCIA (National Coalition for Independent Action) (2015) *Fight or fright: Voluntary services in 2015*, London: NCIA.

Norman, W. (2012) *Adapting to change: The role of community resilience*, London: Barrow Cadbury Trust/Young Foundation.

Oppenheim, C., Cox, E. and Platt, R. (2010) *Regeneration through co-operation: Creating a framework for communities to act together*, Manchester: Co-operatives UK.

OTS (Office of the Third Sector) (2008) *Draft guidance: National Survey of Third Sector Organisations 'Nnder the Radar' Pilot*, London: OTS.

OTS (2010) *Thriving third sector: Creating an environment in which charities, voluntary and community groups and social enterprises can thrive*, London: OTS.

Parker, S. (2015) *Taking back power: Putting people in charge of politics*, Bristol: Policy Press.

Phillimore, J. and McCabe, A. (2015) *Luck, passion, networks and skills: The recipe for action below the radar?*, Birmingham: Third Sector Research Centre.

Phillimore, J. and McCabe, A. with Soteri-Proctor, A. and Taylor, R. (2010) *Understanding the distinctiveness of small scale, third sector activity: The role of local knowledge and networks in shaping below the radar actions*, Birmingham: Third Sector Research Centre.

Putnam, R. (2000) *Bowling alone: The collapse and revival of American community*, New York, NY: Simon & Schuster.

Rochester, C., Paine, A. and Howlett, S. (2009) *Volunteering and society in the 21st century*, Basingstoke: Palgrave Macmillan.

Rogers, E. and Robinson, B. (2004) *The benefits of community engagement: A review of the evidence*, London: Home Office.

Rowson, J., Broome, S. and Jones, A. (2010) *Connected communities: How social networks power and sustain the Big Society*, London: RSA.

Sampson, A. and Weaver, M. (2010) 'Community anchors: securing their position', in *Rising East Essays, Vol 2, Series 1*, London: University of East London.

Sayer, A. (2015) *Why we can't afford the rich*, Bristol: Policy Press.

Silver, D. (2012) 'Open to all: does the Big Society promote equality, human rights and equal participation?', in M.-S. Abbas and R. Lachman (eds) *The Big Society: The Big Divide?*, Bradford: JUST West Yorkshire.

SEU (Social Exclusion Unit) (2001) *A new commitment to neighbourhood renewal: National strategy action plan*, London: SEU.

Smith, M. (2013) 'Asset Transfer: the path to success and pitfalls of failure' *The Guardian*, 15 April, available at: www.theguardian.com/social-enterprise-network/2013/apr/15/asset-transfer-success-failure

Somerville, P. (2011) *Understanding community: Politics, policy and practice*, Bristol: Policy Press.

Tam, H. (2010) *Against power inequalities*, London: Birkbeck Publications.

Taylor, M. (2011) 'Community organising and the Big Society: is Saul Alinsky turning in his grave?', *Voluntary Sector Review*, vol 2, no 2, pp 571-86.

Taylor, M. (2012) 'The changing fortunes of community', *Voluntary Sector Review*, vol 3, no 1, pp 15-34.

TSRC (Third Sector Research Centre) (2013) *Unity in diversity: What is the future of the third sector?*, Birmingham: Third Sector Research Centre.

Wilkinson, R. and Pickett, K. (2009) *The spirit level: Why more equal societies almost always do better*, London: Penguin.

FIVE

Lost to austerity, lost in austerity: rethinking the community sector in Ireland

Niall Crowley

Chapter aims

This chapter aims to:

• assess the impact of austerity on the community sector in Ireland and the responses of the community sector in the context of ongoing austerity;
• rethink the purpose and strategies of the community sector in the context of long-term economic crisis and austerity in Ireland;
• contribute to debate, drawing on the experience in Ireland, on the implications of austerity measures for the community sector at the international level.

Introduction

Threats to society and to the community sector

Despite narratives of turnaround and recovery, these remain times of crisis in Ireland. The threats are multiple. Levels of deprivation and poverty continue to be higher than European averages (Eurostat, 2014). Private debt and mortgage defaults have not been adequately addressed and homelessness has reached crisis proportions (Peter McVerry Trust, 2016). Growing inequality is the norm. Diminished public services cause hardship and disadvantage. Precarious work results in low pay and is no safeguard against poverty.

The community sector involves groups organised around a particular geographical area or around shared identity or interests, engaged in diverse activities, and operating independently, on a not-for-profit basis and with a public good aim. Those involved in the sector and committed to its potential are challenged to address the question of how the community sector should be responding to this continuing crisis. This, however, is also a period of crisis for the community sector itself. A further question must be addressed as to what the community sector should be doing to respond to its own crisis.

The withdrawal of funding is central to the crisis faced by the community sector. However, threats of co-option by the state, of dissent precluded by the state, and of loss of direction and role by the community sector are also at issue. The first instinct in a crisis is to survive. All energies get redirected to the task of survival. People and organisations turn in on themselves, go back to what they know best, and try to hang on until the crisis has passed. This crowds out imagination, analysis and innovation.

This situation is not unique to Ireland – see Chapter Four and, for example, NCIA (2015) and Kenny et al (2015) for UK and international comparisons. It is useful to share emerging analysis and experience across jurisdictions to enable learning and new insights. This analysis of the Irish experience is offered, from a practitioner perspective, with this objective.

About this chapter

The different crises mentioned here have the potential to undermine the community sector in Ireland. They threaten its very existence in some instances. They challenge its purpose and strategy in most instances. However, these crises also offer opportunities to the sector. They provide a stimulus for a rethinking of the community sector and its place as an actor for social change.

This chapter aims to contribute to a process of rethinking the community sector, its purpose and strategy. It explores the impact of the crises on, and key challenges resulting for, the community sector. It seeks to be analytical and grounded but is concerned with dominant trends rather than an examination of the full diversity of individual initiatives. It seeks to provoke debate rather than offer any premature finished analysis.

The chapter tells the story of the community sector in the boom times that preceded the economic and financial crisis, during the crisis, and in its current phase. It is concerned with introducing ideas for a thriving community sector that will contribute to defining and achieving an Ireland of equality and environmental sustainability.

The community sector

The community sector has been talked about and researched for decades (Powell and Geoghegan, 2004). However, it is an entity that has never been easy to define. Its diversity almost defies the label of 'sector' (Alcock, 2010). While it seems to be clear what it is, it can be hard to define its boundaries. Who is 'in', who is 'out', and why?

Organisations would be expected to have some purpose, interests or issues in common if they are to be understood as a sector. However, the community sector is made up of a diverse range of organisations. What shared purpose, interests or issues unites these organisations? What links large service provider organisations and small community development projects? What unites national network organisations engaged in a policy dialogue with powerful interests and those local organisations developing alternative and more ecologically sound ways of living? What unites identity-based groups championing an end to discrimination and inequality with area-based groups developing responses to poverty and exclusion in their communities?

If purpose unites this diversity of organisations, purpose would have to be defined in some broad form of 'doing good works' to get everyone behind it. If shared interests unite organisations, interests would have to be narrowed to funding, accessing grants and sustaining financial viability to include all of them. If common issues unite them, these would need to be narrowly understood in terms of funding sources, charity regulation, or management capacity to be inclusive. The concept of sector appears unhelpful if considered in this way.

The notion of a community sector, defined in this way, locates organisations alongside those they have little in common with, such as groups of people with disabilities promoting independent living and large organisations providing services to people with disabilities. This does not allow for any broad shared agenda for social change to be pursued as a sector. It also divides organisations from others they might have more fruitful relationships with but are in some other sector, such as migrant rights organisations working to improve the situation of migrant workers and trade unions. This limits the power base that could be developed by the sector.

The shared value base of equality of outcomes, social justice, solidarity, environmental sustainability and participative democracy offers a more useful foundation for the community sector. This understanding of a values-based community sector enables mobilisation and growth behind the banner of shared values. It lays the ground for alliance building that might secure the prioritisation and full realisation of such values in policy and practice.

There are complexities with this approach. There are organisations that clearly form part of the broadly defined community sector that have little time for such values. There needs to be mobilisation and education within the sector around these values. These values are open to interpretation. There are those who define them in such limited terms that they serve no purpose in shaping a community sector, let alone in progressing social change. There is work to be done in exploring and building common and shared meanings for these values.

Analysis and debate

Social partnership

It is necessary to explore what happened to the community sector in boom times to better understand where it now finds itself in a time of crisis. There were two significant trends for the community sector during the boom times. First, there was an expansion of service provision by the community sector on behalf of the state. Second, there was an evolution of a policy role for the community sector to be pursued within a partnership with the state.

The former trend was a product of plentiful funding from a state with additional resources and from philanthropic organisations spending down large resources over a short period of time. The number of organisations in the sector multiplied and expanded their service provision capacities with little thought for long-term implications. At its peak, in 2008, the estimated level of employment in the sector was 53,098 full-time equivalents; the value of the voluntary and community sector to the economy was €6.5 billion, or between 3.52% of gross domestic product and 3.97% of gross national product, the annual level of state funding for the sector was in the order of €1.89 billion and there were about 6,100 voluntary and community 'charitable' organisations (Harvey, 2012).

The trend of policy partnership involved the eventual entry of the community sector into a social partnership. Social partnership was the process developed between the Irish government, the business sector, the farming sector and the trade unions for regular wage negotiations that included significant focus on a social wage (Larragy, 2014). The community sector entered the process in 1996. It is of interest that it was the community sector that was invited rather than the more formal and larger voluntary organisations. Government sought legitimation for the social partnership process with this invitation.

Social partnership provided an opportunity to extend the range of tools deployed by community organisations in seeking social change. Research found that noteworthy gains were made, even if the scope of the gains was limited. These included a broadening of the national agreements resulting from the negotiations and a deepening of the coupling of economic and social issues. This has to be seen, however, in the context of a government 'flush' with revenue (Larragy, 2014).

Larragy places his analysis within an understanding of asymmetric engagement that 'describes the patterns of engagement between small mobile organisations and the political establishment and state bureaucracy' (Larragy, 2014, p 219). Community organisations were too small for symmetric engagement or bargaining. Their power lay in a policy entrepreneurship based on the knowledge they held, the innovation they offered, and their tactical flexibility (Larragy, 2014).

The campaigning work of the organisations made a contribution to changing public perspectives on issues, which in turn enabled headway to be made in social partnership. A key gain, for example, in the first national agreements in which the community sector participated, was an agreement to implement the Commission on Social Welfare (1983-86) recommendations on social welfare payment levels. The Irish National Organisation of the Unemployed, one of the participating groups, had been campaigning on this issue for years. The influence of community organisations in social partnership was found to fluctuate with shifts in wider societal perspectives on the issues involved (Larragy, 2014).

The community sector in crisis

The main focus for research on what is happening to the community sector in times of economic and financial crisis has been on funding cutbacks. During the period 2008-12, government spending overall fell by 2.82%, while funding for the community and voluntary sector fell by over 35% in this period (Harvey, 2012). The largest decreases were in the health-related funding for voluntary services (a drop of between 3.4% and 6.7% for different services), voluntary social housing (−54%), support for national voluntary and community organisations (−48%), the local community development programme (−35%), drugs initiatives (−29%) and family support projects (−17%) (Harvey, 2012). There is little evidence of change in this scenario since this research was conducted, despite a 'recovery' situation being identified for the national exchequer.

The impact of these cutbacks included a reduction in staff, estimated at 11,150 jobs lost by 2013. A drop to 36,638 full-time equivalent jobs was estimated for 2015 (The Wheel, 2014). The cutbacks have led to the closure of organisations or reductions in the services offered. They have led to increased pressure on remaining staff to meet needs, a deterioration in working conditions and damage to staff motivation (Harvey, 2012). This research was commissioned by the trade union sector and not the community sector. This reflects valuable solidarity across sectors and limited attempts within the community sector to take a sectoral perspective in reflecting on its situation beyond that as individual organisations.

The ideological shift that underpinned these cutbacks is captured in an analysis by Crowley (2010) of the experience of the Equality Authority, the statutory equality body in Ireland, whose budget was cut by 43% in 2008. This ideological shift, while analysed in relation to a statutory body, has immediate relevance to the experience of the community sector.

Three factors were identified as being at play. First, at a political level, the enthusiasm for equality had waned. Second, there was something counter-cultural about the work of the Equality Authority in Celtic Tiger Ireland. It challenged the 'anything is possible and everything is allowed' ethos of the boom times and became an awkward witness to inequality and discrimination. The third and decisive factor was the resistance of the statutory sector, which did not accept the Equality Authority's independence and saw its activities as a threat. In 2007, 67% of the case files of the Equality Authority under the Equal Status Acts related to allegations of discrimination by public sector services (Crowley, 2010).

Future perspectives

There has been limited academic exploration of future perspectives for the community sector. The need for movement building has been highlighted along with the need for civil society to act as a transformative agent in demanding and securing a 'new republic' based on values of equality, inclusion, democracy and ecological sustainability. This is based on an understanding that without significant demand from below, this level of ambition for change is unlikely from above (Kirby and Murphy, 2011).

A range of barriers to movement building are identified, including the following: a substantive proportion of Irish people do not as yet share the values espoused; social partnership has weakened the capacity of trade unions to mobilise; parties on the Left, generally, do not have a good record of cooperation with civil society; civil society is characterised by intense cross-sectoral fragmentation; there are difficulties in developing practical pragmatic reformist agendas that move beyond sectoral defensive campaigning and build a cross-sectoral movement; and there is a lack of clarity as to who will provide leadership to develop more powerful horizontal alliances and common agendas (Kirby and Murphy, 2011).

Sectoral fragmentation within civil society is a barrier to movement building that has intensified through the crisis. It is rooted in the different traditions, ways of working and language of different sectors. It is intensified by competition between sectors for status and space within public and political discourse (NCIA, 2015). It has become hostile where political dispositions, values and analyses dominant within different sectors clash, particularly within a public debate that increasingly presents issues in terms of conflicting parties.

Public debate

Public debate on the community sector is limited. Internal debate on these issues is equally inadequate. A number of organisations, such as Claiming Our Future, have offered space for the sector and the wider civil society to deliberate on these issues. However, this has been hard to sustain. *Village* magazine has provided a published format for the exchange of ideas. A number of strands emerge from the debates in the magazine.

Local government reform and the impact of the Local Government Reform Bill 2013 have been examined for their impact on the community sector. The Bill established Local Community Development Committees under the auspices of the local authorities with a mandate to achieve alignment between local development and community development and the work of local authorities. The committees are responsible for the coordination, governance, oversight and planning of all publicly funded community development work. Irwin concluded that 'the changes proposed will give ultimate control over local and community development to local authorities' (Irwin, 2014, p 40).

The evolving nature of philanthropy and its impact on the community sector has also been tracked. Crowley examined proposals to further grow philanthropic giving. He noted the following:

> Civil society is sadly malleable. It feels it has to shape up to the funding available and, only then, look to what really needs doing in our society. The philanthropy of tax exiles will not, self-evidently, fund many campaigns for tax justice. The philanthropy of big business will not fund actions to develop a de-growth agenda. The philanthropy of the wealthy will not enable a more equal society. (Crowley, 2013, p 54)

Further, Connolly identified that 'the trend towards privatisation, whether through outsourcing, procurement, public tendering or other means, has intensified' (Connolly, 2014, p 54). He reported on the privatisation of the JobPath employment service and the decisions to put local development programmes and the local employment services to public tender. He concluded that these decisions 'fundamentally alter the operating environment' for all service delivery through the voluntary and community sector (Connolly, 2014, p 54). Privatisation shifts the value base of services and introduces profit as a driving force in service design and delivery. Public tendering intensifies competition within the community sector, and creates an internal hierarchy where the capacity of an organisation to tender effectively is more important than its capacity to advance social change.

The potential of community arts to combat disadvantage and revitalise work on equality and human rights issues is another strand of this debate. Carroll reported:

> Many artists and cultural activists are at the forefront of creative work nested in initiatives seeking equality and human rights. But they are not seen or heard. Community art is a field of practice that must be given a new status in policy and funding – at least if arts and culture are to be for all. (Carroll, 2015, p 56)

The community sector prior to austerity

Roots of the community sector

The story of the community sector in Ireland in the 1980s was purposefully gathered in a seminar report (Combat Poverty Agency, 1990). This is a useful reminder that the roots of today's community sector lie in local actions to mobilise people who experience inequality and poverty. Community organisations provided the space within which individual hardships could become collective interests. They offered a platform from which to articulate these collective interests and the means to agitate for an effective response to these interests.

The agendas for these local organisations were developed with the active participation of people experiencing inequality and poverty. The skills in these organisations were those of politicising, mobilising and campaigning. Organisations were directly accountable to those who experienced poverty and inequality.

State funding was important for the ongoing survival, growth and impact of these organisations. This always carried the risk of co-option by the state and the displacement of unpaid activism. However, organisations were adept at combining the meeting of funding requirements with the creation of space for advocacy work and dissent.

Organisational networks emerged at the national level and a national community sector voice was developed. Its power lay in its ability to articulate accurately the concerns of local disadvantaged communities, to mobilise local organisations behind national campaign, and to convince policymakers and the general population of the importance of these concerns. Their agendas were formed from the engagement of disadvantaged communities in local organisations that made up the national networks.

The shift to partnership with the state

The community sector evolved as a policy-focused lobby. It sought to foster a closer relationship with decision makers at national level and, ultimately, to bring its agendas into social partnership. Opportunities for participation and partnership with the state opened up at local level too. The early experiences of partnership between the community sector and the state were documented (CWC, 1992). These experiences ranged from local-level partnerships specifically established to address local development in disadvantaged communities to national-level partnership in planning for, and monitoring the use of, European Union Structural Funds.

This ultimately led to the inclusion of the community sector as a pillar within national social partnership arrangements from 1996. A division emerged between those organisations engaged in social partnership and those outside the partnership process. Some inside social partnership saw those outside as irrelevant. Some outside social partnership saw those inside as compromised. The lobbyists were distanced from the campaigners, which diminished both.

Participation within social partnership was weaker for not being linked to protest and agitation from outside. Protest and agitation were easily marginalised where social partnership had no means of communication and negotiation with the decision makers. This failure meant the sector in effect voluntarily and unnecessarily traded in one source of its power, public mobilization, in demanding change. It also weakened its negotiating position as its work on influencing public perspectives diminished.

In becoming a policy lobby, the skills base within the sector changed. Policy analysis and policy development skills dominated to the exclusion of the earlier skills of politicising, mobilising and campaigning. The agenda was eventually set not out of the experience of local action but out of the knowledge of policy experts. Accountability to those experiencing poverty and inequality became more tenuous as the technical level of the positions developed became increasingly complex. Further problems emerged as participation ultimately became the goal at national and local level rather than a means to an end.

The shift to service provider

The boom time meant the state had funds to dispense and the community sector secured significant access to these funds, principally to provide services within disadvantaged communities at the local level. Previously the sector had used state funds not only to provide the service funded but also as a subsidy to the activities of politicisation, mobilisation and agitation. The boom times changed this because of the scale of the funds on offer and closer state scrutiny of their use.

While at the national level the community sector transformed itself into a policy lobby, at the local level it developed into a service provider. Local organisations took on the interests of a service provider and began to network around these interests locally and nationally. The sector developed a skills base as an employer, a service provider and a manager to the exclusion of its earlier skills of campaigning.

This was accompanied by a significant bureaucratic workload for the organisations involved. Regular reports to funders had to be provided. Financial controls had to be implemented and reported on. Impact had to be demonstrated and measured. This diminished the space available for these organisations to take on other roles, such as advocacy, beyond that of service provider. In some instances, roles of dissent or protest were expressly excluded in contracts signed by the organisations in question (Harvey, 2013). There was also a gradual shift in accountability; organisations were no longer accountable to their local communities, but to their funders, the state.

Changing roles and priorities meant that the links of communication and solidarity between organisations at the national and local levels were broken. National policy expertise was not informed by local action and experience. Local service provision was not supported in national policy development work.

Philanthropy

Two large philanthropic funds (Atlantic Philanthropies Ireland and One Foundation Ireland) decided to spend down their resources over the lifetime of the philanthropist involved during the boom times. This was one particular and unwelcome approach evident within philanthropy. It led to a surge of funding into the community sector, particularly at national level. Activity expanded in terms of quality of campaigning work, the range of issues being pursued and the number of organisations involved. However, the issue of sustainability loomed large, with a funding 'cliff' in prospect once the spend-down was completed. Both funds have now been spent down and organisations have closed, merged, cut back their activities, and invested heavily in the search for new resources.

The philanthropic funding sources came out of the business sector. They demanded an intensive and particular accountability from funded organisations, and required them to take on business methodologies in planning, managing finances, measuring progress and reporting. These demands distracted organisations from their principal purpose. This had an impact on the nature and culture of the organisations themselves. Key personnel moved from being activists to becoming managers and the culture of their organisations changed with them.

The community sector in austerity

Funding crisis

Since the onset of the economic crisis there has been a constant whittling away of the resources available to the community sector (Harvey, 2012). At best this is a reflection of the limited status of the sector. Politicians see it as expendable and a source of quick and easy savings. At worst it is a reflection of political hostility to the sector.

At the same time organisations in the sector are faced with increasing demands on their services. Poverty and inequality are deepening. Public services are being diminished. Organisations in the sector are challenged to do much more with much less (Aiken 2014). They end up doing things that they would normally be critical of: making staff redundant; reducing services to people in increasing need; and serving as a transmission line for delivering austerity at the local community level.

The voice of most community sector organisations has grown cautious. Funding relationships must be sustained. The state, as the core funder for most of the sector, is no longer challenged in any substantial manner. Protest, with some honourable exceptions, remains largely unvoiced in the public arena and dissent is diminished (Harvey, 2013).

This situation has intensified competition within the sector for diminished funding. There is greater competition for status, media space, access to decision makers and even 'market share' in disadvantaged communities. The sector, already fragmented by its diversity, is further divided by this competition.

Status crisis

Alongside this funding crisis, the community sector has experienced a loss of status and influence in its engagement with the state. There has been a political insistence that there is no alternative to austerity. Even in the current period of supposed 'recovery', the insistence that there is no alternative to a model of development based on market-led dominance and inadequate public service funding remains. This shapes a political unresponsiveness to any challenge or demand for alternatives.

This leaves the community sector with a limited audience for its lobbying work, whether this policy work is confined to defending particular groups and services from austerity, or ambitiously setting out and demanding alternatives to austerity. This has been exacerbated by the dismantling of the structures for social partnership that had involved the community sector. The potential and impact of policy work have been diminished. This has further distanced disadvantaged communities from any say in decisions that affect them.

Public administration, government and many politicians are often hostile to dissent and advocacy from the community sector (Harvey, 2013). Alongside this there has been a lack of public support for equality of outcome, social justice and solidarity, environmental sustainability and participative democracy. This was found to be key in the advances made on its policy agenda by the community sector in social partnership. The community sector also becomes less and less focused on influencing public sentiment as it invests more of its resources in policy work and service provision. The absence of public demand, combined with a lack of media coverage, contributes to political disinterest in engaging with the community sector in these areas.

The failure of philanthropy

Philanthropy has, generally, failed to offer effective support to the community sector in finding a way out of crisis. It has other concerns, principally with legacy as the key philanthropic funds pursue their spend-down strategy. Legacy is about the concrete achievements and the societal changes that funds can point to as a result of their support. It involves responding to the interests of the philanthropist rather than those of the sector.

Philanthropic funding sources may became somewhat desperate in their search for this legacy. This has led them to take a more hands-on approach with the organisations they fund and the issues they support. This, in some instances, involves imposing agendas on organisations and taking places on their boards. In other instances, funding sources set up new organisations that parallel activity already being developed by community sector organisations. While this has been justified in terms of adding value, it is experienced as controlling. It also involves cuts to the funding of less malleable organisations that could have provided the foundations for a different future for the sector.

The survival agenda

Advocacy by many organisations now focuses on sustaining much-needed services in increasingly disadvantaged communities. It is important to keep the show on the road when the communities served by these organisations are in ever greater need. Organisations are, in part, trapped into an agenda of survival because of their role as service providers. However, at times, this advocacy for their own survival has been reduced to a demand to save jobs in the sector.

The agenda and voice of many in the community sector have had a limited role in focusing public attention on the crisis in society and the economy and on the quality of the government's responses to this. The agenda to contest the dismantling of public services, to challenge stifling austerity policies, to promote investment in jobs and public services and to advance alternative models of social and economic development is only articulated sporadically.

Politics is changing, the state and the role of the state are changing, popular values are changing, and yet the agenda of survival has the community sector ever more determined to stay the same. The sector has not explored how it is currently structured and the extent to which its structures still serve action for equality of outcome, social justice and environmental sustainability. It has not explored how its role could evolve so as to promote a society based on these values.

While there are some examples, few organisations in the community sector have put forward an agenda for transformation that goes beyond their specific focus and mandate (Cannon and Murphy, 2015). There has, generally, been an ineffective engagement with, and response to, questions such as: what are the alternatives to policies that transfer huge amounts of public money to international bondholders, reduce public services to balance the books and purport to create jobs through the expansion of precarious forms of work? What are the parameters of a new model of economic and social development that would make real the values held by the sector?

Furthermore, the community sector has not seen the need for, nor imagined the content of, an agenda for its own transformation. What forms of organisation could progress social change for those experiencing inequality and poverty in this new context? What types of activity could mobilise people and advancing the values-based agenda of the sector?

Moving beyond the survival agenda

There are some signs of the community sector looking beyond this survival agenda at the national level. Claiming our Future was established in 2010 to build an empowered civil society base using a cross-sectoral and deliberative approach. It is committed to values of equality, environmental sustainability, participation, accountability and solidarity. It has hosted large deliberative events to develop agendas based on these values, including those on income equality, developing an economy for society, democratic reform, and budgetary priorities. It promotes new forms of action to engage and convince the general public about the values it espouses (Murphy, 2012).

The Community Platform, originally created by some national community sector organisations to coordinate and enable a broad participation in the social partnership process, has published policy directions for a future Ireland based on its values of economic equality, social inclusion, social justice, dignity, sustainability and participation (Community Platform, 2015).

Right2Water is a largely community-based campaign opposing the introduction of a water tax. A number of trade unions, playing leadership roles within the campaign, convened two national meetings to build a broader policy agenda out of this single issue and to secure political engagement with this broader agenda. This is based on the rights to water, jobs and decent work, housing, health, debt justice, education and democratic reform, equality, sustainable environment, and national resources. Town hall meetings were held around the country to discuss this agenda, a fiscal framework on how the proposals could be implemented was published, and new types of relationships for the campaign with political parties are being explored (Right2Change, 2015). This new work is being pursued under the name to Right2Change.

At a local level, the Spectacle of Defiance and Hope is a broad alliance of community sector organisations, mainly from Dublin. In 2010 a large number of communities came together to protest and challenge the programme of cuts that was imposed on youth and community organisations and to draw attention to the broader economic injustices taking place. A powerful and creative event was organised through the streets of Dublin. The Spectacle has sustained its engagement in creative protest and in mobilising local communities throughout Dublin.

On a more thematic basis, the Values Lab was developed to provide support to the community sector and others to pursue more values-based approaches to social change. This is rooted in an analysis of the motivational power of values and of the need to engage in what is essentially a cultural battle in relation to the values that get prioritised in society and within organisations and key institutions. In particular, the Values Lab works towards a new statutory duty on the public sector to have regard to the need to eliminate discrimination, and to promote equality and protect human rights in carrying out its functions. It also encourages the prioritisation of the values of social justice, dignity, democracy, inclusion and autonomy in public sector organisations and in publicly funded policy planning (Blehein et al, 2015).

Challenges to the community sector

The nature of the crisis

As noted, the immediate crisis for the community sector is one of surviving funding cutbacks. But at a more fundamental level, it also faces a crisis of purpose and capacity. The sector has lost the decision-maker audience required for its role of policy analysis and policy development. It has lost the means necessary to adequately play a role in service provision. The skills base it needs to imagine, develop and pursue new roles is lacking.

It is also a crisis of values. Organisations have had to take on roles of business planning and management, of reducing staff levels and of rationing or closing crucial services. These roles leave little room for expressing the values of equality of outcome, social justice and solidarity, environmental sustainability and participative democracy that have characterised the work of the sector in the past.

A challenge of imagination

The community sector faces a challenge of imagination in defining a new purpose and establishing an agenda fit for that purpose. Organisations that espouse the shared values of the sector need to change from being a partner of the state or from being a servant of the state. Their primary roles now need to be oppositional to the dominant policy positions being pursued by the state at national and local levels and inspirational in influencing public opinion about alternative policies.

Organisations need to build and pursue new agendas that are broader than their immediate mandate, go beyond what they stand against and establish the alternatives they are for, and engage a wider proportion of the population. These new agendas should come from the experience and situation of people experiencing inequality and poverty. They should reach beyond these groups to build solidarity with those higher up the income scale who still experience barriers to wellbeing. They should include an understanding of the threats posed by climate change and the alternatives required to secure a planet fit for future generations. These agendas should hold some resonance for all who espouse the values of the sector if cross–sectoral alliances, with the power to achieve change, are to emerge.

A challenge of organisation

There is another challenge – one of organisation – that involves identifying and establishing the institutional structures that are required within the sector to enable it to effectively pursue its new purpose and agenda. New relationships of cooperation and collaboration need to be brokered. Fluid alliances are needed across the strict sectoral boundaries that have divided organisations that share the value base of the sector. The issues being pursued need to be framed in a manner that enables and gives effect to such alliances.

The relationship between national and local-level organisations needs to be repaired and redeveloped. Agendas at national level need to come from local experience and situations of poverty and inequality if they are to have resonance. Local action needs to give expression to values, analysis and priorities agreed at national level. In this way local opposition has the possibility of being part of something greater than the efforts of small individual organisations. Effective communication, trust building and resource sharing are required to rebuild this relationship.

This challenge of organisation must also address the excessive numbers of organisations operating within the community sector. Where there is overlap of function and of values, mergers need to be considered.

A challenge of approach

A final challenge is one of approach – to establish how and where the community sector needs to focus its efforts. A combined oppositional and inspirational purpose, a context of political unresponsiveness and a situation where values of equality of outcome, social justice and solidarity, environmental sustainability and participative democracy have only limited popular traction suggest an approach rooted in building public engagement with the values of the community sector and in stimulating new forms of public demand on the political process.

There is a need to convince people of the importance of these values in shaping society and of their potential to contribute to a resolution of the crises that confront society. Key activities would include initiatives of conscientisation and politicisation to secure broad popular traction for the values of mobilization, to articulate the political demands they give rise to, and of demonstration, to establish what these values look like in real life. Community arts initiatives would have a particular contribution to this.

The approach of civil society organisations to the recent marriage equality referendum is instructive in this regard. They campaigned on the basis of values, in particular espousing the value of equality. Their call for support was based on equality as a shared value and their strategy was based on people telling their own stories as a trigger for this value (Healy et al, 2015).

Conclusion

The community sector is struggling in a context of austerity and supposed 'recovery'. Many of its problems lie in funding regimes and in the roles it pursued in boom times. It faces an immediate crisis of funding alongside a more fundamental crisis of purpose, direction and values. It needs to imagine and develop new agendas for change, new ways of organising, and new approaches to engaging the public with its values.

Table 5.1: The community sector as an agent of social change: advantages and disadvantages

Advantages	Disadvantages
• Community sector organisations have a capacity to engage, provide platforms for, and amplify the voice of those experiencing inequality and poverty. • Community sector organisations have a capacity to engage with the general public and policymakers to raise awareness of the values of the sector. • Community sector organisations can deploy a range of tools for change and strategies to engage with decision makers.	• Community sector organisations are vulnerable to pressure from funders. • Community sector organisations are fragmented and distant from other civil society actors. • There is a lack of self-analysis among community sector organisations.

Key learning

• The community sector can be considered lost to austerity. The funding crisis it is experiencing diminishes its level of activity. Its role as a policy partner to the state has been lost, with the structures for social partnership dismantled and political unresponsiveness precluding alternatives to austerity. Its role as service provider has been compromised by funding reductions and it runs the risk of being a transmission belt for austerity into local communities.

- The community sector can be considered lost in austerity as a result of being confined largely to pursuing a survival agenda. It has failed to review its role and purpose in a context that has changed radically. The voice of the sector has been quieted and no convincing alternative to austerity has been effectively articulated by the sector.
- The community sector is being challenged to redefine its purpose in opposition to a state committed to austerity and market-led development. It faces the challenge of expanding this purpose to encompass ways of influencing public sentiment with convincing alternatives and of inspiring people with the values of the sector: equality, social justice, environmental sustainability, solidarity and participation. It needs to reorganise in a manner that links the sector both at the national level and at the local level and that pursues fluid alliances across civil society.

Reflective exercises

- Why/should the state fund dissenting voices?
- What steps need to be taken by the community sector and community organisations to better contribute to social change for equality and environmental sustainability?
- Given the diversity in terms of values, strategies and structures of community organisations in Ireland, can they be described as 'a sector'?
- How do the arguments presented in this chapter resonate with experience beyond Ireland?

References

Aiken, M. (2014) *Voluntary services and campaigning in austerity UK: Saying less and doing more*, London: NCIA.

Alcock, P. (2010) 'A strategic unity: defining the third sector in the UK', *Voluntary Sector Review*, vol 1, no 1, pp 5-24.

Blehein, T., Crowley, N., Donohue, K. and Mullen, R. (2015) *A values-based approach to incorporate an equality and human rights perspective in work with children and young people*, Dublin: Values Lab.

Cannon, B. and Murphy, M. (2015) 'Where are the pots and pans? Collective responses in Ireland to neo-liberalization, learning from Latin-America', *Irish Political Studies*, vol 30, no 1, pp 1-19.

Carroll, E. (2015) 'Reducing the art's regressiveness', *Village*, March, no 35, p 56.

Combat Poverty Agency (1990) *Community work in Ireland: Trends in the 80s, options for the 90s*, Dublin: Combat Poverty Agency.

Community Platform (2015) *The future perspective of the community platform*, Dublin: Community Platform.

Connolly, D. (2014) 'Our communities go under the hammer', *Village*, April/May, no 28, p 54.

Crowley, N. (2010) *Empty promises: Bringing the Equality Authority to heel*, Dublin: A&A Farmar.

Crowley, N. (August/September 2013) *'Corrupting Philanthropy'*, *Village,* Issue 24.

CWC (Community Workers' Cooperative) (1992) *Consensus or censorship? Community work in partnership with the state*, Dublin: CWC.

Eurostat (2014) *Living conditions in Europe*, Luxembourg: Eurostat.

Harvey, B. (2012) *Downsizing the community sector: Changes in employment and service provision in the community and voluntary sector in Ireland 2008-2012*, Dublin: Irish Congress of Trade Unions Community Sector Committee.

Harvey, B. (2013) *Funding dissent: Research into the impact of advocacy on state funding of voluntary and community organisations*, Dublin: Advocacy Initiative.

Healy, G., Sheehan, B. and Whelan, N. (2015) *Ireland says yes: The inside story of how the vote for marriage equality was won*, Dublin: Merrion Press.

Irwin, A. (2014) 'Town hall power grab', *Village*, February/March, no 27, p 40.

Kenny, S., Taylor, M., Onyx, J. and Mayo, M. (2015) *Challenging the third sector: Global prospects for active citizenship*, Bristol: Policy Press.

Kirby, P. and Murphy, M. (2011) *Towards a second republic: Irish politics after the Celtic Tiger*, London: Pluto Press.

Larragy, J. (2014) *Asymmetric engagement: The community and voluntary pillar in Irish social partnership*, Manchester: Manchester University Press.

Murphy, M. (2012) 'Participation and deliberation: a case study of Claiming Our Future', in G. Carny and C. Harris (eds) *Citizens' voices: Experiments in democratic renewal and reform*, Dublin: Political Studies Association of Ireland/Irish Centre for Social Gerontology, available at: www.psai.ie/specialist/psai-ebook-citizens-voices.pdf

NCIA (National Coalition for Independent Action) (2015) *Fight or Fright: Voluntary services in 2015*, London: NCIA.

Peter McVerry Trust (2016) *Homelessness in Ireland: Facts and figures*, Dublin: Peter McVerry Trust.

Powell, F. and Geoghegan, M. (2004) *The politics of community development: Reclaiming civil society or reinventing governance?*, Dublin: A&A Farmar.

Right2Change (2015) *Right2Change: Equality, democracy, justice*, Dublin: Right2 Change.

The Wheel (2014) *A portrait of Ireland's non-profit sector*, Dublin: The Wheel.

SIX

All change? Surviving below the radar: community groups and activities in hard times

Angus McCabe and Jenny Phillimore

Chapter aims

Whereas Chapter Four reflected on key changes in policy towards communities and community groups, this chapter, which draws on 85 interviews and six focus groups conducted in 2010, 2012 and 2015, asks the following questions:

- How have these groups responded to change over the past six years?
- What was the impact of policy shifts and, in particular, what was the effect of central and local government budget cuts below the radar?
- What are the challenges for both communities and government itself in delivering the agendas of localism, 'social action' and open public services?

Introduction

Participants in the research that informs this chapter were recruited at a number of levels, and comprise representatives from national community network organisations and from regional and local infrastructure agencies, staff in small community-based voluntary organisations, and unpaid activists in volunteer-led organisations. Care was taken to involve a wide range of groups and perspectives, those active in communities of interest as well as at a neighbourhood level, 'single-cause' groups, such as black and minority ethnic (BME) and women's organisations, and advocacy organisations as well as service providers.

Table 6.1: Summary of participating groups/organisations

Year	National community network organisations	Regional/ sub-regional network organisations	Small/ community-based voluntary organisations with paid staff	Below the radar/ volunteer-led organisations	Total
2010	4	5	12	15	36
2012	4	4	9	12	29
2015	2	2	8	8	20
Total	10	11	29	35	85

Source: Phillimore and McCabe (2010; 2015), McCabe and Phillimore (2012).

Resource constraints meant that interviews were undertaken in three regions in England – West Midlands (35), London and the South East (30) and the North West (20) – rather than offering national coverage. The relative decline in the number of organisations involved between 2010 and 2015 reflects a wider trend of groups either closing or lacking the capacity to participate (for example, because of losing paid workers and being staffed only by volunteers).

At each stage of the research, reference groups consisting of practitioners, policymakers, activists and academics reviewed the findings to reflect on their accuracy in terms of lived experience below the radar and their applicability. All those organisations and individuals involved have been anonymised to comply with ethical requirements.

Background: austerity in policy context

For all the talk of 'community engagement' over the past decade or so, in practice, it has tended to mean little more than consultation with the community. The term 'community' has tended to be adopted in an uncritical fashion and assumed to relate to a coherent set of individuals or groups who share common goals, interests or geographies. Community activists in the study who had previous experience of Area Based Initiatives reported that far too often 'engagement' has felt like a tick-box exercise, a gesture towards dialogue rather than a genuine attempt to listen and change. Engagement instead was said to feel tokenistic, masking the real aim of government, which was perceived as the imposition of its own agendas.

Since 2010, it has been possible to identify two very different debates on community and community groups. First, there was the transformational language adopted in the early stages of the coalition government. The 'Big Society' was meant to be about genuine community 'empowerment ... freedom ... and responsibility', according to former Prime Minister David Cameron in a speech on 19 July 2010. Big Society was intended to involve social action for local change rather than community development as a tool for governance and consultation (Home Office, 2011). It was about the ending of imposed 'top down diktats from Whitehall',[1] creating 'the UK's biggest mutual to which all citizens will be able to belong'[2] and fundamentally changing the relationship between communities, individual citizens and the state.

Second, the concept of a 'Big Society' (and subsequently localism) was met with a degree of scepticism, if not cynicism. The term was argued to be little more than an empty policy strapline which, like the Back to Basics campaign before it, would be short-lived (McCabe, 2010). Commentators argued it lacked substance, bore little relevance to people's lived experience, was not grounded in the realities of community and was little more than a smokescreen for public spending cuts (Chanan and Miller, 2010; Coote, 2010; Stott, 2010; Ishkanian and Szreter, 2012), with the Archbishop of Canterbury condemning the concept of Big Society as 'aspirational waffle' and an attempt to hide a 'deeply damaging withdrawal of the state from its responsibilities to the most vulnerable' (Williams, *Daily Telegraph*, 24 June 2012).

Others pointed out that the Big Society, in stressing the importance of associational life, was not a 'new' concept but bore resemblances to the social theories of Adam Smith and Alexis de Tocqueville dating from the 18th and 19th centuries (Harris, 2012).

Big Society as a policy headline has subsequently disappeared and, in hindsight, has been described as 'an English political discourse with different policy developments ... taking place within the devolved administrations in Scotland, Wales and Northern Ireland' (Alcock, 2012, p 1). It did inform subsequent coalition government agendas: hence the 2011 Localism Act, the *Open public services* White Paper and its 2012 update (HM Government, 2012). Further, in terms of expectations placed on communities, there were, in the early years of the coalition, certain philosophical continuities with previous Labour administrations, albeit from different political starting points. Community, under New Labour, was a vehicle for reconnecting people to political process as so-called 'active citizens'. Under the coalition administration, community organisers were envisaged as change agents challenging existing power structures and vested interests: 'a means of addressing economic and political decline or crisis and is based on a philosophy' and beyond any political programme, 'it rests on a bold conjecture, that lying beneath the surface of British society today is a vast amount of latent and untapped energy' (Norman, 2010, p

195). The notion of community organisers as community disruptors, using social action to effect change may be seen as "different to the interventionist state where New Labour was using community as a governance vehicle" (umbrella organisation representative).

Some of that rhetoric of fundamental change, generated at a community level, remained throughout the coalition government's term of office. Commentators spoke of a new relationship emerging between the state and citizens. At one level, this was aspirational – shaped by a belief that the state, in its current form, was no longer fit for purpose and a new relationship between an 'enabling state, active individual and linking institution' was needed (Norman, 2010, p 7). In the face of continuing austerity, for some, involving community groups more in service delivery was seen as a purely pragmatic, rather than aspirational, response in that an 'austere fiscal climate will require a transformation in the role that citizens play in shaping public services and the places in which they live' (McLean and Dellot, 2011, p 7).

Indeed, the idea of seeking increased community involvement took hold in some quarters more traditionally associated with left of centre politics. With continued austerity, the 'normal service' of a big state doing for citizens in no longer seen as tenable (Parker, 2015). Co-production became the new, at least rhetorical, orthodoxy (Bovaird et al, 2015) as 'a new paradigm [with community groups] equipped to deliver co-design and co-delivery in public services and a new relationship between citizens and the State' (Blume, 2012, p 214).

Responses to austerity 2010-16: policy rich and resource poor?

There were different responses from interview respondents to the coalition's early agenda for activating communities and community groups (see also Stott, 2010). Some welcomed the initial direction of travel. Localism, for example, was seen as offering the opportunity of a real transfer of power to communities. The *Open public services* White Paper might, they contended, in the medium to longer term, enable even small community groups to expand as policy recognised the value and importance of grassroots activity (Coote, 2010).

Such optimism has, in perhaps most cases, over the final years of the coalition government and on into the current Conservative administration, given way to a resigned pragmatism at one level, and cynicism at another. Just as the Big Society was seen as a smokescreen for cuts, so co-production "is just a mechanism for passing any responsibility, and any blame when things go wrong, on from the state to the individual, the community" (Faith leader representative). Indeed, advocates of co-production at a community level have yet to explore, in any critical depth, its potential in an environment of growing public distrust of the state and its institutions. There has been a move away from engaging in any political discourse at the level of co-production and social action to a dominant focus on the continuing cuts to government funding, their impact on the voluntary sector and the increasing role of the private sector in the delivery of public services (Rees and Mullins, 2016).

The National Council for Voluntary Organisations (Clark et al, 2012; Kane et al, 2014) has consistently estimated those cuts to the voluntary and community sector globally in 2010 to 2012 to have been £1.3 billion with at least a further £1.2 billion over 2015. These are, however, only estimates as there is a lack of refined, real time data from government, both central and local, which means that proxies and estimates have to be adopted instead (Kane and Allen, 2011).

Problems estimating the level of cuts also exist in the online mechanisms for recording the impact of cutbacks such as self-reporting (www.voluntarysectorcuts.org.uk) and through requests made under the 2000 Freedom of Information Act (www.falseeconomy.org.uk). Both provided a partial picture of the changes underway and have now fallen by the wayside. More local surveys of community-based organisations have provided a consistent picture across regions in England but are often small scale and rely on organisations' statements about cuts to services they have experienced (rather than hard financial data) and/or their views about the anticipated outcomes of any future cuts (Chapman et al, 2010; London Voluntary Service Council, 2011; Davidson and Packham, 2012). For example, South West Foundation has argued that 'small community groups are being affected in many ways by the current economic climate but much of this is invisible and unrecorded' (Crawley and Watkin, 2011, p 4). Still others suggest that the cuts have had a disproportionate effect on specific parts of the sector – for example, BME organisations and those with an advocacy role (ROTA, 2011; Stokes, 2011; Lachman and Malik, 2012). However, large-scale national research (Alcock, 2012) suggests that groups in poor communities (with a reliance on local authority or the former Area Based Initiatives funds) were most affected 'across the board', with austerity cuts exacerbating pre-existing inequalities (Slocock, 2012).

Substantially less is, therefore, known about the impact of austerity on small community groups (Hemming, 2011). Studies have instead focused on the registered and regulated voluntary sector, examining the impact on registered charities and groups with other legal statuses.

Surviving below the radar?

Given that below the radar groups are not heavily dependent on central or local grants as a form of income (arts and sports groups, and local community support groups, generate their own income or need very few external financial resources), cuts in central and local government funding may have little or no impact on their activities. However, participants interviewed in this (and related research exploring skills and knowledge in below the radar groups – see Chapter Twelve) identified a number of other recession- and austerity-related factors that had affected their activities in addition to cuts in public expenditure. These are discussed in the next part of this chapter.

Time and resources

Those running or volunteering in community activities are frequently employed elsewhere, earning the income that enables them to volunteer. With increased concern about security in their day job, community activists felt the pressure of increased workloads, which limited the spare time they had available for voluntary activity: "If I'm still in the office at 8, I can't make the meeting that starts at 7" (faith group representative).

Further, the rapidity with which policy changed in the early years of the coalition government gave groups little opportunity to respond to those changes. For example, reflecting on asset transfer, one participating group secured substantial capital prior to austerity measures to extend the village hall and take on its management. However, even in this relatively affluent community, the process had taken nearly eight years, whereas:

> "Because of all the financial pressures and so on, there isn't time for that sort of timed process to happen. What's happening at the moment on assets is that local authorities are disposing of them very rapidly. Even where there is a commitment, in principle, to consider asset transfer, there's a real danger that local groups will be unable to respond within the required timescales and assets will either close or move to the private sector." (Regional network organisation representative)

Other interviewees noted that unrealistic timescales had been placed on those involved in the locally managed Community Organisers programme with the expectation that substantial change could be effected by such organisers in the communities selected within 51 weeks. Indeed, initial research by Richardson (2011) in Bradford suggested that community organisers were engaged in informal/ small-scale activity rather than working towards substantive, structural change either at a local or policy level – the scale of their actions did not respond to government expectations.

For community activists in low-paid jobs, the issue was a lack of both time *and* resources:

> "The main crux of it being is that the people that are involved in all of this are volunteers. I personally over the years, I'm easily about £3,500 down because I couldn't make a claim against things and I couldn't claim for this and I couldn't claim for that. I don't do it no more. I can't afford it.... It's all very well £1.80 to town and £1.80 back, but when you've got two or three meetings a week, straight away that's £10 wiped off, so over a month that's £40. It's an awful lot of money. Between times you've got letters to write and phone calls to make and you've got to buy the envelopes. All this kind of stuff, it all adds up." (Tenants' and residents' association representative)

The expectation that activists would cover their own costs, regardless of their financial situation, was seen as having a potential 'knock-on' effect in terms of their capacity to organise:

> "Each member was paying a membership fee, they were charging £20 for a membership for a year and then they ran very specific events, and each event people had to pay to participate in, so obviously now with people losing jobs and stuff and people having less money, I can see that that's a massive impact on them not being able to run their own activities." (National network organisation representative)

For a number of interviewees, particularly those active in inner-city community groups, lack of time, energy and personal resources were exacerbated by welfare reform:

> "Just survive in their own families, in their own houses, and so I think it's going to be a lot harder because I think people's energy is going to go, for some it's going to go more

into trying to survive." (Sub-regional network organisation representative)

Places and spaces for community activity

Many community organisations are dependent on access to affordable or free space in order to meet and run their activities. Indeed, the Office of the Third Sector, commenting on the National Survey of Third Sector Organisations, noted that:

> Third Sector organisations without premises of their own – the great majority – rely on cheap or free meeting space at council-run or council-supported venues such as community centres, village halls and sports clubs. This is a fundamental contribution to the groups' ability to function. (OTS, 2010, p 19)

However, our respondents outlined how, since 2010, local authorities experiencing high levels of cuts in central government income and forced to make cuts to local services had closed community centres or had started to charge for room hire in libraries and other public buildings at commercial rates, which were too expensive for small groups. Talking about a community group that managed the local tenants' hall, one activist noted:

> "Not only is their lease going up a lot but also they're finding that maintenance arrangements are becoming less much favourable as pressures are put on local authorities to make money out of those assets or get rid of them." (Sub-regional network organisation representative)

Beyond the local authority context, the closure of voluntary sector community anchor organisations following the loss of government grants also means the loss of 'invited spaces' and 'claimed' or 'popular' spaces (Cornwall, 2004; Hutchinson and Cairns, 2010).

Between 2010 and 2016, below the radar groups appeared to experience a multiplier effect, or compound disadvantages (where different adverse factors impact at the same time), coming into play that went beyond the effects of cuts to funding. Combined, these could have a devastating impact on groups' ability to operate, as was the case for Crumley Pensioners' group (see case study 1).

Case study 1: Crumley Pensioners' group

Crumley Pensioners is a long-established group that meets weekly at the local library. Its activities include social events and invited speakers. Members come from a variety of surrounding villages. Public transport links are poor and the group has received a small grant for community transport to take people to their meetings. The group has been highlighted in the local press as important in tackling the isolation felt by older people in rural communities.

Crumley Pensioners recently lost its community transport grant of £500 per annum. Members approached the Rural Community Council's (RCC) development worker, who informed them that the RCC no longer had the capacity to support them in applying for other funding due to reductions in its own budget. They had previously received 'pro bono' advice from the local authority but were told that this was no longer available due to restructuring.

The library is also threatened with closure. As part of its survival strategy, it is exploring income generation and has told the group that it will need to pay a commercial rate (£1,000 a year) for the room it previously used on a grace-and-favour basis.

The group is currently considering its own future. While members want to maintain weekly meetings, their view is that it is not feasible for members to cover their own travel costs as well as pay for the rental of space at the library. Recruiting volunteer drivers has also proved problematic.

Scaling up to survive?

An inherent expectation in the Big Society and subsequent agendas has been that community groups should grow in order to engage with the opportunities they are being offered to get more involved in service provision.

> For smaller voluntary and community sector groups, there has been an added driver of needing to come together to be big enough to be able to access external resources, whether in the form of service contracts or grant-funding. (Evison and Jochum, 2010, p 7)

'Scaling up' – getting bigger – is seen by some in the sector as a key survival strategy (Moore and Mullins, 2013). Growing, it has been argued, is likely to be a more successful approach to sustainability than relying on reserves and hoping for Big Lottery Fund money – or hanging on to the apparently vain hope that 'things can only get better'.

There are two fundamental problems with this model of survival. First, the data collected in interviews found there was very little appetite for small organisations to scale up. For example, in one case the village shop did not want to manage community shops in other villages or the local library, despite such an approach being suggested by the local authority. The tenants' and residents' association was in the process of moving into the management of its own housing estate, but it was not interested, when approached by the local housing department, in offering those services to other estates. The village hall committee recognised that there were other assets at risk in the community, but felt that its focus had to be on making the hall itself sustainable rather than expanding into other areas. The groups interviewed focused on the immediate issue in their community and did not want to move out of their local sphere of action (McCabe, 2010; McCabe et al, 2016). For them, local connection and embeddedness were more important than growth.

Second, even if small groups (particularly community-based organisations with some funding) were motivated to scale up, they faced a number of barriers. The trend in contracting out public services has been towards fewer and larger contracts (for example, the Work Programme), which, because of their terms and conditions, effectively exclude even larger formal voluntary organisations. The financial requirements, set out in pre-qualifying questionnaires (PQQs) for organisations bidding for such contracts, require that the total contract value is less than 25% of annual turnover. If the third sector were to get involved at all, such contracts would favour, under the coalition, the large, national, charities that have high levels of turnover. Since 2015, conditions in PQQs on monitoring, financial reporting and standards systems (as well as ideology) have benefited the corporate sector, with, for example, large multinationals winning all the prime contracts for the delivery of the Work Programme elements of the probation service. Where third sector organisations are involved in large state contracts, they are partners to – or more cynically (Third Sector, 2011) 'bid candy' for – the corporates that take the leading role and determine the terms, conditions and remuneration that reach non-corporate sub-contractors. The experiences of tendering recalled by the Advice Shop illustrate how the processes of the contract culture effectively exclude local voluntary organisations – never mind community groups (see case study 2). Further, this reflects the decline in the number of small community-based organisations (and infrastructure/network bodies) involved in the research between 2010 and 2015. Of 20 organisations contacted for interview in the final phase of the research, 12 had either ceased to exist or had lost all their paid staff, were continuing on a volunteer basis and felt they lacked the capacity to participate.

Case study 2: the Advice Shop

The Advice Shop was established in 1972, initially on a voluntary basis, then with a series of small grants and later securing contracts with the local authority and Legal Services Commission (LSC). The organisation grew from two to 22 staff and served a diverse inner-city area working in nine community languages with over 40,000 users annually. However, reductions in local authority budgets and revisions to LSC contract conditions resulted in a reduction of income and staffing. The local authority decided to tender out advice services to a single, city-wide, provider in 2012. By this point, the Advice Shop's annual turnover had fallen below the threshold required in the bidding process. As a result, it further reduced staff numbers and limited opening times. Accumulated reserves and a Big Lottery Fund grant enabled the Advice Shop to survive, on a restricted basis, for a further four years until closure in 2016.

Shifting attitudes and ideologies

Beyond the immediate, practical, issues of funding, time and affordable meeting places, it has been possible to identify key shifts in attitudes within voluntary and community organisations post-2010. In the first wave of interviews, just after the 2010 general election, research participants expressed a view that 'we are all in this together'. By 2015 this expression of mutuality had given way to a feeling of 'them' and 'us': 'them' being the large voluntaries that, rightly or wrongly, were seen as 'doing all right' and 'us' being the small community groups who were struggling or had ceased to operate. As one community activist with a long history of collaborative working in Area Based Initiatives expressed it: "We [names group] used to work in partnership with some of the big players around here. But now we know who our real enemies are." This feeling of 'them' and 'us' is not, however, confined to voluntary and community groups but reflects a wider disillusionment with 'the establishment' (whoever the establishment is perceived to be) that was evident in the results of the UK's so-called Brexit referendum in June 2016, when 51.9% of the British population voted to withdraw from the European Union.

In addition, community groups active in particularly marginalised communities (whether neighbourhoods or communities of interest) reported working within the context of a very different debate about community and social needs. Austerity measures were, in their view, no longer a purely fiscal matter, and were not engendering greater levels of solidarity. Instead austerity had prompted an attitude of hostility to vulnerable individuals and groups that was argued to have been further exacerbated by television programmes such as Benefits Street, described as 'poverty porn' (Jensen, 2014), and Channel 4's My Big Fat Gypsy Wedding (see also Jones, 2011). This ideology of what Jensen (2013) has termed 'the new thrift', a culture of blaming the poor for their plight (Kyprianou, 2015), has made the task of small community groups within, and of, deprived neighbourhoods, even harder.

Conclusion: all change below the radar?

As noted, much research has focused on the impact of the coalition and subsequent Conservative administration's deficit reduction strategy on the formal, funded, voluntary sector.

However, for below the radar community groups, the findings outlined herein offer an insight that is complex and suggests a potentially more invidious picture than simply 'the cuts'. Small community groups have not only experienced the loss of grants/funding but also the loss of affordable places and spaces to meet, of access to pro-bono advice, increasing difficulties in recruiting members or volunteers and the pressures of time in the face, for many, of increasing levels of need. The short timescales associated with any potential opportunities around, for example, asset transfer or right to manage are also seen as problematic. These compound disadvantages may also be overlaid by the virtual exclusion of smaller voluntary organisations, let alone community groups, from bidding for contracts that may have enabled them to be sustainable and to ensure that communities do have a genuine role in shaping and providing services for themselves. As Taylor (2011, p 260) notes,

'In local ecologies where organisations are interdependent, cuts to one part of the sector – as well as to the public sector itself – can have significant ripple effects.'

Such ripple effects were certainly felt by those small community-based voluntaries interviewed that, as noted, either closed over the life of this research or have survived (at least for a while) on reserves or grants from the Big Lottery Fund. Beyond access to finance, however, what was being played out in the period of intense change during which the interviews took place was a profound shift in the relationship between communities, community groups, larger charities and the state. Yet, with the closure of community sector infrastructure bodies (for example, the Community Development Exchange and Community Matters) opportunities to potentially influence some of those debates about communities and public policy have been lost.

Some remain optimistic, arguing that, despite the changes, voluntary action has not been driven out by the state or withered on the vine of austerity. Rates of participation have remained constant over time (Hall, 1999; Hemming, 2011; Mohan, 2011). Austerity for some provides an opportunity to rethink the landscape of communities and develop a new mutualism:

> Focus on active participation and social responsibility ... holds a normative appeal. It speaks to people from across the ideological spectrum who believe that British politics and public policy has for too long lacked an animating vision of the 'good society' based on shared obligations of citizenship and self-government. (McLean and Dellott, 2011, p 7)

Co-production has come to be seen as the way forward in changing services and relationships:

> "Listen to people, engage them, help them to find connections, give them simple steps and simple tools to get things going themselves. After time they'll start seeing things differently and will challenge the council and a more mature relationship will develop between them and the local authority." (Policy worker)

The research, however, found no real appetite for co-production at the community level. Instead, the term, while not explicitly used, was seen as a way of passing risks on to communities and, rather than a means of reforming public services, being a smoke-screen for cuts to those services. Further, some of the groups interviewed (see Chapter Twelve), feeling overwhelmed by increasing and competing demands, had 'retreated' from wider engagement to supporting core members

(McCabe et al, 2016). Others had given up or burnt out in the face of adversity.

Some interviewees remained relatively optimistic about the future, arguing that, in continuing austerity, "Everything might become an opportunity because local authorities are helpless and the resulting power vacuum allows for community groups to take initiatives and risks that local authorities cannot take" (focus group, community activist).

For some, the current climate could 'force' change while not being McLean and Dellot's 'animating vision':

> "In adversity, people do come together and actually find the bonds between them, which can happen. I have experienced that. Yes, that could be a positive thing. Now, you know, potentially this is the time to do that. It's just that danger, if people just think about only their own interest." (Focus group, funder)

Others caution that community groups and activities have come to mirror, rather than addressing or challenging, wider social changes, with Danny Dorling arguing that 'British society ... [has been] moving towards demographic segregation and economic polarisation, social fragmentation and political disengagement since at least the late 1960s' (Dorling et al, 2008, p 35).

Indeed, the majority of below the radar research participants felt that policy over at least the past decade had exacerbated this. New groups may form but, because wider solidarities are so weak, they would be homogeneous and narrow in their membership, reflecting 'the fragmentation of society into neighbourhoods of similar income, age groups and lifestyles' (Jordan, 2010, pp 202-3).

The opportunities afforded to some by both the 2011 Localism Act and the *Open public services* White Paper would effectively empower the already powerful, in the words of one national network organisation, increase social division and leave communities increasingly anxious, prone to depression, anxious about friendships and driven as consumers with little community life (Wilkinson and Pickett, 2010).

Others (NCIA, 2015) worry that:

> "It has become a land grab or a money hunt or some sort of beauty contest about who does something better or so on, then it actually poisons some of the goodwill and social solidarity or social capital and trust that kinds of needs to make things grow really." (Funder)

So, in summary, community groups continue in austere times 'thriving, surviving, dying' (Davidson and Packham, 2012), but was this not always so?

> Those organisations that sit more closely with their communities of interest and place, especially if they have been established for a long time, will have the momentum and tenacity to keep going. (Chapman and Robinson, 2011, p 35)

They continue in part because they are misunderstood by policymakers:

> People usually choose to participate in community activities when they find them optional, small scale, convivial and life-enhancing, but many of the Government's plans … are conditional, formalised, complicated and hard graft. (Coote, 2010, p 18)

They survive because government initiatives and funding have passed them by and they rely on their own money, efforts and skills. But at what costs to those community groups – and to the activists involved – financially, emotionally and in terms of solidarity?

Key learning

- Much of the recent literature on the third sector has focused on cuts to funding for voluntary organisations. This is evident amongst community groups as well. Other forces are, however, at play in terms of their health and survival. The loss of pro-bono/face to face advice, the struggle to attract activists and volunteers with the growth of in-work poverty and the closure of no/low cost places to meet.
- There has been an emphasis on community groups 'scaling up' their activities and diversifying their funding base to survive or thrive. Community groups, however, exist and operate on a human, person to person scale and do not have the desire to expand simply as a means of survival. This would be a diversion from their original purpose.
- The closure of small scale civil society groups may seem insignificant in terms of the scale of austerity measures and the reductions in mainstream, statutory services. Those closures do, however, have a significant impact on the quality of community and associational life.

Reflective exercises

- Reflecting on the two case studies in this chapter, what strategies might the Crumley Pensioners Group and the Advice Shop have adopted to survive and what might the benefits and costs of those strategies be?
- Community activity has been seen as the social glue that binds people together. Consider this argument in the light of concerns that communities and community groups are becoming more fragmented, self-interested and reflect pre-existing social and economic divisions.
- This chapter offers two different arguments about the future of community action. Some see co-design and co-production with communities as the way forward in developing more responsive and effective services – others see these ideas as a way of passing responsibility and blame from government to communities. To what extent do you agree with these views? Can they to some extent coexist?

Notes

[1]   Open letter to the voluntary, community and social enterprise sectors, Frances Maude and Nick Hurd, Cabinet Office, 12 November 2010.

[2]   www.thebigsociety.co.uk/square-mile.html

References

Alcock, P. (2012) *The Big Society: A new policy environment for the third sector?*, Working Paper 82, Birmingham: Third Sector Research Centre.

Blume, T. (2012) 'Creative disruption: community organising and a chance for positive transformation', in M.-S. Abbas and R. Lachman (eds) *The Big Society: The Big Divide?*, Bradford: JUST West Yorkshire.

Bovaird, T., Van Ryzin, G., Loeffler, E. and Parrado, S. (2015) 'Activating citizens to participate in collective co-production of public services', *Journal of Social Policy*, vol 44, no 1, pp 1-33.

Chanan, G. and Miller, C. (2010) *The Big Society: How it could work. A positive idea at risk from caricature*, PACES, available at: www.younglancashire.org.uk/webfm_send/185

Chapman, T. and Robinson, F. (2011) *Taking Stock: Moving On: A summary report and position statement at the end of the first phase of study* (Third Sector Trends Study), Newcastle upon Tyne: Northern Rock Foundation.

Chapman, T., van der Graaf, P., Bell, V., Robinson, F. and Crow, R. (2010) *Keeping the show on the road: Findings from a survey of third sector organisations in North East England and Cumbria*, Middlesbrough: Social Futures Institute.

Clark, J., Kane, D., Wilding, K. and Bass, P. (2012) *UK civil society almanac 2012*, London: NCVO.

Coote, A. (2010) *Cutting it: The 'Big Society' and the new austerity*, London: New Economics Foundation.

Cornwall, A. (2004) 'Spaces for transformation: reflections on the issues of power and difference in participation in development', in S. Hickey and G. Mohan (eds) *Participation: From tyranny to transformation*, London: Zed Books.

Crawley, J. and Watkin, R. (2011) *Crisis and contradiction: Research into the current issues facing small voluntary and community organisations*, Bishop Sutton: South West Foundation.

Davidson, E. and Packham, C. (2012) *Surviving, thriving or dying: Resilience in small community groups in the North West of England*, Manchester: Manchester Metropolitan University.

Dorling, D., Vickers, D., Bethan, T., Prichard, J. and Ballas, D. (2008*) Changing UK: The way we live now*, available at: www.sasi.group.shef.ac.uk/research/changinguk/Changing_UK_report _sheffield_webv1.pdf

Evison, I. and Jochum, V. (2010) *Learning about the impact of the recession on communities, community cohesion and community empowerment*, London: CDF.

Hall, P. (1999) 'Social capital in Britain', *British Journal of Political Science*, vol 29, no 3, pp 417-61.

Harris, J. (2012) '"Big Society" and "Great Society": a problem in the history of ideas', in A. Ishkanian and S. Szreter (eds) *The Big Society debate: A new agenda for social welfare?*, Cheltenham: Edward Elgar.

Hemming, H. (2011) *Together: How small groups achieve big things*, London: John Murray.

HM Government (2012) *Open public services 2012*, London: HM Government.

Home Office (2011) *Our vision for safe and active communities: A report by Baroness Newlove*, London: Home Office.

Hutchinson, R. and Cairns, B. (2010) 'Community anchor organisations: sustainability and independence', in D. Billis (ed) *Hybrid organisations and the third sector: Challenges for practice, theory and policy*, Basingstoke: Palgrave Macmillan.

Ishkanian, A. and Szreter, S. (2012) *The Big Society debate: A new agenda for social welfare?*, CheltenhamL Edward Elgar.

Jensen, T. (2013) 'Riots, restraint and the new cultural politics of wanting', *Sociological Research Online*, 18 (4) 7, pp 1-20, available at: www.socresonline.org.uk/18/4/7.html

Jensen, T. (2014) '"Poverty porn": public perceptions of social housing', *Inside Housing*, 12 November.

Jones, O. (2011) *Chavs: The demonization of the working class*, London: Verso.

Jordan, B. (2010) *Why the Third Way failed: Economics, morality and the origins of the 'Big Society'*, Bristol: Policy Press.

Kane, D. and Allen, J. (2011) *Counting the cuts: The impact of spending cuts on the UK voluntary and community sector*, London: NCVO.

Kane, D., Bass, P., Heywood, J., Jochum, V., James, D. and Lloyd, G. (2014) *UK civil society almanac 2014*, London: NCVO.

Kyprianou, P. (2105) *Getting by? A year in the life of 30 working families in Liverpool*, Liverpool: Praxis.

Lachman, R. and Malik, F. (2012) *West Yorkshire public sector cuts: The impact on the BME voluntary and community sector*, Bradford: JUST West Yorkshire.

London Voluntary Service Council (2011) *The big squeeze: The squeeze tightens: The economic climate, Londoners and the voluntary and community groups that serve them*, London: LVSC.

McCabe, A. (2010) *Below the radar in a Big Society? Reflections on community engagement, empowerment and social action in a changing policy context*, Working Paper 51, Birmingham: Third Sector Research Centre.

McCabe, A. and Phillimore, J. (2012) *All change? Surviving 'below the radar': Community groups and activities in a Big Society*, Birmingham: Third Sector Research Centre.

McCabe, A., Buckingham, H. and Miller, S. with Musabyimana, M. (2016) *Belief in social action: Exploring faith groups' responses to local needs*, Working Paper 137, Birmingham: Third Sector Research Centre.

McLean, S. and Dellot, B. (2011) *The civic pulse: Measuring active citizenship in a cold climate*, London: RSA.

Mohan, J. (2011) *Mapping the Big Society: Perspectives from the Third Sector Research Centre*, Working Paper 62, Birmingham: Third Sector Research Centre.

Moore, T. and Mullins, D. (2013) *Scaling-up or going viral: Comparing self-help housing and community land trust facilitation*, Birmingham: Third Sector Research Centre.

NCIA (National Coalition for Independent Action) (2015) *Fight or Flight? Voluntary Services in 2015*, London: NCIA.

Norman, J. (2010) *The Big Society: The anatomy of the new politics*, Buckingham: University of Buckingham Press.

OTS (Office of the Third Sector) (2010) *Thriving third sector: A user guide for the National Survey of Third Sector Organisations*, London: OTS.

Parker, S. (2015) *Taking back power: Putting people in charge of politics*, Bristol: Policy Press.

Phillimore, J. and McCabe, A. (2010) *Understanding the distinctiveness of small scale third sector activity*, Birmingham: Third Sector Research Centre.

Phillimore, J. and McCabe, A. (2015) *Luck, passion, networks and skills: recipe for action below the radar*, Birmingham: Third Sector Research Centre.

Rees, J. and Mullins, D. (eds) (2016) *The third sector delivering public services. Developments, innovations and challenges*, Bristol: Policy Press.

Richardson, L. (2011) *Working in Neighbourhoods in Bradford*, York: Joseph Rowntree Foundation.

ROTA (Race on the Agenda) (2011) *BAME women's sector: Fighting for survival*, London: ROTA.

Slocock, C. (2012) *The Big Society audit 2012*, London: Civil Exchange.

Stokes, E. (2011) *The impact of the economic downturn on BAME education services*, London: MiNet.

Stott, M. (2010) 'The Big Society in context', in M. Stott (ed) *The Big Society challenge*, Cardiff: Keystone Development Trust Publications.

Taylor, M. (2011) 'Community organising and the Big Society: is Saul Alinsky turning in his grave?', *Voluntary Sector Review*, vol 2, no 2, pp 259-66.

Third Sector (2011) *Analysis: The Work Programme. Are charities proper partners or just bid candy?*, Third Sector, available at: www.thirdsector. co.uk/analysis-work-programme-charities-proper-partners-just-bid-candy/finance/article/1076895

Wilkinson, R. and Pickett, K. (2010) *The spirit level. Why equality is better for everyone*, London: Penguin.

Williams, R. (2012) Archbishop of Canterbury: speech reported in the Daily Telegraph 24/6/12, 'Rowan Williams: Big Society is not just "aspirational waffle"', available at: www.telegraph.co.uk/news/religion/9352412/Rowan-Williams-Big-Society-is-not-just-aspirational-waffle.html

PART THREE

Under-explored radars

The UK Gypsy, Traveller and Roma third sector: a Gypsy industry or route to empowerment?

Andrew Ryder and Sarah Cemlyn

Chapter aims

This chapter aims to:

- explore the historical and contemporary condition of the Gypsy, Traveller and Roma civil society movement;
- analyse its varied, evolving and often overlapping forms, including oppositional campaigns, service-oriented organisations and, more recently, bridging or advocacy organisations;
- suggest how wider alliances within social justice movements are potentially shifting the forms and focus of struggle for Gypsies, Travellers and Roma.

Introduction

This chapter reviews the strengths, achievements, threats and pitfalls facing Gypsy, Traveller and Roma (GTR)[1] civil society, and the role GTR voluntary and community organisations have played in defending and enhancing the political and cultural rights of these marginalised groups. Drawing on historical and contemporary analysis, we explore the motivation, dynamism and tensions inherent in varied manifestations of GTR community activism and the struggles against, and impact of, assimilatory and discriminatory policy. Finally, we explore the way community bonds and diverse aspects of identity interplay in the growth of community activism and the survival and development of the sector, often against the odds.

The roots of the Gypsy, Traveller and Roma third sector

In 1966, the Gypsy Council was formed in the UK as a campaigning organisation. Among the leading catalysts was the non-Gypsy campaigner Grattan Puxon, who, prior to this, had honed his skills in community mobilisation in Ireland by working with Irish Travellers in a campaign centred on resistance to eviction. In both the UK and Ireland, a growing body of restrictions on nomadism and the breakdown in the symbiotic economic relationship between farmers and nomadic communities greatly diminished the supply of stopping places and scope for Traveller lifestyles. Hence eviction became a pronounced feature of Gypsy/Traveller life (Acton, 1974). As in Ireland, Puxon (through the Gypsy Council) helped thread a network of charismatic community leaders and extended families into a coherent campaign. The Gypsy Council presented a landmark moment, being the first formal national GTR non-governmental organisation (NGO) in the UK and indeed one of the first in Europe. The Gypsy Council was later weakened by disputes and fissures. Many of these centred on what role non-community members should play, debates about the value and danger of being linked too closely with services and centres of power and the tensions caused by charismatic leadership (Acton et al, 2014).

As this chapter demonstrates, these are themes that continue to have resonance with reference to the development and progress of the UK GTR third sector. Today there are about 30 GTR community organisations (Ryder et al, 2014). Organisationally they are heterogeneous and many can be described as below the radar, a term used to describe loosely constituted community groups undertaking informal or semi-formal activities in the third sector (McCabe et al, 2010). As quickly as some spring up, others disappear, taking root among the day-to-day struggle of the communities to maintain their lifestyle and then maybe succumbing to the pressures of this struggle in a hostile environment. Their demise often stems from being ground down by lack of financial support or activist 'burn-out' caused by the Herculean demands of trying to meet the huge needs of highly marginalised communities.

Further restraints have been placed on development by the increasingly complex, legalistic and bureaucratic tasks that even a small NGO now requires in the context of sometimes limited levels of formal education among GTR activists. Added to this is the conservatism of many funders worried about the media fallout associated with supporting GTR causes (Alexander and Greenfields, 2014).

Somewhat contentiously, Hawes and Perez (1996, p 174) note: 'The very notion of Gypsydom is antipathetic to the creation of a coherent programme of action or campaign for recognition and respect for Gypsies in the modern world.' Such an assertion bolsters a perception that third sector/social movement organisation in effect constitutes an imposition on the cultural orientation of GTR communities. Indeed, some critics within GTR communities as well as academia go so far as to contend that there is a 'Gypsy industry', a collection of primarily non-GTR service providers and community organisers who wish to guide, direct and corral GTR communities into narrow integrationist policy agendas based on conceptions of normative behaviour that seek to integrate and 'civilise' (Matras et al, 2015). While the authors of this chapter accept that paternalistic forms of community development have, and continue to be, present within the landscape of the GTR third sector, it is our view that such critique constitutes a rigid and narrow view that holds the inherent danger of stifling emancipatory agendas by failing to appreciate the good practice that is being developed in the third sector. Moreover, it oversimplifies the reality of community support and struggle, including the development of service organisations that are able to engage in meaningful partnerships with service providers and also develop forms of national advocacy.

Assimilation, emancipation or empowerment

GTR communities, being among the most prominent victims of economic, political and social instability and inequality, can be considered as a bellwether (indicator) reflecting the orientation of the society they are located in. They may also be a screen on which power elites project a vision that is deeply revealing of their own core philosophy and values. So it has been the case that GTR communities have been subject to policies of persecution, ranging from genocide to assimilation, over at least a 500-year span of history. More subtle forms of coercion have involved religious conversion, sedentarisation (being forced to abandon nomadism) and education as tools of conformity and civilisation (Mayall, 1988; McVeigh, 1997).

Correspondingly, community development has often been paternalist and outsider driven. In the 1960s, Communist regimes in Central and Eastern Europe sought to 'proletarianise' the Roma through narrow integrationist policy agendas (Stewart, 1997), while in the West of Europe equally assimilative social policy sought to sedentarise nomadic communities; in the UK this was initiated primarily through council-controlled caravan sites and compulsory school attendance (Okely,

2001), although educational provision was also often discriminatory, stigmatising or effectively denied. In addition charities and community support groups also veered into such assimilatory agendas. In Ireland, for example, after the departure of Puxon, Irish Traveller activism was subverted from the latter part of the 1960s by the Catholic Church, service providers and charities, which Acton and colleagues (2014) argue emasculated the nascent radicalism of the Irish Traveller civil rights movement. The charity sector sought such encroachments in the UK in the 1960s but was rebuffed by a Gypsy Council that wished to preserve its autonomy (Acton, 1974). During the 1970s and 1980s, some of the charity-supported work with Gypsies and Travellers was seen as outsider driven and paternalistic. For example, in the educational sphere, family support, literacy and pre-school projects were uncritical of the educational system for which children were being prepared and of the discriminatory context of Gypsies' and Travellers' lives.

More recently, Trehan (2001) raised concerns about the funding and donor-driven agendas in Europe of philanthropists like George Soros and how these run the danger of creating forms of managerialism ('NGOisation') that disempower or distract activists. The UK GTR third sector has not been immune from such processes. It has at times found itself having to run parallel projects with one strand pleasing the funders and the other more covert strand doing the job it really wants to do (Vanderbeck, 2009). The UK GTR sector has also at times been vulnerable to what Alinsky (1971) cautioned as the danger of activism being hijacked by a service-driven agenda. This can result in what can be termed a 'shadow state', leading to the subversion of autonomy and radicalism. Reflecting such fears, a policy briefing by the University of Manchester (2014) stated that interventions by third sector agencies entrusted with managing interaction between Roma and local institutions held the long-term risk of perpetuating the Roma's dependency on outside mediators and support provisions. Instead it was argued that intervention should take the form of capacity building within the Roma community. This critique mirrors the thoughts of theorists such as Foucault (1998), who argued that development theory constituted a form of control through the concept of governmentality, which normalises neoliberal and assimilative policy agendas, and 'responsibilisation', individualising and pathologising the victims rather than the structural agents of exclusion.

With reference to GTR communities some of these concerns are more intensely theorised by Vanderbeck (2009) and Powell (2010), who contrast two interpretations of intervention/development related to GTR communities. One perspective perceives social policy intervention as assimilationist, based on the imposition of normative and civilising values that discard and deride Gypsy and Traveller norms and values, while another, by contrast, sees such intervention as a means to promote empowerment through emancipatory processes. According to Vanderbeck and Powell, the emancipatory perspective has been projected onto children from Gypsy and Traveller communities, in particular through the notion that participation in formal schooling is to be preferred to the practice of in-family socialisation, where children learn gendered adult roles through work with their parents, which involves boys working with their fathers and girls conducting domestic work. The emancipatory perspective argues that formal education broadens horizons and opportunities, allowing children to escape and reformulate the stifling straightjacket of tradition.

The cultural fear of education is one reason why traditional Gypsy and Traveller families have been apprehensive about the effect of sending their children to school, with some seeking to limit and curtail this influence by withdrawing children at the end of their primary schooling (Derrington and Kendall, 2004). Indeed, given the static and mono-cultural curricula and intense bullying to be found in some schools, some parents have had legitimate concerns about school attendance. However, choices do not need to be so stark; inclusive institutions should and in some cases do enable a more intercultural approach, where services or projects are shaped through dialogue and deliberation that allows for flexibility but also for tradition and identity to be treated as an asset. Such a dialogic approach, where those at the margins have a say and steer of policy, can be termed inclusive community development (Ryder et al, 2014).

A danger of post-development theory is that the concept of progress may be lost and an unquestioning exaltation of ethnic cultures can promote static and narrow versions of identity. Powell (2010) may fall into this trap envisioning a rather static view of Gypsy and Traveller culture that fails to fully accept the fluidity of identity and GTR propensity for 'bricolage' or cultural borrowing and innovation. In addition, Powell fails to adequately recognise that some manifestations of identity may be 'reactive', shaped and formed through bonding social capital honed as a defensive mechanism in response to the hostility of mainstream society. Powell (2010) notes, as influenced by Bauman (2001), that emancipatory development can be individualising and may fragment group cohesion. More nuanced post-development theory contends that a new way of development should be inspired from within those social groups that are socially, politically and geographically outside of hegemonic power. Hence there is a need for empowerment and for these groups to look inwards and self-organise and mobilise, avoiding the pitfalls of narrow donor-driven control and manipulation (Udombana, 2000). The authors of this chapter argue that such a concept is at the heart of inclusive community development. While we share concerns about misinformed and paternalistic policy interventions, we contend that GTR civil society, although small and fragile, has made an important contribution to empowerment and emancipatory processes. Rather than eroding tradition and identity, GTR community organisations may be among the most effective weapons in defending and maintaining GTR culture, actions that in effect are in accordance with notions of inclusive community development.

UK GTR activism: ladders or scaffolds

Arnstein's highly influential ladder of participation creates a stepped gradient of empowerment, with 'citizens' control' at the pinnacle and where communities are given real agency and choice in determining their affairs; at the median level, communities are afforded 'tokenistic' forms of say and determination; and at the lowest rung, communities are subject to 'manipulation' and indeed 'therapy', where hierarchical and outsider forms of power seek to civilise (Arnstein, 1969).

However, such a linear scale may oversimplify a process that is more complex. The reality is that people, depending on backgrounds, skills, pressures and opportunities, may need to have a range of starting points; in this respect, it might be more apt to envisage empowerment as a scaffold rather than a ladder (Ryder, 2013). Experience and involvement in the third sector tells us that for some community members from more bonded communities, the first tentative steps towards activism have come through forms of volunteering performing basic tasks. Using Arnstein's scale, such work may be derided as tokenistic. However, it has enabled GTR community members to gain the experience and confidence of working in a new and sometimes strange environment and has provided the foundations for skills progression (Ryder and Greenfields, 2010). It should be noted that in some cases traditional families, especially in the case of young single women, are extremely cautious about the potential impact on family members of working in a non-traditional work environment (McCabe et al, 2014). It is also the case that where projects and community groups have been too zealous in empowering the community by inviting members of GTR communities to become trustees or hold other central positions in an organisation, in contexts where there has been an unaddressed skills deficit, such participants have floundered and in extreme cases failed. This can lead to demoralisation and low expectations and negative stereotypes being reaffirmed.

As will be demonstrated, effective support and training environments, often utilising forms of positive action and inclusive community development, have enabled community members to develop and progress. It is important to note that GTR women have been the most forthcoming in taking up the opportunities presented by activism. This is a dramatic contrast to the Gypsy Council politics of the 1960s, which were male dominated. This reversal of fortunes possibly reflects the fact that, in traditional communities in particular, men have focused on economic activities, leaving women to manage the domestic household but also to liaise with and navigate the various bureaucracies that now touch the communities' lives, encompassing health workers, schools and site managers. This pattern is also evident in activism in other communities (Mayo, 1977). Women's mediatory role has been enhanced by the fact that education levels and literacy are often higher among GTR women than among GTR men and these factors combined mean that it is easier for some GTR women to develop bridging forms of social cultural capital that are more disposed to developing wide and diverse networks, while carving out for themselves new and innovative cultural, political and economic roles that touch the sphere of the third sector.

Cemlyn and colleagues (2014) note that, for many GTR female activists, planning cases have been a major point of mobilisation. An important field of struggle and conflict for GTR communities is seeking to get planning permission for Traveller sites, a process that arouses deep hostility and opposition from the settled community, which in turn influences councils to wilfully obstruct and unfairly deny GTR planning applications (Richardson and Ryder, 2012). Thus, extended families within the GTR community often find themselves dragged into hugely complex and expensive legal battles. In these disputes families have often looked to matriarchs not just to hold the family together but to mobilise their case. This has resulted in women networking within communities and forming alliances within the GTR third sector, learning from them and mastering not just planning law but wider social policy. A number of these formidable women have found themselves taking up lead roles in the GTR third sector through the national organisations or through establishing their own local groups.

In the 1990s and first decade of the 21st century, the GTR issue climbed the media and political agenda (Ryder, 2015). New funders became interested in supporting GTR issues, most notably Comic

Relief, the Rowntree Charitable Trust and Foundation and Capacity Builders. In turn, this prompted an intense spurt of activity where new groups were formed. In some cases, new funding streams appeared as a consequence of policy that increasingly emphasised the value of partnership and engagement. This was most evident in the field of health. Friends, Families and Travellers is a national organisation that has secured a number of NHS contracts providing tailored outreach for local health services or mediation and liaison services.

However, it appears that such service links have not muted the advocacy work of these organisations. On the contrary, they assert that their frontline experiences of services informs and shapes their local and national campaign work and has also enabled them to challenge service discrimination by assisting GTR service users who have suffered racial discrimination from health providers to navigate official channels of complaint to seek redress and policy change (McCabe et al, 2014). Friends Families and Travellers also operates a national helpline and undertakes a great deal of casework, but the organisation argues that this gives its advocacy work informed insights as to what is happening in real communities. In fact, the organisation has managed to mobilise and empower some of its clients, enabling them to become trainers and advocates, an example that illustrates the potential connection between offering a service and constructing change agendas.

A valid argument is that services genuinely committed to inclusion should welcome challenges that ultimately will improve service quality even if the challenges are facilitated and supported by community organisations that have been sub-contracted in service delivery. The specific duty in the NHS to eradicate inequality, coupled with the former Pacesetters programme, which aimed to enable service users to influence the service provided and improve outreach, may be policy levers unique to the health service that have facilitated particularly fruitful collaboration between service providers and community organisations (Van Cleemput, 2012).

Personalisation within social care was initially heralded as empowering service users to achieve greater control and more flexible services. Hodges and Cemlyn (2013) found that outreach and personalised approaches within the Supporting People (SP) programme did enable greater equality of services for Gypsies and Travellers, but funds withered after SP ring-fencing was withdrawn in 2009 (House of Commons Library, 2012). Critics have pointed to the narrowing of personalisation to a neoliberal framework of consumer choice, its inherent inequalities, and, most significantly, the context of massive cuts to local authority social care budgets (Lymbery, 2012). This leaves minimal optimism for improved social care without the input of GTR community organisations. Aside from national organisations like Friends Families and Travellers, a number of local community organisations have secured important service contracts to work in partnership with a range of services. Leeds Gypsy and Traveller Exchange and the London Gypsy and Traveller Unit are among the most established. These have been joined by organisations for the new Roma migrant communities such as the Roma Support Group and Roma Community Care Derby. Both these organisations have played an invaluable role in liaison, improving understanding and relationships between service providers and clients in health and education for instance, but they have also challenged and highlighted the exploitation Roma are suffering as a result of unscrupulous landlords, gang masters and zero-hour work contracts (Decade for Roma Inclusion Secretariat Foundation/Ryder and Cemlyn, 2014). Another relatively recent development has been a drive to establish residents' associations on local authority Traveller sites. It is held that such organisational units might be more conducive to family networks and or forms of bonding social capital found on many sites and be a good starting point in the training of GTR activists, enabling them to challenge immediate and pressing inequalities connected to the national network of 320 local authority sites, many of which occupy marginal space and suffer from substandard services and management (Ryder, 2012).

Conversely, there are other GTR organisations that have not actively sought large grants. For instance, the Gypsy Council, after the death of its chair Charles Smith, decided to jettison his strategy of trying to attract major grants to build up a large staff team to service case work and advocacy. The Council returned to an earlier conception of the Gypsy Council as existed during its formative years in the 1960s, where it was primarily run on goodwill and unpaid activism (Acton and Ryder, 2012). Although this may make the Gypsy Council's reach and support rather 'amateurish' and less uniform than the other more professionalised national GTR organisations, it could be argued that such informality has enabled the Gypsy Council to be more agile and possibly even more radical than those dependent on the strictures of funders. Hence, the Gypsy Council was able to play a lead role in the monitoring of and political resistance to the eviction of 80 families, which took place in 2011 at the Dale Farm Traveller site.

It is evident therefore that the GTR third sector is highly diverse and heterogeneous yet the diverse different strands also complement each other, enabling particular groups to fill particular niches. Yet, for much of the time the groups are prepared to cooperate, overcome rivalries and competition for scarce resources and come together in short- and long-term alliances and collaborations. Some of the family-based GTR organisations have remained rather informal, yet others have evolved into highly organised and staffed community groups providing a range of services and advocacy work. In some cases, GTR activists have gained skills in national organisations and then gone on to develop their own projects. In others, informal mentoring takes place where newer NGOs have been guided and advised on funding applications and or conforming to the bureaucratic procedures necessary to be a registered charity or social enterprise. Alongside these informal support networks, for many years the Travellers' Aid Trust provided small start-up capital and advice for new groups.

It was through the Travellers' Aid Trust that forms of support and collaboration were provided for the wide range of GTR community groups that were emerging at the start of the 21st century. Such support included pooling expertise and experience into an effective coalition that lobbied the New Labour Government for more sites. The Gypsy and Traveller Law Reform Coalition, as it became known, was successful in persuading the government to return to a form of obligation on local authorities to provide sites (Ryder and Cemlyn, 2014).

Later, a new umbrella group emerged, called the National Federation of Gypsy Liaison Groups, which focused on supporting local groups. It should be noted that an important funnel for UK advocacy has been the All Party Parliamentary Group for Gypsies, Roma and Travellers, which brings together a range of politicians from across the political spectrum interested in GTR issues and which frequently meets representatives of the third sector. Other initiatives that have threaded together the broad array of Gypsy, Traveller and Roma NGOs and communities include Gypsy Roma Traveller History Month, which promotes the history and culture of these communities. In fact, arts-focused community organisations are emerging, like the Romani Cultural and Arts Company based in Wales (Acton and Ryder, 2012).

Within this wave of GTR third sector development, some organisations have proven to be adept at enabling community members to set the agenda of campaign and support work, rather than leaving donors to map out what needs to be done and risking misinformed outsiders setting a course of action that problematises GTR communities and imposes narrow integrationist agendas. Another important development is the range of activists representing different generations and the unique and respective strands of the misleadingly homogenising umbrella term 'GTR' that are organising in a way that blends tradition and innovation. These important traits could be termed asset-based community development in the sense that they allow community members to frame campaign directions that draw from the strengths of their tradition but also build networks and partnerships and innovate by blending the old with new approaches, in effect practising bricolage. Leeds GATE is currently developing an asset-based approach in its work on health inclusion and justifies this as a more holistic, whole-system and person-centred approach as opposed to a needs-based approach that frequently lacks coherence, only works on part of the system and is centred on external policy goals rather than people and their aspirations (Jones, 2013).

One aspect of such an approach is the Gypsy/Traveller tradition of interactive learning, learning through participation and observation (Jordan, 2001). A number of community members, in particular women, often lacking formal education, have managed to expand and develop their literacy and cultural capital through forms of activism initially centred on immediate problems challenging them in their lives and those of their communities and in response rapidly developing and improvising a series of skillsets (Cemlyn et al, 2014). Three activists (known to the authors) who started out with primary school level education have returned to education and acquired various certificates and diplomas and are now near completion of doctorates.

An important feature of the GTR third sector has been large gatherings, often in the form of conferences, most notably those organised by the Gypsy and Traveller Law Reform Coalition and the Pride not Prejudice events to counter discriminatory practices within police forces organised by the National Federation of Gypsy Liaison Groups. The organisation of these events has tended to be based on what are termed 'search conferences'. These provide community-friendly forums where GTR community members have been able to describe personal experiences of discrimination and exclusion and where activists and policymakers have gathered such information to understand and try to connect practice with experience (Ryder, 2013)

In the forums organised by the Gypsy and Traveller Law Reform Coalition (2002–2006), meetings did not follow rigid agendas. They were be long and sprawling to provide space for personal narrative and deep deliberation, avoiding organisational management processes that curtail and circumvent the connection between decision making and real experience. In other words, decision-making processes were invested with grounded experience, emotion and even passion. The process was felt by participants to be close and meaningful to their lives and in that sense to be uniquely Gypsy/Traveller in nature, as the essence of the campaign was not lost in a fog of abstraction.

The various meetings and gatherings of the GTR third sector have also replicated another important aspect of GTR culture, namely emotional capital. According to Nowotny (1981), this is a form of social capital that provides psychological and emotional support through networks that foster a sense of relatedness. Emotional capital gives people the 'will to carry on' and has always been a central resource for those at the very margins. It is for this reason that family gatherings and traditional meeting places such as fairs and markets have held such importance for GTR communities, offering not only collective opportunities for cultural expression but also a chance for emotional sustenance. It is not surprising, therefore, that community leaders fighting planning cases or engaged in casework and other struggles have found such events an ideal forum for networking, giving or receiving peer support and sharing experiences, as well as expressing intense feelings of fear, frustration and occasionally jubilation.

The GTR third sector under the coalition and Conservative governments

GTR community development suffered a series of reverses in the wake of the financial crisis, leading to reduced funding as charities' ability to offer financial support became diminished and governmental donors at national and local level became restrained through the culture and economics of austerity and cutbacks. This, in turn, has reduced partnership opportunities for the GTR third sector and inclusive services. In addition to this, a more combative approach was adopted by the coalition government on GTR issues, which scrapped the Labour Government's regional spatial strategies that had set regional targets for pitches, backed up by an obligation on local authorities to provide/ facilitate site provision. Instead, localism gave local authorities and local residents greater scope to thwart and obstruct site provision. Relations were further inflamed by a number of ministers issuing confrontational and provocative statements. The Department for Communities and Local Government, under the aegis of Eric Pickles MP, issued a press release that referred to unauthorised Traveller sites as a 'blight' on the countryside (Decade for Roma Inclusion Secretariat Foundation/ Ryder and Cemlyn, 2014). Simultaneously, in a televised interview, Pickles said he expected Gypsies and Travellers to "obey the law like you and I do" and not to come on to the green belt and "trash it" (Mason, 2013).

Indicative of the poor relations between government and GTR groups is governmental management of the UK's participation in the European Union Framework for National Roma Integration Strategies. The framework was established in 2011 in the hope that EU member states would devise National Action Plans to improve inclusion for GTR communities. The Cross Ministerial Working Group for Gypsies and Travellers (CMWG), established to facilitate governmental coordination on the EU Framework for National Roma Integration Strategies, met, with little or no input from NGOs or other stakeholders, before producing a progress report in April 2012. This contrasts with a key emphasis in the framework on partnership with GTR communities in the design, delivery and monitoring of resulting policies. It was thus felt by GTR groups that the CMWG had not worked within the spirit of the framework. Chris Whitwell, Director of Friends Families and Travellers, stated with reference to the CMWG progress report for the framework:

> The report was met with considerable disappointment by the key Gypsy/Traveller/Roma stakeholders since it contained little that was new.... The Department of [sic] Communities and Local Government agreed to hold meetings with a stakeholder group of the key NGOs but these meetings are only attended by civil servants and do not amount to any meaningful dialogue between the Gypsy, Traveller and Roma communities and Government Ministers. (Decade for Roma Inclusion Secretariat Foundation/Ryder and Cemlyn, 2014, p 28)

The Department for Communities and Local Government in fact refused to respond to Whitwell's request to let GTR groups know how often the CMWG had met, and Friends Families and Travellers was forced to issue a freedom of information request. This was initially refused by the government but was overturned by the Freedom of Information Commissioner. It materialised that the CMWG had not met since the publication of its progress report (Brown, 2014).

The general election result in May 2015, which delivered a Conservative majority government, left GTR organisations and communities feeling highly apprehensive given the continuation of localism, which undermines any equality agenda by granting greater power to local, often prejudiced, majorities (Parvin, 2009; Ryder et al, 2012). The Conservatives' stated intention to stipulate that if a Gypsy or Traveller stops travelling permanently for reasons of health, education or old age they will no longer be within the planning definition of Gypsy and Traveller was implemented in September 2015 alongside a number of other restrictive measures (DCLG, 2015), causing great concern to the communities (Johnson and Ryder, 2015). In addition, austerity including further welfare cuts will have an impact on GTR families and the lack of social housing and continuance of zero hours contracts are expected to have a negative effect many Roma families. Also on the horizon is the potential abolition of the Human Rights Act 1998, which is even more likely now that the UK has voted to leave the European Union.

A pedagogy of hope

Nevertheless, the following dialogue from two GTR third sector activists on Facebook the day after the general election reveals a sense of defiance.

> Maggie: I won't give up – but will fight the good fight, we have some great groups in our corner folks – and we all of us want the same thing – we shall put our heads together and work out what to do for the future of our people ... so we are far from down and out.
>
> Ryalla: Well said Maggie xx there is a new dawn and a fresh horizon. We have an indomitable spirit which will see us through anything when we work together in the same direction. I remember the old Pride not Prejudice days [see the earlier discussion on GTR activism] when we would have so many Gypsy people together in one big hall and the buzz was amazing. We got our voices heard and our message across.[2]

Since the 1960s, the shoots of grassroots community activism within GTR communities have continued to spring up, reseed, sometimes fade but then flourish elsewhere and anew, often struggling against huge odds. Strengths include the mostly unpaid work on planning applications (Cemlyn et al, 2014), the growth of arts-related activism, the use of social media, especially by young people, and the growing engagement between GTR, sympathetic service providers and other minority groups. Such strengths were evident at a gathering of Roma NGOs to share and review their work on Roma rights in the UK in March 2015, which also highlighted the importance and vibrancy of alliances within and outside the sector, working collaboratively with other marginalised and minority groups. Liz Fekete from the Institute of Race Relations pointed out how the GTR third sector had taken the lead among anti-racism groups to highlight the dangers of localism in giving greater scope to prejudiced local majorities, but also how crucial it was to maintain a focus on anti-racism rather than allowing it to be diluted by slippage to generalised anti-discrimination. The centrality and challenges of intercommunity solidarity and intersectionality are also being championed and debated across Europe (Bogdán et al, 2015).

Freire (1998) recognised the centrality of a 'pedagogy of hope', a sense of idealism and belief that there is a way out. In the coming years, the GTR third sector will continue to articulate hopes and concerns for communities that will feel deeply hounded and harassed. As is evident from this chapter, the challenges will be immense and the external resources available will be sorely lacking, but, if those policies are to be challenged and ultimately reversed, the GTR third sector will have a profound part to play and offer a greater chance to celebrate, develop and build outwards from community identity, rather than resort to cultural retreatism, isolation and reactivity.

Key learning

- There have been a number of policy initiatives, often prompted and guided by the European Union, to address the social and economic exclusion of Gypsy, Traveller and Roma communities. These have largely failed as those communities have largely been marginalised in, or actively excluded from, the policy making process and or states have failed to provide sufficient commitment and resources to deliver meaningful change.
- The principle of 'nothing about us without us', is critical if Gypsy, Traveller and Roma policy initiatives are to be experienced as something other than attempts at assimilation rather than integration.
- Although the Gypsy, Traveller and Roma third sector in the UK has been underfunded and undervalued by policymakers, it represents a crucial resource that can harness civil society expertise and guidance to deliver inclusive policies. What is critical in addressing the exclusion of Gypsy, Traveller and Roma communities is the building of partnerships and alliances, based on the principles of equality, which promote a pedagogy of hope – things can change.

Reflective exercises

- A recent report demonstrated that people (of all ages and different social classes) are more likely to make discriminatory comments about GTR communities and asylum seekers than about other marginalised groups. Why might this be and how might it be countered?
- To what extent do the leading and innovative roles of GTR female activists in their communities' campaigns exemplify the value of female emancipatory agendas in wider struggles against oppression?
- How can allies and sympathetic professionals support communities or community members in actively challenging internal group behaviours among some GTR communities that might be deemed oppressive without accentuating negative external stereotypes and increasing overall discrimination towards the group?
- What are the policy and practice implications of 'homogenising' diverse GTR communities?

Notes

[1] The term GTR is adopted as this is the favoured term of civil society groups reflecting the closer cultural connections between Gypsies and Travellers with particular reference to preferences for caravan dwelling and nomadism. At the same time, it reflects the desire to show solidarity with Roma communities, which, although practising different customs and practices, share with Gypsies and Travellers a propensity to being scapegoated and marginalised.

[2] Maggie Smith-Bendell is an author, campaigner and founder of Romani Gypsy associations in the West of England. Ryalla Duffy is chairperson of the Lincolnshire Gypsy Liaison Group. Both are long-term activists and core members of the Federation of Gypsy Liaison Groups.

References

Acton T. (1974) *Gypsy politics and social change*, London: Routledge Kegan Paul.

Acton, T. and Ryder, A. (2012) 'Recognising Gypsy, Roma, Traveller history and culture', in J. Richardson and A. Ryder (eds) (2012) *Gypsies and Travellers: Accommodation, empowerment and inclusion in British Society*, Bristol: Policy Press, pp 135-49.

Acton, T., Mercer, P., Day, J. and Ryder, A. (2014) 'Pedagogies of hope; the Gypsy Council and the National Gypsy Education Council', in A. Ryder, S. Cemlyn and T. Acton (eds) (2014) *Hearing the voice of Gypsies, Roma and Travellers: Inclusive community development*, Bristol: Policy Press, pp 29-48.

Alexander, S. and Greenfields, M. (2014) 'Below the Radar – Gypsy and Traveller self-help communities and the role of the Travellers Aid Trust', in A. Ryder, S. Cemlyn and T. Acton (eds) (2014) *Hearing the voice of Gypsies, Roma and Travellers: Inclusive community development*, Bristol: Policy Press, pp 137-53.

Alinsky, S. (1971) *Rules for radicals: A political primer for practical radicals*, New York, NY: Random House.

Arnstein, S. R. (1969) 'A ladder of citizen participation', *Journal of the American Institute of Planners*, vol 35, pp 216-24.

Bauman, Z. (2001) *The individualized society*, Cambridge: Polity Press.

Bogdán, M., Dunajeva, J., Junghaus, T., Kóczé, A., Rövid, M., Rostas, I., Ryder, A., Szilvási, M. and Taba, M. (eds) (2015) 'Nothing about us without us? Roma participation in policy making and knowledge production', *European Roma Rights Centre Journal*, available at: www. errc.org/roma-rights-journal

Brown, C. (2014) 'DCLG forced to release Gypsy and Traveller group information', *Inside Housing*, 5 November, available at: www. insidehousing.co.uk/dclg-forced-to-release-gypsy-and-traveller-group-information/7006679.article

Cemlyn, S., Smith-Bendell, M., Spencer, S. and Woodbury, S. (2014) 'Gender and community activism: the role of women in the work of the National Federation of Gypsy Liaison Groups', in A. Ryder, S. Cemlyn and T. Acton, (eds) (2014) *Hearing the voice of Gypsies, Roma and Travellers: Inclusive community development*, Bristol: Policy Press , pp 155-76.

Communities and Local Government (2012) Progress report by the ministerial working group on tackling inequalities experienced by Gypsies and Travellers. London, CLG, available at: www. gov.uk/government/uploads/system/uploads/attachment_data/file/6287/2124046.pdf

DCLG (Department for Communities and Local Government) (2015) *Planning policy for travellers sites*, London: DCLG, available at: www. gov.uk/government/uploads/system/uploads/attachment_data/file/457420/Final_planning_and_travellers_policy.pdf

Decade for Roma Inclusion Secretariat Foundation/Ryder, A. and Cemlyn, S. (2014) *Civil society monitoring on the implementation of the National Roma Integration Strategy in the United Kingdom in 2012 and 2013*, Budapest: Decade for Roma Inclusion Secretariat Foundation, available at: www.romadecade.org/cms/upload/file/9773_file15_uk_ civil-society-monitoring-report_en-1.pdf

Derrington, C. and Kendall, S. (2004) *Gypsy Traveller students in secondary schools: Culture, identity and achievement*, Stoke-on-Trent: Trentham Books.

Foucault, M. (1998) *The history of sexuality: The will to knowledge*, London, Penguin.

Freire, P. (1998) *Pedagogy of hope: Reliving pedagogy of the oppressed*, New York, NY: Continuum.

Hawes, D. and Perez, B. (1996) *The Gypsy and the state: The ethnic cleansing of British society*, Bristol: Policy Press.

Hodges, N. and Cemlyn, S. (2013) 'The accommodation experiences of older Gypsies and Travellers: personalisation of support and coalition policy', *Social Policy and Society*, vol 12, no 2, pp 205-19.

House of Commons Library (2012) *The Supporting People programme. Research Paper 12/40*, available at: http://researchbriefings.files. parliament.uk/documents/RP12-40/RP12-40.pdf

Johnson, C. and Ryder, A. (2015) 'New government measures on Gypsies and Travellers on a collision course with human rights', Institute of Race Relations, available at: www.irr.org.uk/news/ new-government-measures-on-gypsies-and-travellers-on-a-collision-course-with-human-rights

Jones, H. (2013) As easy as ABCD! (Asset Based Community Development), Leeds: Leeds GATE, available at: http://leedsgate. co.uk/easy-abcd-asset-based-community-development

Jordan, E. (2001) 'Exclusion of Travellers in state schools', *Educational Research*, vol 43, no 2, pp 117-32.

Lymbery, M. (2012) 'Critical commentary. Social work and personalisation', *British Journal of Social Work*, vol 42, pp 783-92.

Mason, R. (2013) 'Eric Pickles accused of using Travellers as political football', *The Guardian*, 9 August, available at: www.theguardian. com/world/2013/aug/09/eric-pickles-travellers-political-football

Matras,Y., Leggio, D.V. and Steel, M. (2015) ''Roma education' as a lucrative niche: ideologies and representations', *Zeitschrift für internationale Bildungsforschung und Entwicklungspädagogik*, vol 38, pp 11-17.

Mayall, D. (1988) *Gypsy-Travellers in nineteenth century society*, Cambridge: Cambridge University Press.

Mayo, M. (ed) (1977) *Women in the community*, London: Routledge and Kegan Paul.

McCabe, A., MacNamara, Y. and Mann, S. (2014) 'Building bridges, shifting sands: changing community development strategies in the Gypsy and Traveller voluntary sector', in A. Ryder, S. Cemlyn and T. Acton (eds) (2014) *Hearing the voice of Gypsies, Roma and Travellers: Inclusive community development*, Bristol: Policy Press, pp 99-117.

McCabe, A., Phillimore, J. and Maybin, L. (2010) *'Below the radar' activities and organisations in the third sector: A summary review of the literature*, Birmingham: Third Sector Research Centre.

McVeigh, R. (1997) 'Theorising sedentarism: the roots of anti-nomadism', in T. Acton, (ed) *Gypsy politics and traveller identity*, Hatfield: University of Hertfordshire Press, pp 7-25.

Nowotny, H. (1981) 'Women in public life in Austria', in C. Fuchs Epstein and R. Laub Coser (eds) *Access to power: Cross-national studies of women and elites*, London: George Allen and Unwin, pp 147-56.

Okely, J. (2001) 'Non-territorial culture as the rationale for the assimilation of Gypsy children', *Childhood*, vol 4, pp 63-80.

Parvin, P. (2009) 'Against localism: does decentralising power to communities fail minorities?', *The Political Quarterly*, vol 80, no 3, pp 351-60.

Powell, R. (2010) 'Gypsy-Travellers and welfare professional discourse: on individualisation and social integration', *Antipode*, vol 43, no 2, pp 471-93.

Richardson, J. and Ryder, A. (eds) (2012) *Gypsies and Travellers: Accommodation, empowerment and inclusion in British society*, Bristol: Policy Press.

Ryder, A. (2012) *'Hearing the voice of Gypsies and Travellers: The history, development and challenges of Gypsy and Traveller tenants' and residents' associations'*, Birmingham: Third Sector Research Centre.

Ryder, A. (2013) 'Snakes and ladders: inclusive community development and Gypsies and Travellers', *Community Development Journal*, vol 49, no 1, pp 21-36.

Ryder, A. (2015) 'Gypsies and Travellers: a big or divided society?', *Policy & Politics*, vol 43, no 1, pp 101-17.

Ryder, A, and Cemlyn, S. (2014) 'The Gypsy and Traveller Law Reform Coalition', in A. Ryder, S. Cemlyn and T. Acton (eds) (2014) *Hearing the voice of Gypsies, Roma and Travellers: Inclusive community development*, Bristol: Policy Press, pp 119-36.

Ryder, A. and Greenfields, M. (2010) *Roads to success: Routes to economic and social inclusion for Gypsies and Travellers*, London: Irish Traveller Movement in Britain.

Ryder, A. Cemlyn, S. and Acton, T. (eds) (2014) *Hearing the voice of Gypsies, Roma and Travellers: Inclusive community development*, Bristol: Policy Press.

Ryder, A., Cemlyn, S., Greenfields, M., Richardson, J. and Van Cleemput, P. (2012) 'A critique of UK coalition government policy on Gypsy, Roma and Traveller communities', Equality and Diversity Forum, available at: www.edf.org.uk/blog/?p=19051

Stewart, M. (1997) *The time of the gypsies*, Boulder, CO: Westview Press.

Trehan, N. (2001) 'In the name of the Roma', in W. Guy (ed) *Between past and future: The Roma of Central and Eastern Europe*, Hatfield: University of Hertfordshire Press, pp 134-49.

Udombana, N. (2000) 'The third world and the right to development: an agenda for the next millennium', *Human Rights Quarterly*, vol 22, no 3, pp 753-87.

Van Cleemput, P. (2012) 'Gypsy and Traveller health', in J. Richardson and A. Ryder (eds) *Gypsies and Travellers: Accommodation, empowerment and inclusion in British society*, Bristol: Policy Press, pp 43-60.

Vanderbeck, R.M. (2009) 'Gypsy-Traveller young people and the spaces of social welfare: a critical ethnography', *Acme: An International E-Journal for Critical Geographies*, vol 8, no 2, pp 304-40.

University of Manchester (2014) 'Roma migrants from Central and Eastern Europe', available at: www.policy.manchester.ac.uk/media/projects/policymanchester/Policy@Manchester-briefing---Roma-Migrants.pdf

EIGHT

Understanding grassroots arts groups and practices in communities

Hilary Ramsden, Jane Milling and Robin Simpson

Chapter aims

This chapter aims to:

• consider the distinctive elements of the amateur and grassroots arts sector;
• assess current understandings of the impacts and experiences of grassroots arts groups in communities;
• question the current critical framing of amateur and grassroots arts activities and groups;
• reflect on the direction of future research in amateur and grassroots arts in communities.

The amateur and grassroots arts sector

The most recent assessment of the scale of amateur arts participation in England came in the study *Our creative talent*, commissioned by the Department for Culture, Media and Sport (DCMS) and Arts Council England in 2008. The report judged that:

> [T]here are 49,140 groups across the country with a total of 5.9 million members. An additional 3.5 million people volunteer as extras or helpers – a total of 9.4 million people taking part. (Dodd et al, 2008, p 10)[1]

Given this scale of informal arts participation and activity at grassroots level within communities, it is surprising how little research there has been on the sector.[2] Cultural policy, and arts and cultural scholarship, has been primarily focused on formal, subsidised arts provision, artists and facilitators, while amateur arts groups and arts participation have been little considered in voluntary and community studies literature. The amateur and grassroots arts sector is diverse, rich in passion, knowledge and skills. While there is much actual crossover between amateur and commercial or state-subsidised culture in terms of shared aesthetic pleasure and social benefit, the amateur sector tends to be defined as a distinct sphere on the economic basis of its activities: that makers and participants are not paid for their creative labour. Holden's useful report *The ecology of culture* (2015) is a recent illustration of this distinction. In charting the wider cultural landscape in Britain, Holden identifies three spheres of culture: the publicly funded, commercially funded and 'homemade' cultural activities (2015, p 2).[3] We should be cautious of accepting this distinction too readily. While the amateur and grassroots arts sector frequently has a different economic underpinning, this is not an absolute or clear-cut distinction, as we shall see, and the idea of its economic difference by no means fully characterises or describes activity in the sector. Rather the challenge, as Edensor and colleagues have suggested, is to come to 'an understanding of vernacular and everyday landscapes of creativity [that] honours the non-economic values and outcomes produced by alternative, marginal, and quotidian creative practices' (Edensor et al, 2010, p 1). In other words, the challenge is to understand grassroots arts practices, and the sector, in ways that extend usefully beyond a definition or evaluation simply in economic terms.

One of the main ways in which this is occurring, as Robin Simpson, Chief Executive of Voluntary Arts observes, is that amateur arts activity is being recognised as an integral part of civil society that brings benefits to communities and individuals. Research from sociology, cultural studies and social policy has tended to cluster analysis around questions of community formation and social efficacy. In particular, research has asked questions about the development of relationships between people and groups within communities who would not normally, in the round of their everyday lives, meet 'different others', international as well as national, through a shared interest in an arts activity. Thus, the lens through which amateur, informal or 'homemade' arts are viewed has been focused on evaluation and assessment of social impacts and public good, such as health and wellbeing benefits, social cohesion, individual and community empowerment, and increased social capital. We suggest in this chapter that, while these areas of focus are useful for understanding some of the possible relationships between grassroots arts practices and communities, such a framework does not capture the extent and intricacies of grassroots arts activities and the sector as a whole.

Evidence in this chapter arises from desk-based research that was carried out in partnership with the Third Sector Research Centre at the University of Birmingham, the University of Exeter and the University of South Wales, and supported by Voluntary Arts, funded under the Arts and Humanities Research Council's Connected Communities programme.[4] The study examined literature from 2005 onwards, with some additional reference to earlier key texts, in order to develop a contemporary picture of the state of research into amateur and voluntary arts in the UK. In addition to a wide range of academic literature from different disciplines such as ethnography, music and the visual arts, the study drew on policy documents, voluntary arts literature, and grassroots arts groups' membership publications and newsletters. We were explicitly looking at voluntary and amateur arts, where groups self-organise and are participant initiated and governed, and therefore we did not focus on community arts or art as therapy where groups are initiated or facilitated by professional artists. In this chapter, we set out to examine the way in which the informal arts sector has been defined and valued in these studies and policy documents, and to question some of the ways in which the arts practices within the sector have been framed.

Framing informal arts practices

The broader context for considering amateur and grassroots arts activities might be found in the remarkable recent increase in user-generated content and the evolution of the creative commons in social media and within the creative industries. Parallel to the outpouring of self-created work on social media, British television output has found repeated audience success with revamped entertainment talent contests featuring 'ordinary' people, and in programming competitions that follow individuals and their hobbies in craft arenas such as cooking, baking, sewing and pottery. This impetus has been picked up and extended through nationwide initiatives such as the BBC's Get Creative campaign and the Big Painting Challenge. Individual engagement in informal leisure, hobby and grassroots activities is highly visible in contemporary British popular culture. One of the interesting aspects of this development is the concomitant increase in awareness that cultural engagement is not just about the consumption of formal culture. Calhoun and Sennett in their collection *Practicing culture* (2007) reminded cultural sociology and cultural studies that:

> The production and reproduction of culture is not confined to a specialized realm of official cultural artefacts; it is vital to all aspects of social life. [...N]ot only as an abstract system of norms or knowledge, but also as implicit, often embodied understandings of how things work ... both available in part to actors' explicit knowledge and reflection and in part disclosed only in performance. (Calhoun and Sennett, 2007, pp 5, 8)

In taking a broader canvas for thinking about cultural activity, there has been a turn from viewing cultural participation in terms of the consumption of or being an audience for public art work, and a move towards understanding arts participation as creative making by the widest range of individuals, and as an activity in itself a crucial part of all social life.

Participation in the informal, amateur and grassroots arts covers an enormously wide range of arts practices and levels of involvement. The characterisation of the sector as alternative, marginal or quotidian, as Edensor et al (2010) identify, is by no means the whole story. An important element in understanding the sector as a whole must be in judging the extent to which common characterisations hold true. For example, grassroots arts groups are often described as operating at the small or micro-scale, both in terms of group participant numbers and localised contexts. However, our research examined the grey literature from the multiple national organisational bodies that connect groups, and provide a national and international visibility and overview. In post-World War II discourses, amateur arts' perceived distance from formal and subsidised arts agendas and funding has been constructed in contrast to the rising professionalisation of the artist figure or company where expertise and talent are denoted by an emphasis on innovation and aesthetic difficulty (Hewison, 1995; Florida, 2002). Yet recent studies on the precarity of remunerative artistic labour (Taylor and Littleton, 2012), and the impetus for all workers to become 'creative' (Stebbins, 1992, 2004; Sennett, 1998), have blurred boundaries between work and leisure, professional and amateur in the aesthetic realm. Moreover, discussions of the amateur and grassroots arts sector have to grapple with the extensive range of practices and activities included in this sector. Beyond artistic practices that might connect in some way to formal or commercial culture, amateur arts participation has sometimes emerged from traditions of autonomy and resistance to commodified arts production (see the Craftivist Collective website, https://craftivist-collective.com; McKay, 1998; Gauntlett, 2011; Greer,

2014). Conversely, many amateur cultural practices have a strong connection with traditional or folk arts, rather than adhering to notions of aesthetic modernity, and some quotidian practices may fall outside classification as art, craft or cultural activity. So, defining the amateur and grassroots arts sector itself has thrown up some interesting critical challenges for researchers.

Beyond amateur-professional binaries

Feist and Hutchison's 1991 study of *Amateur arts in the UK* suggested that amateur and professional art activities are 'intertwined and interdependent', as a 'complex amateur-professional continuum or spectrum of ambition, accomplishment and activity' (p 294). Defining amateur participation is far more complex than the question of who is being paid: some amateurs might be paid for their services, some professionals might donate their services. Smith's (2006) study of amateur symphonic choruses problematised a simple separation of the 'amateur' and 'professional', when amateur choirs perform with professional orchestras, and *are* the equivalent and standard of a professional chorus (2006, p 299). There is evidence of an increasing connection between amateur and professional arts organisations, for example, Open Stages, a collaboration between multiple amateur theatre societies and the Royal Shakespeare Company, or Making Music initiatives that give amateur music organisations the opportunity to perform and record music as part of the BBC Radio 3 Listen Up or Play to the Nation projects. Not only may personnel mix between amateur and subsidised realms, with amateur arts groups employing professionals for specific roles, but they may also inhabit both realms at different stages of their life course, with amateurs as retired professionals themselves.

This model of the close connection between amateur and professional initially might seem to echo Stebbins' notion of 'serious leisure', which he designates as 'the systematic pursuit of an amateur, hobbyist or volunteer activity that is sufficiently substantial and interesting for the participant to find a career there in the acquisition and expression of its special skills and knowledge' (Stebbins, 1992, p 3). The idea of the amateur sector as a training ground for professional achievement is a perspective that has interested government policy, as *Our creative talent* for the DCMS notes: 'Over the last five years, 34% of amateur groups have had members who went on to become professional' (Dodd et al, 2008, p 11). However, as Smith's (2006) study of amateur choirs reveals, contrary to this sense of 'progression' from untrained amateur to highly qualified professional, many amateur choir members do not aspire to 'professional' status, but are already achieving professional standards and for themselves value performing with professionals in their field.

A recurring trope in discourses around the informal arts is that they should aspire to standards of expertise and achievement set by the professional or publicly subsidised realm. Citing Reid, Jackson-Tretchikoff's (2008) study of amateur operatic societies in Auckland pits an evaluation of an amateur creative practice against the non-professional basis of the organisation: 'Amateurism is a very important element in our artistic heritage ... as long as it is not amateurish' (p 195). Taylor (2008) sees the professional arts sector as 'key to establishing the standards and skills that are transmitted to local neighborhoods through the efforts of amateur and semi-professional artists', although he suggests that no sector is more important than the other, both being 'elements of a more comprehensive ecology that includes both formal and informal acts of activity' (Taylor, 2008, p 11). In these accounts, there appears to be a traditional view of the separation and purpose of these two sectors of arts activities: the professionals set and preserve the standards and quality by which amateurs measure their work. Yet this separation is by no means universal in the informal arts sector. In her study of amateur tap dancers, Lawson (2009) draws on Becker's notion of art worlds and expertise to argue that 'the structural constraint of legitimacy is lessened by the special status accorded to amateurs in a consumerist society. Amateurs, being the aficionados of commercial culture, are leaders' (p 4). Likewise, as Lee (2007) identifies in his study of Chinese street opera in Singapore, amateur *xiqu* groups are bearers of cultural heritage, and 'performing *xiqu* is significant more as a celebration of social status than an achievement of technical expertise' (p 406). In the *xiqu*, scholar-amateur performers are seen as embodying higher levels of 'self-cultivation' and Confucian principles of behaviour appropriate to ideals of Singaporean culture.

Defining the amateur and grassroots arts sector is a complex undertaking but an increasingly important one, with recent cultural and social policy turning its attention to the role that participation in informal arts might make both to British cultural ecology and to broader social participation. Informal arts participation in 'homemade' culture has a key role to play in the democratisation of cultural life for Holden:

> From the historic objects and activities of folk art, through to the post-modern punk garage band and the YouTube upload. Here, the definition of what counts as culture is

much broader; it is defined by an informal self-selecting peer group, and the barriers to entry are much lower. (Holden, 2008, p 11)

For Hewison, grassroots culture has an 'essentially spontaneous and democratic nature', although he goes on to suggest that much of this grassroots cultural production 'will be trivial and self-referential' (Hewison, 2014, p 221).[5] There remains a gently pejorative romanticism lurking in Hewison's and Holden's characterisation of 'homemade' culture, which appears as less significant than subsidised and professional culture, but which is activated on behalf of funded culture as part of 'building the holistic case for arts and culture', as Chair of Arts Council England, Peter Bazalgette, suggested in his annual report *The value of arts and culture to people and society* (ACE, 2014, p 7). It is difficult to sustain a framework of values that can encompass both the justification of public subsidy for artistic excellent policed by cultural elites, and the participatory enthusiasm of a Morris side, amateur painting group or sewing bee. Indeed, Hewison's recent study of *Cultural capital* (2014) argues that the 'cultural capitalism' of recent discourses of the creative industries has done little to alter the restricted gatekeeper of official culture. The informal arts sector has tended to be seen within cultural policy as a training ground for professional practice, as audience building for publicly subsidised cultural provision, or as an echo of developments in publicly subsidised arts practice that has turned to interactional or participatory processes as examined by artist Hutchinson (2010) or curator Bourriaud (1998) and academics such as Bishop (2012) and Kester (2004; 2011). Those few social and cultural policy studies that have engaged with the informal arts sector and that have begun to examine participatory arts practices, have tended to use discourses of evaluation that consider arts practices in terms of their social impacts and benefits. This approach is not without its difficulties, as we will examine in some detail.

Social impacts and benefits: a dominant discourse

A central discourse in scholarly studies of amateur arts practices is the argument that participating in the arts leads to wider individual and social benefits and impacts. This chimes with the evolution, in cultural policy circles, of a defence of ongoing public subsidy for the arts because of the arts' instrumental benefits. Belfiore and others have argued that there are significant problems with valuing artistic activity, usually facilitated by a professional artist, predominantly as a means of developing individual wellbeing or social cohesion (Belfiore, 2012). Beyond individual benefits, participatory arts projects led by professional artists have been framed as cultural interventions key to successful neighbourhood regeneration. Given that arts *participation* is central to these understandings of publicly funded community arts or professionally led projects, it is clear to see that similar claims might effectively be made for projects guided and initiated by amateur arts groups (Howard-Spink, 2004; Gray et al, 2010). Grassroots arts-led regeneration has been less studied, but it draws on a similar range of precepts (Wohlheim, 1998; Taylor, 2008; Dunin, 2009). Many of the studies examined followed the experience of Wali and colleagues' research, *Informal arts: Finding cohesion, capacity and other cultural benefits in unexpected places* (2002), which considered the informal arts a key part of the arts continuum and found evidence that they were 'an important reservoir of social capital, significant for life-long-learning, building civic engagement and strengthening communities' (p ix). Most recent scholarly studies of informal and grassroots arts groups examine or celebrate amateur cultural participation as contributing to community development, social cohesion and developing a sense of social belonging, whether the aim is to reinforce the norms of the given social context or to offer an alternative or radical intervention for community development (ACE, 2007; Meade and Shaw, 2007; Hui and Stickley, 2009; Burt and Atkinson, 2011).

The concentration on public good, impacts and benefits in the discourses used about informal arts groups draws on Bourdieu's framing of arts participation as producing, and produced by, social and cultural capital (Bourdieu, 1986). Bourdieu's construction – that individuals benefit socially from participating in the cultural field, acquiring social capital from demonstrations of their cultural taste – has furthered an argument that an individual might alter their relationship within a social hierarchy by leveraging their acquisition of embodied cultural capital:

> The work of acquisition is work on oneself (self-improvement), an effort that presupposes a personal cost, an investment, above all of time, but also of that socially constituted form of libido, *libido sciendi*, with all the privation, renunciation, and sacrifice that it may entail.... The specifically symbolic logic of distinction additionally secures material and symbolic profits for possessors of a large cultural capital. (Bourdieu, 1986, pp 243, 244)

In other words, for Bourdieu, cultural participation has an explicit utilitarian value for an individual. Putnam's interpretation of this model in *Bowling alone* (2000) suggested a decline in American associational life. He saw a concomitant reduction in Americans' participation in shared creative activities bringing about a decline in their bridging social capital, the ability of individuals to reach out to different others, and an increase in self-same, bonding social capital. Sennett's recent work, particularly *The craftsman* (2008) and *Together* (2012), has emphasised that the value and significance of culture for participants lies not in the consuming of culture but its making, doing and practising (Sennett, 2008). Sennett argues that craftsmanship offers bridging social capital, and, in *Together*, he suggests that individuals rehearse cooperation in the social and political realm in part through participating in shared creative activities; that is, creative participation is training in bridging social capital that can prepare us to embrace cooperation with different others. In part, this debate around questions of social and cultural participation and practice has drawn sociology and humanities scholars' attention back to informal, vernacular and grassroots arts participation. This is because the social capital argument has become a dominant discourse. The sense that arts intervention might facilitate enhanced social networks and enhanced social cohesion has percolated down to the previously unrecognised and unnoticed arenas of informal and grassroots arts groups.

Indeed, amateur participants in many of the studies of amateur arts practices report that they commit considerable time and energy to their activities and from which they derive 'durable benefits' such as 'self-esteem ... feelings of accomplishment ... social interaction and belongingness' (Smith, 2006, p 295). In his study of the anime music video scene, Ito (2010) examines the intricacies and nuances of grassroots arts activity:

> Non–commercial, amateur, and peer-based production scenes thrive on models of open participation and access, but processes for differentiating participation, recognizing leadership, and developing status and reputation are also central to the scene.... The value people get out of participation is a complex alchemy of community participation, recognition, and the pleasures of creation and connoisseurship. (Ito, 2010, p 6)

Much of the research into grassroots arts activities in communities examined by our review followed this agenda and charted evidence for individual wellbeing, public good and social benefit arising from participation in informal arts activities.

Understanding informal arts groups in communities

Perhaps the clearest and most significant example of the utilitarian discourse of social benefit from arts activities comes through the evolution of the notion of 'impact'. Measuring social impact has become not just part of an agenda, but the agenda itself. Not only do most scholarly studies of amateur arts participation chart the questions of impact and social outcomes, but membership organisations in the amateur arts are also frequently turning to this language in articulating their aims. Discussions of the social impacts of arts and cultural participation usefully draw on Guetzkow's work (2002) on the mechanisms of arts impact, which distinguishes between impacts on the individual and those on the community. Guetzkow highlights the shortcomings of arts impact studies that make generalisations about impact on the overall population from small sample studies. The recurring topics of interest in the scholarly and grey literature we reviewed were the impacts and outcomes from informal arts participation that result in enhancements for individual wellbeing, the evolution of beneficial social networks and the possibilities for enhancing social cohesion.

Individual wellbeing

Amateur and grassroots arts are seen as having particularly powerful impact capabilities in the areas of health and wellbeing, exploring a multitude of elements from an individual's self-confidence and self-esteem to the quality of life in a particular neighbourhood or geographical community (Hui and Stickley, 2009; Burt and Atkinson, 2011). The articulation of these wellbeing benefits is drawn from studies of professional artists' interventions. The Arts Council England report, *The arts, health and wellbeing*, recognised 'that people's health and wellbeing is influenced by a range of interconnecting factors' (ACE, 2007, p 4) and that art interventions 'produce, at their best, startling artistic, personal and social outcomes' (p 7). In other words physical, mental and social wellbeing are interlinked and art can work on all these levels. In the Arts Council England report, it is professional artists who create and facilitate the projects with participants as 'recipients'. Amateur arts activities, on the other hand, have the agency of the process firmly in the minds and bodies of the participants themselves. In a study of Australian amateur arts groups, Bendle and Patterson (2009) found that volunteering and leisure activities have positive effects on 'people's physical and mental vitality' (p 273). A study by Burt and Atkinson (2011) argued that 'creative craft hobbies such as quilting can be a meaningful vehicle for enhancing wellbeing' (p 54) particularly for older people, with the activity helping their 'cognitive, creative and emotional well-being' (p 58). The authors went further to argue that:

> Whether it is growing vegetables, knitting a jumper or discovering a new scientific formula creativity may be fundamental for wellbeing and has received little attention so far within Public Health. Exploring creativity and what people do in their everyday lives, which they deem creative, may be an important avenue for wellbeing promoters. Additionally, more consideration needs to be given to all hobbies, from reading to train-spotting, and their potential for enhancing wellbeing. (Burt and Atkinson, 2011, p 59)

Drawing on findings from professionally facilitated arts intervention, the language of wellbeing outcomes from creative participation has been extended into the amateur and informal arts fields. An increasing number of studies are using these indicators to assess ways in which hobbies such as knitting or vegetable growing produce enhanced physical, mental, emotional and social wellbeing for a wide range of participants of different ages and abilities.

Studies over the past 10 years show increasing evidence testifying to the positive effects of participation in arts activities on physical health and wellbeing. A study of group singing and performance on two groups of people – one choir created for homeless men, the other for middle-class singers – showed singing had a positive physiological effect on levels of hormones that facilitate emotional balance (Bailey and Davidson, 2005, p 271). Hui and Stickley's report, *Guidelines to Art* (2009), found improvements in Alzheimer's patients' memory and independence over a number of painting sessions. There are also arts projects, such as the Tremble Clefs, an American amateur music group for Parkinson's disease sufferers, that have claimed success in countering some of the physical effects of illness (http://endo-education.com/tremble-clefs). Participants in Burt and Atkinson's (2011) UK study observe that quilting 'helped to maintain cognitive abilities', which is borne out by empirical research (Geda et al, 2010) showing that 'participating in hobbies ... reduced the rate of cognitive decline in older individuals' (Burt and Atkinson, 2011, p 59). Amateur participants in a number of membership journals make the connection between physical and mental health and wellbeing, and one article focuses on the organisation Diabetes UK, which suggests that participation in dance can help prevent and educate people about diabetes (James, 2010, p 29). The editorial in *Highnotes* makes quite specific connections between improvement of the capacity of breath and lungs and wind and brass instrument playing (Cardy, 2011, p 3). Many of these studies also note that improved physical wellbeing not only benefits the individual but also arguably the rest of the community through a reduction in demand on health services.

Overall, the literature claims that participation in informal arts activities has demonstrable positive benefits for individuals in terms of their mental, emotional and social wellbeing. Unsurprisingly, these findings are supported and mirrored by the extensive user art movement, which uses art in therapeutic contexts. Bailey and Davidson (2005) found that, for the homeless men in their study group, singing 'seemed to facilitate emotional balance' (p 277). Participants overall found their self-confidence and self-esteem improved. They were able to make 'positive changes in their lives' as a result of gaining confidence from participating in the choir. Similarly, the lifestyle of ageing homeless men who formed a Musubi storytelling troupe in Osaka 'changed dramatically' (Nakagawa, 2010, p 21) through their performances two to three times per month and the media coverage they received as a result of their work. Nakagawa (2010) maintains they are now 'certain of their raison d'être and now possess a connection to society' (p 21). Hui and Stickley's (2009) study shows that working with the Guidelines to Art scheme created a sense of achievement and a 'huge boost to ... self esteem and confidence' (p 14). The work reinforced participants' self-worth and they appeared to 'have the confidence to carry on trying more things at home' (p 14). One of the nurse managers involved in the scheme suggested that "creativity creates confidence and with confidence comes choice" (p 14). Participants in Burt and Atkinson's (2011) study felt that 'finishing a quilt and receiving praise from others boosted confidence' (p 5). One participant observed that she felt she was 'still valuable' and that the activity of quilting "brought back confidence ... because you begin to learn new skills ... you begin to become a person rather than a machine" (p 3). Another participant felt that receiving affirmation from others was important: "to get appreciation back is good" (p 4). Individuals in Smith's study (2006) of symphonic choirs listed 'self esteem ... feelings of accomplishment' among the 'durable benefits' of participation (p 295). These individual mental and emotional benefits and outcomes were also linked to social interaction and were formed in part through the participation in more densely configured social networks.

Relationships and social networks

Whether it is joining a dance class, a knitting group or being part of an anime music video network, the social aspect of participation figures prominently in individuals' reasons for taking up an arts activity. Lawson's study (2009) found that 'seeking a sense of community' was one of six motivations for taking up a dance class. Additionally she observed that the 'affectual element' of the activity 'develops ties amongst participants and serves social ends' (2009, p 14). Reynolds (2010) also identifies staying connected and involved as being an important motive for older women for making art. For the homeless men in Nakagawa's study (2010), their choir provided a kind of social support system. An anime music video network provides a similar social connection, one participant referring to it as a "community type effort, village minded" (Ito, 2010, p 6). A member of the Knitting and Crocheting Guild remarked that in addition to the inspiration and learning that she had received, the friendships emerging from belonging to a 'cafe knitting group' provided a 'glue' to keep the group going (O'Connell Edwards, 2007, p 7). Participants learning Celtic traditional music found that in teaching others who were less proficient players, they had to develop their people skills to communicate in constructive ways (Waldron and Veblen, 2009, p 63). Likewise, Bailey and Davidson found that performing in a choir enabled homeless men 'to connect to the larger society from which they have been estranged' (2005, p 277). Successful communication through an arts activity that may not be based on verbal or oral skills may increase an individual's confidence to subsequently communicate through those skills.

The social networks of grassroots arts organisations extend widely. In addition to the local networking opportunities offered by arts activities, there are reasonably extensive regional and national networks representing all the types of activity examined in our initial study. Newsletters and magazines issued by amateur arts groups and societies have substantial sections dedicated to lists of regional and local groups, reports from regional groups, meetings and events organised in the regions (*Slipknot*, 2007, pp 59-63; O'Neill, 2008, pp 31-5; Smith, 2008, pp 81-6;). Beyond these are the multiple and complex web-based networks that use fora such as chat rooms, etc., in addition to an increasing variety of social media that create and proliferate networks and structures for communication and exchange.

Social cohesion and place identity

Much of the literature makes an argument that participation in arts activities can lead to improved communication and social skills. A desire to engage members of an older generation in conversations about their Harlem neighbourhood enabled two young African American adults to develop their communication and social skills through an arts activity that included photography, poetry and painting (Kinloch, 2007). The young adults in Kinloch's (2007) study were developing a sense of community and cohesion through a collective process of conversation with older residents and information gathering, creating stories, poetry, documentaries and exhibitions. Kinloch suggests that these conversations resulted in a learning that 'became reciprocal, active, and transformational for both the adults and the youngsters', enriching and affirming a sense of identity and belonging in those Harlem neighbourhoods: 'Youth activism was met with adult learning' (p 46).

Residents of Ravensthorpe, Western Australia (Mayes, 2010) engaged in the production of local postcards that they sold to tourists. What began with residents' desire to put their community on the map has developed over a period of 20 years into a local small arts industry that offers individual and local views of Ravensthorpe distinct from the images on commercial postcards. In addition to creating revenues for themselves and the community, the 'lay' or amateur postcard production has contributed to the creation of a local rural place identity for residents and tourists alike. Such activities and processes can lead to improved community image and identity, with amateur creativity taking a place of increased visibility within a town. Taylor (2008) suggests that the correlation between arts activity and neighbourhood stability is evidence of magnetisation – 'an increase in the desirability, commitment, social integration, and quality of life in a community area' (p 1). He maintains that arts have the ability to create enjoyable public spaces, to create shared experience, and to encourage intergenerational activity. Further, amateur, informal arts contribute to this as well. It may be through such formal and informal networking and the development of a located identity for participants that a strong sense of independence and desire for self-governance emerges. The scholarly literature and policy documentation of informal arts groups' activities builds a picture of the social connectivity and networks that develop for participants and for the wider community, generating a sense of cohesion and an enhanced sense of place.

Conclusion

Much of the policy and scholarly literature on the informal arts sector uses an impact or benefit framework, and identifies some of the valuable and valued elements of participation in informal arts groups. However, this provides a rather limited focus on those groups, and some recent literature is seeking to explore how we might reframe our perspectives on the grassroots arts activities. Matarasso's Regular Marvels project centres on informal arts in which, following his long resistance to instrumentalist approaches to cultural development, he is looking for new modes of perceiving and valuing informal cultural activities. In his study of a West Bromwich Operatic Society production, Matarasso states:

> The arts are not divided into two separate and antagonistic worlds: the amateurs and the professionals. It is better understood as a complex ecosystem in which people may play different roles at different times or in different aspects of their careers. (Matarasso, 2012, p 76)

Foreshadowing Holden, he argues that the conception of a cultural ecology has been helpful in transposing a focus from official culture and economic assessments of value. In drawing attention to the prevailing force of discourses of instrumentalism or economic benefit, Matarasso returns us to the recognition of the value of amateur arts by participants themselves:

> Its value comes from doing, from understanding something from the inside, experientially, and its greatest prize is not applause, joyous as that is, but nurturing skill, ability and understanding in community. (Matarasso, 2012, p 81)

Recent scholarship focuses on those unique elements of informal *arts* activities – as distinct from sports, charity or environmental volunteering – creative, imaginative and improvisatory *experience* and creative skills development. As Ito suggests, amateur arts participation offers 'a complex alchemy of community participation, recognition, and the pleasures of creation and connoisseurship' (Ito, 2010, p 14). Although it is rarely the focus of scholarly studies, the grey literature from membership groups and amateur art organisations reveals that many participants take part in arts activities for the art itself. Rather than simple assertions of the inherent aesthetic value of informal art forms or products, the aesthetic remains a key, under-examined, element of an agreed social imaginary. For example, art work renders a community more aesthetically pleasing, through public artwork, murals and mosaics, and beautified community gathering places; it promotes and enhances an individual's and community's sense of 'beauty' and/ or aesthetics; it inspires and develops individual and community openness to the usefulness of art within everyday life; it encourages more people to become involved in arts activities that exist within a community. As Ruiz (2004) eloquently suggests, further research on the 'intrinsic nature of art and its capacity to provide meaning to different individuals and different cultures' might enable us to better understand why participating in amateur and informal arts is important for individuals and communities. Extending beyond the predominant trend in scholarship that focuses on social impacts and that sets up firm distinctions between the commercial or subsidised arts sector, and the amateur, informal arts sector, further research is needed into the areas of experience, pleasure and aesthetics. Such investigations will permit a re-evaluation of the diversity of contemporary arts practices experienced in the UK, and integrate our understanding of the informal, amateur arts sector within Hewison's call for 'a more generous and open conception of culture ... [and] a reassertion of the value of the public realm' (Hewison, 2014, p 225).

Key learning

- The amateur and informal arts sector has tended to be characterised by its economic difference from the professional or subsidised art worlds.
- Hierarchical structures of cultural value continue to evolve a pejorative view of the informal arts sector.
- Much of the current discourse around the amateur arts sector is characterised by a focus on social benefits and impacts drawn from a social capital model.
- This focus overrides other, more diverse, avenues that might be explored around aesthetic participation itself: the idea of experience and questions of aesthetics.

Reflective exercises

- What are the distinctive features of informal arts activities in communities, as opposed to professionally facilitated arts projects?
- What does participation in informal arts activities offer that is not available through other forms of participation in voluntary or charity organisations?
- How can, or should, the value of the voluntary arts be measured?

Notes

[1]   These figures apply to England, not the UK as a whole, thus the estimation of the scale of grassroots arts participation is larger again.

[2]   There have been a number of commissioned surveys of amateur arts participation and policy documents surrounding the sector, for example Feist and Hutchison's (1991) *Amateur arts in the UK* for the Policy Studies Institute, Giesekam's (2000) report for the Scottish Arts Council, *Amateur and community theatre in Scotland*, and Lowe and Simpson's (2010) *Achieving great art for everyone: Voluntary Arts England response to achieving great art for everyone.*

[3]   There may be a suggestion of the relative significance attributed to the sector reflected in the number of interviewees in this report: only three interviewees from the 'homemade' sector compared with 22 from the public or public-commercial sector, and 15 from the commercial or public-commercial sector.

[4]   Jenny Phillimore, Hamish Fyfe, Angus McCabe, Jane Milling, Hilary Ramsden and Robin Simpson, *The Role of Grassroots Arts Activities in Communities: A Scoping Study* (AHRC grant AH/I507590/1), see Ramsden et al, *The role of grassroots arts activity*, TSRC Working Paper 68, (Dec 2011).

[5]   This implicit value judgment chimes with Holden's *Democratic culture* report that still determines that 'popular literature, television and crossovers on the whole produce rubbish (they do, although they occasionally produce brilliance)' (2008, p 23).

References

ACE (Arts Council England) (2007) *The arts, health and wellbeing*, London: Arts Council England, available at: www.artscouncil.org.uk/media/uploads/phpC1AcLv.pdf

ACE (2014) *The value of arts and culture to people and society: An evidence review*, Manchester: Arts Council England, available at: www.artscouncil.org.uk/what-we-do/research-and-data/value-arts-and-culture-people-and-society-evidence-review

Bailey, B.A. and Davidson, J.W. (2005) 'Effects of group singing and performance for marginalized and middle-class singers', *Psychology of Music*, vol 33, no 3, pp 269-303.

Belfiore, E. (2012) '"Defensive instrumentalism" and the legacy of New Labour's cultural policies', *Cultural Trends*, vol 21, no 2, pp 103-11.

Bendle, L.J. and Patterson, I. (2009) 'Mixed serious leisure and grassroots organizational capacity: a study of amateur artist groups in a regional Australian city', *Leisure Sciences*, vol 31, no 3, pp 272-86.

Bishop, C. (2012) *Artificial hells: Participatory art and the politics of spectatorship*, London: Verso.

Bourdieu, P. (1986) 'The forms of capital', in J. Richardson (ed) *Handbook of theory and research for the sociology of education*, New York, NY: Greenwood, pp 241-58.

Bourriaud, N. (1998) *Relational aesthetics*, Paris: Les presses du reel.

Burt, E.L. and Atkinson, J. (2011) 'The relationship between quilting and wellbeing', *Journal of Public Health*, vol 34, no 1, pp 54-9.

Calhoun, C. and Sennett, R. (2007) *Practicing culture*, London: Routledge.

Cardy, K. (2011) 'Editorial', *Highnotes*, no 15, February, p 3.

Dodd, F., Graves, A. and Taws, K. (2008) *Our creative talent: The voluntary and amateur arts in England*, London: DCMS.

Dunin, E.I. (2009) 'Village "folklor" [dance] integrated as a touristic commodity in the Dubrovnik area: an overview 1948-1977-2008', *Nar. umjet*, vol 46, no 1, pp 61-75.

Edensor, T., Leslie, D., Millington, S. and Rantisi, N. (eds) (2010) *Spaces of vernacular creativity*, London: Routledge.

Feist, A. and Hutchison, R. (1991) *Amateur arts in the UK*, London: Policy Studies Institute.

Florida, R. (2002) *The rise of the creative class*, New York, NY: Basic Books.

Gauntlett, D. (2011) *Making is creating: The social meaning of creativity*, London: Polity.

Geda, Y., Roberts, R., Knopman, D., Christianson, T., Pankratz, V., Ivnik, R., Boeve, B., Tangalos, E., Petersen, R. and Rocca, W. (2010) 'Physical exercise and mild cognitive impairment: a population-based study', *Archives of Neurology*, vol 67, no 1, pp 80-6.

Giesekam, G. (2000) *Amateur and community theatre in Scotland*, Glasgow: Scottish Arts Council.

Gray, N., Oré De Boehm, C., Farnsworth, A. and Wolf, D. (2010) 'Integration of creative expression into community based participatory research and health promotion with native Americans', *Family and Community Health*, vol 33, no 3, pp 186-92.

Greer, B. (2014) *Craftivism: The art of craft and activism*, London: Arsenal Pulp Press.

Guetzkow, J. (2002) *How the arts impact communities: An introduction to the literature on arts impact studies*, Working Paper Series, 2. Princeton, NJ: Centre for Arts and Cultural Policy Studies, available at: www.princeton.edu/~artspol/workpap/WP20%20-%20Guetzkow.pdf

Hewison, R. (1995) *Culture and consensus: England, art and politics since 1940*, London: Methuen.

Hewison, R. (2014) *Cultural capital: The rise and fall of creative Britain*, London: Verso.

Holden, J. (2008) *Democratic culture: Opening up the arts to everyone*, London: Demos.

Holden, J. (2015) *The ecology of culture: A report commissioned by the Arts and Humanities Cultural Value Programme*, Swindon: Arts and Humanities Research Council.

Howard-Spink, S. (2004) 'Grey Tuesday, online cultural activism and the mash-up of music and politics', *First Monday*, vol 9, no 10, 4 October, available at: http://firstmonday.org/ojs/index.php/fm/article/view/1180

Hui, A. and Stickley, T. (2009) *Guidelines to art: Making art available to all, an evaluation report*, Nottingham: Society for All Artists/University of Nottingham.

Hutchinson, M. (2010) 'Four stages of public art', *Third Text*, vol 16, no 4, pp 329-438.

Ito, M. (2010) 'The rewards of non-commercial production: distinctions and status in the anime music video Scene', *First Monday*, vol 15, no 5, 3 May, available at: http://firstmonday.org/ojs/index.php/fm/article/view/2968/2528

Jackson-Tretchikoff, J. (2008) 'Amateur operatics in Auckland: musical theatre's last frontier', *Studies in Musical Theatre*, vol 2, no 2, pp: 195-207.

James, A. (2010) *Animated: the community dance magazine*, 'Diabetes UK embraces Dance', *Autumn*, pp. 29-30, available at: www.communitydance.org.uk

Kester, G. (2004) *Conversation pieces: Community and communication in modern art*, Berkeley, CA: University of California Press.

Kester, G. (2011) *The one and the many: Contemporary collaborative art in a global context*, Durham, NC: Duke University Press.

Kinloch, V. (2007) 'Youth representations of community, art, and struggle in Harlem', *New Directions for Adult and Continuing Education*, no 116, Winter, pp 37-49.

Lawson, H.M. (2009) 'Why dance? The motivations of an unlikely group of dancers', *Music and Arts in Action*, vol 1, no 2, pp 3-15.

Lee, T.S. (2007) 'Chinese theatre, Confucianism, and nationalism: amateur Chinese opera tradition in Singapore', *Asian Theatre Journal*, vol 24, no 2, pp 397-421.

Lowe, M. and Simpson, R. (2010) *Achieving great art for everyone: Voluntary Arts England response to achieving great art for everyone*, London: Voluntary Arts.

Matarasso, F. (2012) *Where we dream*, West Bromwich: Multistory.

Mayes, R. (2010) 'Doing cultural work: local postcard production and place identity in a rural shire', *Journal of Rural Studies*, vol 26, no 1, pp 1-11.

McKay, G. (1998) *DiY culture: Party and protest in nineties Britain*, London: Verso.

Meade, R. and Shaw, M. (2007) 'Community development and the arts: reviving the democratic imagination', *Community Development Journal*, vol 42, no 4, pp 413-21.

Nakagawa, S. (2010) 'Socially inclusive cultural policy and arts-based urban community regeneration', *Cities*, vol 27, no 1, pp 16-24.

O'Connell Edwards, L. (2007) 'Message from the Editor', *Slipknot*, no 117, September, p 7.

O'Neill, C. (2008) 'Running a local area group', *Harmonica World* April/May, pp 31-5, available at: http://harmonica.co.uk/magazine.htm

Putnam, R. (2000) *Bowling alone: The collapse and revival of American community*, New York, NY: Simon & Schuster.

Ramsden, H., Milling, J., Phillimore, J., McCabe, A., Fyfe, H. and Simpson, R. (2011) *The role of grassroots arts activities in communities: a scoping study*, TSRC Working Paper 68, available at: www.birmingham.ac.uk/generic/tsrc/documents/tsrc/working-papers/working-paper-68.pdf

Reynolds, F. (2010) 'Colour and communion: exploring the influences of visual art-making as a leisure activity on older women's subjective well-being', *Journal of Aging Studies*, vol 24, no 2, pp 135-43.

Ruiz, J. (2004) *A literature review of the evidence base for culture, the arts and sport policy*, Edinburgh: Research and Economic Unit, Scottish Executive Education Department, available at: www.gov.scot/Publications/2004/08/19784/41527

Sennett, R. (1998) *The corrosion of character: The personal consequence of work in the new capitalism*, London: W.W. Norton.

Sennett, R. (2008) *The craftsman*, New Haven, CT: Yale University Press.

Sennett, R. (2012) *Together: The rituals, pleasures and politics of cooperation*, New Haven, CT: Yale University Press.

Slipknot (2007) 'Regional reports', *Slipknot*, no 117, September, p 59-63.

Smith, A. (2008) 'Archivist's corner', *Reverberations: Journal of the Handbell Ringers of Great Britain*, Spring/Summer.

Smith, R. (2006) 'Symphonic choirs: understanding the borders of professionalism', in K. Alquist (ed) *Chorus and community*, Urbana and Chicago, IL: University of Illinois Press, pp 293-306.

Stebbins, R.A. (1992) *Amateurs, professionals and serious leisure*, Montreal: McGill-Queen's University Press.

Stebbins, R.A. (2004) *Between work and leisure: The common ground of two separate worlds*, New Brunswick: Transaction.

Taylor, D.G. (2008) *Magnetizing neighbourhoods through amateur arts performance*, Washington, DC: Urban Institute, available at: www.urban.org/research/publication/magnetizing-neighborhoods-through-amateur-arts-performance/view/full_report

Taylor, S. and Littleton, K. (2012) *Contemporary identities of ceativity and creative work*, London: Ashgate.

Waldron, J. and Veblen, K. (2009) 'Learning in a Celtic community: an exploration of informal music learning and adult amateur musicians', *Bulletin of the Council for Research in Music Education*, no 180, Spring, pp 59-74, available at: www.jstor.org/stable/40319320

Wali, A., Severson, R. and Longoni, M. (2002) *Informal arts: Finding cohesion, capacity and other cultural benefits in unexpected places*, Chicago, IL: Chicago Center for Arts Policy at Columbia College.

Wohlheim, B. (1998) *Culture makes communities*, DVD video, Joseph Rowntree Foundation, available at: www.jrf.org.uk/report/culture-makes-communities

NINE

Is there a black and minority ethnic third sector in the UK?

Lucy Mayblin

Chapter aims

This chapter aims to:

- explore definitional issues in the category black and minority ethnic third sector;
- consider what the characteristics of the BME third sector might be, and what types of organisations might be included within the term;
- discuss research on some sub-categories of third sector organisation that are commonly defined as BME.

Introduction

There is a wealth of material on the black and minority ethnic (BME) third sector; much of this is produced by and for BME third sector organisations (TSOs). Despite the plethora of publications, there is little empirical evidence from systematic comparative analyses between the BME and other TSOs. Without this, the (potential) implications of these differences can run the risk of being treated as nothing more than rhetoric. The aim of this chapter is to contribute towards improving the foundations of knowledge on the BME third sector (BME TS) through discussing some of the challenges involved in identifying the BME TS as well as key issues faced by different types of BME organisations, and foregrounding gaps in the literature.

The chapter is structured as follows: the next section explores some of the definitional issues that arise when one begins to discuss the BME TS. Following this is a discussion of some of the defining characteristics of the BME TS, notwithstanding the definitional issues already identified. The next section disaggregates the BME

TS and discusses four different types of organisation in turn: refugee community organisations, diasporic and/or immigrant organisations, 'Black' organisations, and faith-based organisation. The final section identifies some key learning points from the chapter.

The BME third sector

Definitional issues: is there a distinctive BME third sector?

The idea that BME voluntary and community organisations (VCOs) are distinctive from non-BME VCOs appears intuitively correct. This may particularly be the case in the experiential settings of some TSOs, where the unique experiences of BME people, and by the extension the challenges faced by organisations working with them, may appear self-apparent. Yet pinning down what might be meant by the BME third sector as an analytical unit is more difficult. What can and cannot be included in the concept of the third sector has been the subject of extensive debate (see, for example, Halfpenny and Reid, 2002; Alcock, 2010) and the category BME is no different. Therefore, combining these two contested concepts raises many issues, leading some to question the utility of the phrase 'BME third sector' (Butt, 2001; Mayblin and Soreti-Proctor, 2011).

At the heart of the issue is the ambiguity of the terms 'Black' and 'minority ethnic'. In writing on the BME third sector, there is often reference to some combination of skin colour, ethnicity, culture, language, immigration status and religion, but rarely, perhaps understandably, are clear boundaries or definitions imposed. There are two aspects to understanding this ambiguity. First, there are those organisations that are run by, and cater for, communities that are clearly both Black and of a minority ethnic group in the UK, such as African-Caribbeans. These organisations developed as a consequence of the experiences of post-war immigrants arriving in Britain following decolonisation. The relatively large-scale arrival of migrants from the former colonies in a short space of time meant that diasporic communities developed that were all dealing with a combination of racist abuse and discrimination, and poor access to basic services. The commonalities between these groups of people and the organisations that they set up are clear: the need to challenge and resist racism, fight for basic rights, and to provide culturally appropriate health and other welfare services where mainstream services were not set up to do so (Afridi and Warmington, 2009; Ware, 2013). Many also, inevitably, fulfilled cultural functions. The experiences of these organisations make talk of a BME third sector seem entirely logical, though BME VCOs remain relatively under-researched as a collective (Craig, 2011; Ware, 2013).

It is the second aspect, however, which complicates the picture. The diversification of migration patterns in recent decades, combined with a broader understanding of the concept of ethnicity and ethnic minority status, as well as the acknowledgement of xenophobia directed towards 'white' minorities, has made the picture much more complicated. Indeed, this diversity is so great that it leads inter alia to questions around the usability of the unifying umbrella of the BME third sector. Let me provide some examples. Are organisations catering for white European migrant workers, who are not Black, may or may not consider themselves an ethnic minority, and may or may not have religious, cultural or linguistic practices that make them feel marginalised within British society part of the BME third sector? Is class a key variable in the ability of groups to avoid the minority ethnic label? Or perhaps immigration status? For example, are Irish and Polish immigrants both ethnic minorities within this context? Do third sector organisations working with both 'count' as BME third sector organisations when Irish immigrants are so well integrated and accepted, even within the context of a long history of marginalisation? How about Gypsy and Traveller communities, who are also not Black, are indigenous to the UK, speak English, and may or may not identify as an ethnic minority? This group has certainly experienced racism for generations, as well as marginalisation in multiple spheres – is this enough to align them in common cause with third sector organisations supporting newly arrived migrant workers or established South Asian communities? Indeed, they are often treated as a separate 'sector' in their own right (Ryder, 2011). If identifying the core of the BME third sector is relatively straightforward, this brief set of examples demonstrates some of the definitional ambiguities that are encountered when one starts to search for the boundaries of the concept.

In operationalising the term 'BME third sector', researchers and practitioners have taken a broad range of approaches that sit somewhere along a spectrum from those who are inclusive of a vast array of different characteristics and identifications (Reilly, 2004), to those who use tighter definitions such as 'visible minorities' (McLeod et al, 2001, p 2). At the inclusive end, Reilly (2004, p 1) defines BME within this context as 'representative of all the diverse groups within BME communities, not just those mainstream religious and cultural groups within general awareness'. While she notes that 'not all groups who took part [in our research] identify themselves with the term Black and Minority Ethnic

... we have used it as the most representative and recognised term for all those we consulted' (Reilly, 2004, p 1). By including groups and organisations that do not themselves identify with the BME category, Reilly assumes that there is a tacit understanding of what is meant by BME among readers and that its boundaries include a range of cultural associations and religious identifications.

In contrast, McLeod and colleagues (2001, p 2) refer to BME TSOs as those led by 'visible minorities' and state that 'groups such as Jews, Poles, Italians, Cypriots etc. are not included', nor are religious organisations. Similarly, a mapping project on the BME TS in the East Midlands (VEM, 2003) used the term black and minority ethnic to mean 'visible (non-white) minorities'; nevertheless, it indicates the tensions of definition in this field by later stating that '"Black and Minority Ethnic organisations" are defined as organisations primarily led by and servicing people from Black and Minority Ethnic communities, but increasingly to a growing number of white communities' (VEM, 2003, p 2).

The use of visibility as an analytical tool, however, can be problematic. For example, Lai (2000) found that in Aberdeen visible minorities experienced accessing voluntary sector mental health services challenging because these services were delivered in an ethnocentric way that presented cultural barriers to non-white people. Yet the cultural barriers that are identified by Lai are not necessarily limited to those whose skin is not white, non-white people are not necessarily 'culturally different', and white people are not necessarily culturally similar. Exclusion is linked to a whole set of intersecting factors such as gender, age, language and religion, which are lost in the category 'non-white'. Equally, categories can become conflated with one another. For example, Harrison (1998) uses 'Black' and 'ethnic minority' as synonyms so 'minority ethnic' means 'Black' and 'Black people' mean 'ethnic minority'.

Yet while a lack of definitional accuracy or analytical sophistication in terms of analysing the intersecting conditions that lead to marginalisation may be of concern to academics, the deliberate emphasis on skin colour should also be considered in relation to political struggles against the lived reality of exclusion for many non-white people in the UK. Visibility here is a proxy for 'is likely to suffer racism'. Indeed, as Ware (2013) and Craig (2011) have argued, BME TSOs have developed in response to the racism, in various guises, experienced by particular groups of people in the UK and, to that extent, many organisations run by and/or for, ethnic minority people, are working under similar conditions. The usefulness of the visibility approach may well be embedded in this context as opposed to the need for definitional clarity or expansive inclusivity.

It is not the aim of this chapter to propose an argument either way as to whether the BME third sector actually exists as a unified (or loosely connected) collectivity, or whether the category is useful as either an analytical category or political strategy. Indeed, the answer may not be the same to those two questions. However, if one message emerges it is surely that a more nuanced understanding of the complexity of associational relationships that fall within the blurred boundaries of the third sector must be the starting point for any academic research in this area.

Characteristics of the BME third sector

The size of the BME third sector is entirely dependent on how it is measured. This clearly relates to the definitional controversies described above. For example, using a very narrow definition of BME, McLeod et al (2001) estimated that there were 5,500 BME-led voluntary and community groups in England and Wales. Two years later, Voice East Midlands identified 7,000–8,000 BME groups in that region alone (20% of the wider third sector), with its survey covering 1,600 BME TSOs (VEM, 2003). The BME third sector is not, therefore, something that necessarily exists 'out there', ready to be measured; it exists only to the extent that *either* researchers or policymakers define the definitional parameters and bring a sector into existence by virtue of their definition of who is and is not included, or because a number of organisations choose to align themselves for strategic gain (for example, mutual support or increased funding).

Beyond definitional ambiguities, there are those who consider the BME TS to be distinctive within the wider sector, without necessarily defining the limits or content of what is meant by the term. Reference to distinctiveness tends to oscillate between those who claim BME TSOs offer a unique purpose, function and role and those who claim that BME TSOs are at a distinct disadvantage in relation to accessing resources for their work, and to sustain their organisations (see, for example, ROTA, 2009; CEMVO, 2010; Tilki et al, 2015). The former specifically relates to the role of BME TSOs in filling gaps where more mainstream organisations lack capacity or knowledge of particular cultural or religious communities.

The narrative on distinctiveness in which BME TSOs fare worse than other organisations is well documented, albeit primarily in grey literature by and for BME TSOs (exceptions are recent and include

Craig, 2011 and Ware, 2013). Some of these anticipate widening inequalities as a result of the current economic downturn in which already vulnerable BME organisations are more likely to be affected by public spending cuts (ROTA, 2009; CEMVO, 2010). Despite these assertions, there is a continued lack of systematic comparative analyses in which like with like is examined between the BME and the wider third sector. It is well documented that BME TSOs are more likely to be small, and as small VCOs suffer disproportionately in the context of changing funding models for the TS more broadly (not least within the context of the financial crisis and ensuing austerity agenda), many of their challenges may be in common with other small VCOs. Without detailed comparative research, discussion of distinctiveness runs the risk of being largely rhetorical. A notable exception is a study by Graddy and Wang (2009), which looked at community foundations and found that ethnicity in part determined involvement with voluntary sector organisations, the type of involvement and the propensity to charitable giving. Their focus was on charitable giving by ethnicity but their findings did show that ethnicity has an impact on the character of different organisations in the BME TS. Communities with high poverty rates have limited charitable capacity and thus give less to community foundations.

The Deakin report (NCVO, 1996) questioned what it termed 'the myth of separateness' of the BME TS, arguing that its characteristics were similar to those of other organisations that deal with groups with specific needs, such as homeless or disabled people, though this was part of an ideological argument proposing a move towards integrated services. Nevertheless, there is a consensus that the common experience of racism links BME TSOs (bearing in mind the definitional controversies around visibility, discussed earlier). While discrimination is a broad category, one cannot argue that all types of discrimination or prejudice are the same, which gives this argument some weight. For example, in relation to challenges in forming partnerships, McLeod et al (2001, p 5) explain that this is related to societal racism in the form of 'employment barriers, educational marginalisation, linguistic and cultural exclusion, residential segregation and racial harassment', which results in competition between different ethnic groups, rather than promoting collaboration. Efforts in Wales have sought to directly address these challenges, though with mixed success (Chaney and Fevre, 2001).

Reilly (2004) argues that while BME TSOs have much in common with other types of TSOs, they are distinctive to the extent that they usually contain a package of characteristics that together make them unique. Whether this set of characteristics is something that would stand up to interrogation using a very broad understanding of the BME category is uncertain. If labelling a cohort of organisations as BME will benefit them, it is arguably a good thing. However, whether an externally imposed search for distinctiveness is necessarily beneficial is another question. Perhaps a more useful way to view BME TSOs is to understand them in the context of their client group: run by individuals or communities with particular needs that are specific to that client group. This specificity can be considered similar to other organisations or clusters of organisations within the third sector and so the issue is less about distinctiveness and more about all organisations being able to access the funding and support that they require within the context of the challenges faced by their client group.

Disaggregating the BME third sector

As discussed earlier, whether the BME TS is distinct from the wider third sector is contested. Nevertheless there are various different sub-groups of organisations that might be included under the heading BME. This section disaggregates the category and looks at four different types of organisation. Gypsy and Traveller organisations have been intentionally left out but are dealt with at length in Chapter Seven by Andrew Ryder. The four types discussed here are:

- refugee and asylum-seeker organisations;
- diasporic and immigrant organisations;
- Black organisations;
- faith-based organisations.

Some of these, such as Black organisations, are clearly BME; others, such as faith-based organisations fit less comfortably under the heading. Some, such as immigrant organisations and RCOs, have overlapping client groups, while others, such as Gypsy and Traveller organisations, tend to stand apart. There are also differing amounts of research into these various sub-categories of BME TSO, and it is less common for researchers to look at them in the round, as opposed to concentrating on one type of organisation.

Refugee and asylum-seeker organisations

If there is any distinctive characteristic of refugee and asylum-seeker organisations, often called refugee community organisations (RCOs) or migrant and refugee community organisations (MRCOs), it is that the community of service users is constructed as a result of legal definitions. In a legal sense, asylum seekers are people who have made an application for asylum in the UK, and refugees are those whose application has been accepted. RCOs are also likely to serve 'failed' asylum seekers – those whose applications for asylum have been rejected by the state. While these are legal definitions, many argue that all three groups are in fact refugees (Griffiths et al, 2006), hence the name RCO. However, beyond either their legal status, or experience of forced migration, these individuals are extremely diverse in terms of nationality, age, ethnicity, gender, class, religion and the language(s) they speak. In turn, RCOs are also diverse, providing a breadth of services from conversation clubs to legal advice, sometimes targeting all refugees, other times serving a specific nationality or linguistic group. Equally, as Teresa Piacentini (Chapter Ten) observes, service users are often from the same country but hold a different legal status.

There is a growing body of literature on refugee and asylum-seeker TSOs that covers a range of topics, including discussion on the label itself, the function and role of RCOs, and the internal challenges faced by these organisations as well as the wider policy context in which they operate. Turning first to the issue of labels. There are a range of terms used to describe RCOs including 'refugee associations', 'refugee organisations', refugee-based organisations', 'refugee community organisations', 'refugee community-based organisations', and 'migrant and refugee community organisations' (Griffiths et al, 2006). For some, the terminology used is important because it is considered to be an expression of the relationship between the organisations and the communities they are assumed to represent, and because it can contribute towards a clearer conception that may resolve some of the 'conflicting pressures faced by refugee organisations and the ambiguities surrounding their role' (Griffiths et al, 2006, p 884). Griffiths et al (2005, p 188) suggest that the term RCO embraces 'a variety of informal networks and more formalised bureaucratic arrangements' among members of refugee communities. In the work of Carey-Wood (1997), the term 'refugee specific initiative' is used to describe any project that has been developed to work with, or provide a service to, refugees and/or asylum seekers, and is distinct from a service provided to the general population. Similarly, Zetter and Pearl (2000, p 676) define RCOs as 'organisations rooted within, and supported by, the ethnic or national refugee/asylum-seeker communities they serve'. Others have gone further by using categories such as 'cultural', 'political' and 'advice-based' to sub-divide RCOs (Joly, 1996).

RCOs are most often small, operate below the radar, and are led by members of the community they serve. As they form in response to changing international events as well as national asylum policy, it is very difficult to quantify, with any accuracy, the number of RCOs operating at any given time (Zetter and Pearl, 2000). Few RCOs today survive to become enduring organisations. This is likely linked to the fact that communities are smaller and more geographically dispersed than in the past when larger groups of people clustered in a smaller number of places (Zetter and Pearl, 2000). Nevertheless, RCOs are still often organised around national groupings, and some nationalities appear to have been more successful than others in becoming established and engaged with public and governmental structures. For newer RCOs, Zetter and Pearl (2000, p 687) report the positive attribute of dynamism and 'unrivalled range of skills, insight and knowledge of their communities' needs'. However, 'their very diversity and specificity (in terms of location or ethnic group) hamper the development of institutional capacity and organisational sustainability' (Zetter and Pearl, 2000, p 686). In addition, the diversity of the client population may lead to splintering, or to a reliance on organisations or 'community leaders' to speak on behalf of particularly marginalised groups (Kelly and Joly, 1999).

A large number of precarious organisations are thought to exist, providing a wide portfolio of services to sometimes large client groups. Indeed, this portfolio changes over time as groups develop, and even as the immigration status of members changes (Piacentini, 2012). The services provided include housing management and provision, legal and welfare advice, financial and other types of subsistence support, and rights-based advocacy. Often RCOs, like other BME TSOs, are filling gaps in mainstream service provision.

Piacentini has dubbed the coming together within diversity of RCOs a 'fictive unity', which is challenged as some members are granted increasing or decreasing rights. Added to these challenges, over the past 20 years these RCOs have increasingly focused on 'short-term, defensive tasks in a hostile policy environment' (Zetter et al, 2005, p 169). This means that RCOs rarely play a 'community cohesion' or integration role, despite the exclusion experienced by asylum seekers and refugees, because government policy is not to promote integration until refugee status is granted (Daley, 2009). This clearly means further marginalisation, even from the wider BME TS that at times has benefited from government interest in immigrant integration or community cohesion.

The geographical location of RCOs has followed changing national policies. Pre-1999 most RCOs were located in the South East and particularly in London. The 1999 Immigration and Asylum Act introduced enforced dispersal around the UK and consequently there has been growth in the number of RCOs appearing in dispersal cities. Zetter et al (2005, p 171) suggest that the impact of dispersal on RCOs 'has been both profound and enduring' as it has 'consolidated a solid core of established RCOs in London, whilst stimulating a regional periphery of volatile semi-secure and insecure RCOs competing for shrinking support'. There are further local and regional differences that are important in terms of location. For example, the Scottish context is different from that in England owing to both lower numbers of BME residents historically and a contemporary policy approach that seeks to *encourage* immigration to deal with skills shortages and depopulation (Wren, 2007). Official backing in Scotland has resulted in RCOs receiving more support than their English counterparts, which has allowed smaller community organisations to play an integral part 'in community development work with asylum seekers in a way which promotes social cohesion in communities where they have been dispersed' (Wren, 2007, p 396). There remain, however, similar problems in relation to accessing resources and RCOs filling gaps where mainstream service providers fail.

Zetter and Pearl (2000, p 682) suggest that RCOs 'are little different from other immigrant groups and organisations' (see also Kelly and Joly, 1999). Organisations that target specific groups, such as Black migrant and refugee women, address issues that affect women who have had similar experiences and left similar home contexts but who have different legal statuses (Davis and Cooke, 2002), blurring the lines between RCOs and immigrant or diasporic TSOs. What sets RCOs apart, according to Zetter and Pearl (2000, p 682), is 'the extent of social exclusion that asylum seekers increasingly experience in the UK'. Indeed, this is a situation that has only worsened in the years since 2000.

Diasporic and/or immigrant community organisations

Diasporic and/or immigrant community organisations (referred to henceforth as ICOs) are those that serve new or well-established immigrant communities. These are diverse and overlap with several other sub-categories identified in this chapter. Like RCOs, their communities of interest are likely to face immediate challenges in accessing resources and services, as well as facing language barriers, but also longer-term challenges relating to socioeconomic marginalisation and racist or xenophobic abuse. There are significant overlaps between RCOs and ICOs, the only real differences relating to the legal context of immigration status (though bearing in mind that many immigrant organisations will cater for refugees and asylum seekers) and geographical location (only asylum seekers experience enforced dispersal). Much of the literature, however, focuses on the US context, with a dearth of studies into immigrant TSOs in the UK. Indeed, ICOs can be hard to reach or access in order to undertake research, and they may leave few traces when they disband. As a result, most studies focus on formal organisations rather than those (the majority) that operate below the radar (Schrover and Vermuelen, 2005).

In the UK, the character of ICOs, and the approach taken towards them by the state has changed considerably over time. In the literature there is a tendency to begin with the post-war migration of people from Commonwealth countries, though clearly immigrant organisations existed before this period. The story of post-war ICOs reflects the changing approach to immigrant inclusion and race relations. For example, writing in the 1980s, Cheetham (1985) bemoans the lack of attention paid to ethnic associations in the academic and policy literature and puts this down to British assimilationist traditions vis-à-vis immigrants and an assumption that immigrants' welfare provisions should be provided by mainstream services.

Older settled communities tend to also have well-established, often formalised, and better resourced ICOs. Equally, ICOs formed by newer immigrant communities are logically less well established (since their formation is more recent) and consequently they are more likely to be poorly resourced. Established communities can dominate in the shifting hierarchies of power at neighbourhood or city level, giving them greater voice and visibility (Daley, 2009). Newer, smaller, organisations can then consequently become excluded and marginalised in terms of resources and influence, though it should be noted that this may be as a consequence of a wide range of issues beyond competition between ICOs. Daley (2009) nevertheless suggests that competition between ICOs damages community cohesion, as well as preventing collaboration, networking and information sharing. On this theme, Schrover and Vermuelen (2005, p 824) study ICOs as a means of understanding immigration patterns and integration processes 'because the extent to which immigrants cluster in organisations is a critical measure of collectively expressed and collectively ascribed identity'. They suggest that 'the character, number and size of organisations indicate the extent to which immigrants want to profile themselves as being different, or how they are seen to be different by others' (Schrover and Vermuelen, 2005, p 824). Controversially, Schrover and Vermuelen (2005) also argue that immigrants set up ICOs in order to set themselves apart from others, with some seeking to distinguish themselves from the wider population and others seeking to encourage integration. In this way, they take a categorical approach to immigrant associations that does not support the idea of individual autonomy outside of the association, nor does it take into account the complexity of people's lives and the various roles they may play within the blurred boundaries of an immigrant community and an abstract concept of a 'host society'.

Research by Garapich (2008) further complicates the picture by suggesting that ICOs may be less important to settlement and integration than some claim. He argues, in the case of Polish immigrants, that migratory movements within the EU are governed by the expanding free market. Integration and participation of immigrants within society are, for Garapich, strongly determined by market forces, which suggests that economic opportunities for immigrants to create their own 'migration industry' are essential in integration. This is certainly not the case for all immigrant groups and it is clear that different national or community cultures play a significant role the forms of TSO involvement that take place among different groups (Campbell and McLean, 2002; Kelly, 2003)

What is clear is that one cannot simply speak of diasporic or immigrant community organisations, because these communities themselves are so diverse. While some have been in the UK for a long time and yet continue to struggle in the face of racism and marginalisation, such as some African-Caribbean communities (Hylton, 1999), others may pursue an instrumental strategy to access services where language barriers are the main issue that they face. A key issue here is racism. A large number of TSOs that very clearly come under the BME heading pursue activities that in various ways are a response to ongoing racisms. The next sub-section addresses some of these issues.

Black organisations

Many organisations describe themselves as Black TSOs, bringing together identifications around nationality and ethnicity. This self-identification more straightforwardly brings Black organisations under the heading BME TSO. Indeed, when activists speak of a BME third sector, they most often are referring to African-Caribbean heritage and other non-white communities such as South Asians. Black TSOs are often motivated by anti-racist struggles against a white hegemony in access to resources – employment, education, housing and so on

(Britton 1999). There are tensions within this sphere in terms of tactics. For example, Hylton (1999, p 4) writes:

> The African-Caribbean efforts in the area of education are a microcosm of the dilemma confronting African-Caribbeans in the area of public service provision, and connect with the balancing act individuals have to undertake in all areas of their everyday life. The dilemma is whether to opt for involvement in the present rules, regulations, and administration systems [which discriminate against Black people] or for rejecting the status quo and replacing it with alternatives.

A key issue here is empowerment. For Christian (1998), empowerment in the Black TS is distinct from that in white organisations because of the particular history of racist marginalisation that Black people have experienced in the UK. He suggests that for the Black TS this means not only giving such organisations a voice, but also facilitating efforts by Black people to secure self-help programmes (Craig, 2011).

Debates around intersectionality have raised awareness over the past couple of decades of the importance of thinking through how 'Blackness' intersects with other axes of identity, most notably gender (Hill-Collins, 2009). It has been argued that there is a need to maintain a balance between fighting for Black people's rights and fighting for Black women specifically (Bryan et al, 1985). The latter may well require self-reflection and calls for change within the Black community and has led to the creation of many Black women's groups. These groups, though, are often doubly marginalised. For example, Davis and Cooke (2002) found that the Black women's organisations they spoke to highlighted engagement with the authorities as an issue. Black women's organisations across the country said that they were insufficiently engaged with local and regional strategic partnership schemes. The impact of this was reflected in the limited funding given to Black women's groups by regeneration programmes such as New Deal for Communities and Health Action Zones.

Davis and Cooke (2002, p 2) note that of the key underpinning principles of Black organisations (such as Black political identity, self-help, empowerment, justice and social inclusion) 'the most contentious is "Black" as a political identity'. The organisations participating in Davis and Cooke's study took 'Black' to encompass recognition of a shared political identity beyond ethnicity (that is, the anti-racist struggle). However, local authorities did not always follow such a political interpretation of Black. Most preferred BME, in which Black refers to African-Caribbean people and minority ethnic to South Asians. The point being made here is that policymakers often attempt to strip the label Black of the political significance attached to it by self-identifying Black organisations.

Faith-based organisations

Faith is often brought in to discussions around the BME TS, with the implication that BME populations often have special religious needs that are not catered for in mainstream services or organisations. Some faith-based third sector organisations (FB TSOs) may be included in the BME TS, primarily those that consist mainly of BME members. Not only is identifying FB TSOs that might also be considered BME TSOs very difficult, this also brings us back to the tricky issue of defining BME. For example, Polish migrants are often Catholic but Polish Catholic organisations are rare, while Catholic organisations more broadly are common, and Polish, Eastern European, or more broadly immigrant worker organisations also exist. While faith is often implicated in writing on the BME TS, there is little research into the overlaps between FB TSOs and BME TSOs. Furthermore, while the 'special religious needs' that BME TSOs are said to be able to cater for are often implied to be non-Christian (such as prayer rooms and halal food), most of the research into FB TSOs is on Christian organisations, and much of this is in the US context. Where other religions are mentioned, there has been a tendency to focus on Islam within the context of the 'preventing violent extremism' agenda, which has become a key focus of the UK government's engagement with Islamic faith groups (Allen, 2010).

Religious NGOs, according to Berger (2003, p 19), are unique in that they 'represent congregations, denominations, spiritual or political orientations, even the entire membership of a particular religion'. We might think of the operationalisation of these philosophies by FBOs in terms of 'demand-side' and 'supply-side' pressures. Demand-side pressures come from social problems that draw out responses from FBOs. An example of this is the growth of food banks following the government's austerity agenda in the UK. Supply-side pressures come from changes in theology and practice among FBOs and may be related also to their size and resources (McCabe et al, 2016). In addition, FBOs sometimes respond to government policy by campaigning directly against it, with some (such as the Quakers) seeing such activity as integral to their faith identity (see Cairns et al, 2007; Conradson, 2008)

Some ideas cut across religions. As McCabe and colleagues (2016) note, many of the principles associated with Christian social engagement 'such as charity, service, hope and neighbourliness have similarities for example with zakat and sadaqa which are cornerstones of Islamic teaching, with the Sikh concepts of Wand Chhakna and Wand Ke Chhakna, and with dana in Hinduism' (p 4). Despite these similarities, Daley (2009) draws attention to fragmentation in her research into community cohesion in one neighbourhood in the West Midlands:

> Shared religion was felt to bring different people together in the area, but only at the level of sharing of religious practices and values, and alone was not seen as strong enough by participants to bond together people from different cultures and traditions. (p 164)

One of her interviewees commented:

> 'There seems to be, especially within BME communities, a uniting factor, which is religion, which is Islam, which kind of creates an infrastructure for a lot of these communities in the area. That's on the surface, but below the surface they're a lot more fragmented and separated due to either language or cultural differences.' (Daley, 2009, p 164)

Meanwhile, Rochester and colleagues (2007) point out that religious organisations, as well as representing religious communities, have historically played an important role in public service delivery, health and education. They suggest that the Labour government, then in power, expressed a renewed interest in encouraging FB TSOs that operate on a small scale at local and community level. They suggest that this renewed interest was driven by the combination of an interest in community cohesion, extending services to BME communities, and a policy push towards the transferring of responsibility for delivery of welfare services from the state to the voluntary sector. Equally, Lowndes and Chapman (2005) found in their research that the government saw faith-based groups as playing a role in 're-moralising' public life, though whether this applied to all religions is not clear. Indeed, while changing priorities in government policy may be beneficial to TSOs, it may also have negative consequences.

Islamic TSOs have been subject to efforts to involve them in counter-terrorism activities in recent years (Sidel, 2006). However, research on

Muslim communities in England conducted by the Department for Communities and Local Government suggests that ethnicity can be as important as religion for Islamic TSOs. Among the Pakistani Muslim community, for example, it was found that both faith-based (social and educational) and secular (welfare, charitable and political) activities were undertaken (DCLG, 2009a). Mosques and Islamic centres were found to offer a wide range of services, many of which were not necessarily Muslim-specific. The findings of this report foreground the challenge of distinguishing between faith communities and other related categories such as cultural groups and ethnic groups (DCLG, 2009a, 2009b). Equally, Hindus and Sikhs in the UK have tended to establish secular organisations that deliver service provision to diasporas rather than to specific faiths (Warren, 2009). Therefore, there are clearly overlaps between the categories of faith, ethnicity and nationality, and the overall picture is very complex. Nevertheless, the commonality is in FBOs supporting migrant communities, which applies to Christian churches as well as Islamic, Sikh and Hindu organisations. For example, research by Pasura (2013) has highlighted the role of Pentecostal churches in supporting Zimbabwean immigrants in the UK in both integrating into the host society and maintaining transnational ties.

There is some evidence that people who follow an organised religion are more likely than others to engage in volunteering or other charitable activities (Lowndes and Chapman, 2005; Netting et al, 2005) but like other sub-sections of the TS, there is some debate as to whether FB TSOs are distinctive. Arguing in favour of distinctiveness, Smith (2002) identified 10 key themes from his research that, like Reilly's (2004) package of characteristics that make the BME TS distinctive, together demonstrate the distinctiveness of the FB TS. Yet one of these characteristics is Christianity; Reilly suggests that Christianity dominates faith-based community work in England and does not disaggregate by ethnicity, nationality or immigration status, making it difficult to draw any conclusions about the role of faith based organisations within the BME TS. Clearly, Christianity is the dominant religion in the UK, which would make other FB TSOs a minority. There is not enough research to enable us to understand whether alliances are more readily built within an inter-faith framework or on the basis of ethnicity; most likely such organisations take part in both.

Conclusion

Is there a black and minority ethnic third sector? The answer is: yes and no. It is unclear whether the BME TS is indeed wholly distinctive and yet the label BME TS is helpful where it is self-identified within organisations and between groups of organisations, and where it strategically helps BME TSOs in their work. Many of the characteristics of the BME TS might be argued to be characteristics of the sector generally in that all organisations have client groups with specific needs and, often, vulnerabilities. However, at the core of the distinctive experience of BME TSOs are issues around tacking experiences of racism and xenophobia. Such issues might include facing what organisations perceive to be institutional racism in accessing resources such as funding mechanisms, fending off prejudicial attacks on the organisation from members of the public, or supporting clients through the challenges associated with being 'Black' or 'minority ethnic' in the UK today.

As an externally imposed categorisation, the term BME TS does not appear to be especially helpful or meaningful, unless the focus is on combatting racism and xenophobia, and may end up pitting organisations against each other where otherwise they might collaborate. Equally, for researchers the category is perhaps more problematic then helpful, as the discussions in this chapter have shown. This is because if the focus is not on experiences of prejudice, there is an implication that there is something unique about minority ethnic people, communities and organisations that is *internal to them*, rather than their experiences being related to structural and societal phenomena (the response of the majority population to them). Therefore, again, an explicit focus on BME TSOs where organisations have identified themselves as such is likely to be the right approach. Where this is not the case, use of the label has often led scholars into problematic definitional knots around who is 'visible' (that is, not white) or 'culturally different' from the majority population, which inevitably opens them up to criticism. More helpfully, there do appear to be some uniquely identifiable characteristics of faith based organisations – the commonality of faith being an obvious one – and though this is under-researched in the UK context, it is certainly worthy of further study.

Key learning

If we are to understand the BME TS in the context of the wider sector, there is a need for robust analyses to identify and understand empirical trends; findings from these may well have important implications for policy development. On this theme, there are significant gaps in the literature, particularly in terms of research into new migrants from Eastern and Central Europe, Chinese communities and Irish communities. There are, however, a number of key learning points developed in the chapter:

- It is relatively straightforward to identify a 'core' group of organisations that work with BME communities but much more challenging to identify the parameters of the category.
- There are significant intersections and overlaps between the various categories of BME TSO discussed in this chapter.
- BME TSOs often work with immigrant communities and seek to challenge or ameliorate the impacts of racism and xenophobia by providing access to basic services as well as interpersonal support and cultural maintenance.
- Faith is a tricky issue in relation to BME TSOs. Many BME TSOs provide services that are sensitive to religious beliefs and practices and this is an important part of what they do. This is not always the case, however, and more research is needed on the link between the two.
- Legal status is a significant issue for BME TSOs as they often work with immigrants. There are, however, significant differences between the experience of immigrants depending on their legal status and this will have a big impact on the activities of organisations that work with and for them.

Reflective exercises

- Is there a BME Third Sector? What are the shortcomings of categorising Third Sector Organisations in this way?
- What benefit does using the category give us? –As researchers? As practitioners?
- Identify and discuss some of the challenges faced by BME Third Sector Organisations. To what extent are these unique to BME organisations?

References

Afridi, A. and Warmington, J. (2009) *Managing competing equality claims*, London: Equality and Diversity Forum.

Alcock, P. (2010) 'A strategic unity: defining the third sector in the UK', *Voluntary Sector Review*, vol 1, no 1, pp 5-24.

Allen, C. (2010) *Islamaphobia*, Ashgate: Farnham.

Berger, J. (2003) 'Religious nongovernmental organisations: an exploratory analysis', *Voluntas*, vol 14, no 1, pp 15-39.

Britton, N.J. (1999) 'Recruiting and retaining black volunteers: a study of a black voluntary organisation', *Voluntary Action*, vol 1, no 3, pp 9-23.

Bryan, B., Dadzie, S. and Scafe, S. (1985) 'Chain reactions: Black women organising', *Race & Class*, vol 27, no 1, pp 1-28.

Butt, J. (2001) 'Partnership and power: the role of black and minority ethnic voluntary organisations in challenging racism', in *Partnership work: Policy and practice*, S. Balloch and M. Taylor (eds) Bristol: Policy Press.

Cairns, B., Harris, M. and Hutchison, R. (2007) 'Sharing God's love or meeting government goals?', *Policy & Politics*, vol 35, no 3, pp 413-32.

Campbell, C. and McLean, C. (2002) 'Ethnic identities, social capital and health inequalities: factors shaping African–Caribbean participation in local community networks in the UK', *Social Science and Medicine*, vol 55, no 4, pp 643-57.

Carey-Wood, J. (1997) *Meeting refugees needs in Britain: The role of refugee-specific initiatives*, London: Home Office.

CEMVO (Council for Ethnic Minority Voluntary Organisations) (2010) *The impact of the economic downturn on BME VCOs*, London: CEMVO.

Chaney, P. and Fevre, R. (2001) 'Inclusive governance and minority groups: the role of the third sector in Wales', *Voluntas*, vol 12, no 2, pp 131-156.

Cheetham, J. (1985) *Ethnic associations in Britain*, Oxford: Refugee Studies Programme.

Christian, M. (1998) 'Empowerment and Black communities in the UK: with special reference to Liverpool', *Community Development Journal*, vol 33, no 1, pp 8-31.

Conradson, D. (2008) 'Expressions of charity and action towards justice: faith-based welfare in urban New Zealand', *Urban Studies*, vol 45, no 10, pp 2117-41.

Craig, G. (2011) 'Forward to the past: Can the UK black and minority ethnic third sector survive?', *Voluntary Sector Review*, vol 2, no 3, pp 367-89.

Daley, C. (2009) 'Exploring community connections: community cohesion and refugee integration at a local level', *Community Development Journal*, vol 44, no 2, pp 158-71.

Davis, S. and Cooke, V. (2002) *The role of Black women's voluntary sector organisations*, York: Joseph Rowntree Foundation.

DCLG (Department for Communities and Local Government) (2009a) *The Bangladeshi Muslim community in England: Understanding Muslim ethnic communities*, London: DCLG.

DCLG (2009b) *The Pakistani Muslim community in England: Understanding Muslim ethnic communities*, London: DCLG.

Garapich, M.P. (2008) 'The migration industry and civil society: Polish immigrants in the United Kingdom before and after EU enlargement', *Journal of Ethnic and Migration Studies*, vol 34, no 5, pp 735-52.

Graddy, E. and Wang, L. (2009) 'Community foundation development and social capital', *Nonprofit and Voluntary Sector Quarterly*, vol 38, no 3, pp 392-412.

Griffiths, D., Sigona, N. and Zetter, R. (2005) *Refugee community organisations and dispersal: Networks, resources and social capital*, Bristol: Policy Press.

Griffiths, D., Sigona, N. and Zetter, R. (2006) 'Integrative paradigms, marginal reality: refugee community organisations and dispersal in Britain', *Journal of Ethnic and Migration Studies*, vol 32, no 5, pp 881-98.

Halfpenny, P. and Reid, M. (2002) 'Research on the voluntary sector: an overview', *Policy & Politics*, vol 30 no 4, pp 533-50.

Harrison, M. (1998) 'Minority ethnic housing associations and local housing strategies: an uncertain future?', *Local Government Studies*, vol 24, no 91, pp 74-89.

Hill-Collins, P. (2009) *Black feminist thought: Knowledge, consciousness, and the politics of empowerment,* Routledge: London.

Hylton, C. (1999) *African-Caribbean community organisations: The search for individual and group identity*, Stoke-on-Trent: Trentham Books.

Joly, D. (1996) *Haven Or hell?: Asylum policies and refugees in Europe*, Basingstoke: Macmillan.

Kelly, L. (2003) 'Bosnian refugees in Britain: questioning community', *Sociology*, vol 37, no 1, pp 35-49.

Kelly, L. and Joly, D. (1999) *Refugees' reception and settlement in Britain*, York: Joseph Rowntree Foundation.

Lai, C. (2000) 'Reaching out to black ethnic minorities: a voluntary sector perspective on mental health', *Practice: Social Work in Action*, vol 12, no 1, pp 17-28.

Lowndes, V. and Chapman, R. (2005) *Faith, hope and charity: Developing a model of faith group involvement in civil renewal*, Leicester: Local Government Research Unit, De Montfort University, available at: www.dmu.ac.uk/Images/Faith_Report_tcm6-6311.pdf (accessed 16 September 2009).

Mayblin, L. and Soteri-Proctor, A. (2011) *The black minority ethnic third sector: A resource paper*, Working Paper 58, Birmingham: Third Sector Research Centre.

McCabe, A., Buckingham, H., Miller, S. and Musabyimana, M. (2016) *Belief in social action: Exploring faith groups' responses to local needs*, Working Paper 137, Birmingham: Third Sector Research Centre.

McLeod, M., Owen, D. and Khamis, C. (2001) *Black and minority ethnic voluntary and community organisations: Their role and future development in England and Wales*, London: Policy Studies Institute.

NCVO (National Council for Voluntary Organisations) (1996) *Meeting the challenge of change: Voluntary action in the 21st century. The report of the Commission on the Future of the Voluntary Sector*, London: NCVO.

Netting, F., O'Connor, M., Thomas, M. and Yancey, G. (2005) 'Mixing and phasing of roles among volunteers, staff and participants in faith-based programmes', *Nonprofit and Voluntary Sector Quarterly*, vol 34, no 2, pp 179-205.

Pasura, P. (2013) 'Modes of incorporation and transnational Zimbabwean migration to Britain', *Ethnic and Racial Studies*, vol 36, no 1, pp 199-218.

Piacentini, T. (2012) *Moving beyond 'refugeeness': Problematising the 'refugee community organisation'*, Working Paper 85, Birmingham: Third Sector Research Centre.

Reilly, C. (2004) *A way of life: Black and minority ethnic diverse communities as volunteers*, Stirling: Volunteer Development Scotland.

Rochester, C., Bissett, T. and Singh, H. (2007) 'Faith-based organisations as service providers', in National Council for Voluntary Organisations *Faith and voluntary action: An overview of the current evidence and debates. A report*, London: NCVO.

ROTA (Race on the Agenda) (2009) *The Economic downturn and the Black, Asian and minority ethnic (BAME) third sector*, London: ROTA.

Ryder, A. (2011) *UK Gypsies and Travellers and the third sector*, Working Paper 63, Birmingham: Third Sector Research Centre.

Schrover, M. and Vermeulen, F. (2005) 'Immigrant organisations', *Journal of Ethnic and Migration Studies*, vol 31, no 5, pp 823-32.

Sidel, M. (2006) 'The third sector, human security, and anti-terrorism: the United States and beyond', *Voluntas*, vol 17, no 3, pp 199-210.

Smith, G. (2002) 'Religion, and the rise of social capitalism: the faith communities in community development and urban regeneration in England', *Community Development Journal*, vol 37, no 2, pp 167-77.

Tilki, M., Thompson, R., Robinson, L., Bruce, J., Chan, E., Lewis, O., Chinegwundoh, F. and Nelson, H. (2015) 'The BME third sector: marginalised and exploited', *Voluntary Sector Review*, vol 6, no 1, pp 93-101.

VEM (Voice East Midlands) (2003) *Mapping the black and minority ethnic voluntary and community organisations in the East Midlands*, Nottingham: VEM.

Ware, P. (2013) *"Very small, very quiet, a whisper". Black and Minority Ethnic groups: Voice and influence*, Working Paper 103, Birmingham: Third Sector Research Centre.

Warren, M.R. (2009) 'Community organizing in Britain: the political engagement of faith-based social capital', *City & Community*, vol 8, no 2, pp 99-127.

Wren, K. (2007) 'Supporting asylum seekers and refugees in Glasgow: the role of multi-agency networks', *Journal of Refugee Studies*, vol 20, no 3, pp 391-413.

Zetter, R. and Pearl, M. (2000) The minority within the minority: refugee community-based organisations in the UK and the impact of restrictionism on asylum-seekers, *Journal of Ethnic and Migration Studies*, 26(4): 675-697.

Zetter, R., Griffiths, D. and Sigona, N. (2005) 'Social capital or social exclusion? The impact of asylum-seeker dispersal on UK refugee community organisations', *Community Development Journal*, vol 40, no 2, pp 69-181.

TEN

'More than a refugee community organisation': a study of African migrant associations in Glasgow

Teresa Piacentini

Chapter aims

This chapter aims to:

- explore the contested nature of refugee community organisations;
- increase knowledge of the complex nature of migrant organising over time;
- focus on how migrant associations experience and respond to the challenges of immigration policies through identifying informal non-regulated activities;
- examine the effects of diversity within diversity and processes of change on migrant associations.

Introduction

Immigration to Scotland since the early 1990s has been characterised by the multiplicity of immigrants' countries of origin. Most of these immigrants are new to Scotland, and come from countries with no specific historical or colonial links with Britain. Like a number of UK cities, Glasgow has experienced a dramatic increase in immigration particularly since the introduction of dispersal with the 1999 Immigration and Asylum Act. The city was, and remains, the largest dispersal site in the UK. Since the introduction of dispersal policy, although designed to disrupt social networks, considered by politicians to act as a 'pull' to further asylum migration, a number of informal and formal associations and networks have nonetheless emerged in dispersal areas across the UK. This chapter explores processes of change and development within African migrant, asylum-seeker and refugee-led associations in Glasgow from 2004 onwards, presenting new findings from the Scottish context.

Much research into associational practices among people claiming asylum, refugees and migrants generally draws on the concept of social capital (Putnam, 1995, 2002; Home Office 2004, 2009; Ager and Strang, 2008; Scottish Government, 2013). This concept is contested, not least for its lack of attention to power and conflict, its over-positive view of social networks and its conceptual fuzziness, which will be discussed in what follows (but see also Fine, 2002; Griffiths et al, 2005; Hynes and Sales, 2010). Nonetheless the idea of social capital has retained its popularity in policy debates, with varying degrees of rigorous evidence presented on the ways in which bonds, bridges and links enable service users to access a wide range of resources. Conversely, the widely cited literature on bridging and bonding social capital (Putnam, 2002; Cantle, 2004) argues that contact with predominantly co-ethnic, national or religious groups and non-contact with out-groups is harmful to integration, potentially leading to further social fragmentation (Putnam, 2002).

An important critique that contributes to the contested nature of the value of social bonds and bridges is that most studies explore this from a 'top-down' perspective, drawing from more formally regulated associations and their practices, tending to over rely on community leaders, and only really capturing moments in associations that can be packaged up as evidence (or otherwise) of social capital. Moreover, within this model, there are two important silences. First, the effect of differences in immigration status between migrant communities or populations is largely muted and yet has been found to play a significant role in the emergence and sustainability of migrant associations (Piacentini, 2012). Second, the bonding/bridging/linking framework takes very little account of the effects of internal dynamics on social relations between migrants; internal conflicts are generally glossed over or assumed to be non-existent. Subsequently there is very little sense of the extent to which the quality and nature of such dynamics shape migrant associations and how they self-identify beyond policy-imposed labels. So in a departure from a social capital analysis of migrant associations that focuses on bonds and bridges, this chapter seeks to explore the inner workings of associations over time, the processes of change they experience and how this might affect some of the informal activities that address the welfare concerns of their members. The main aims of the chapter are to examine the contested nature of refugee community organisations; bring knowledge of the complex nature of migrant organising over time; focus on how migrant associations experience and respond to the challenges of immigration policies through identifying informal non-regulated activities; and examine the effects of diversity within diversity and processes of change on migrant associations

This chapter draws on the experiences of six mainly Francophone and Anglophone African asylum-seeker and refugee-led associations in Glasgow. Members of these associations are people seeking asylum and refugees and general migrants from Cameroon, Democratic Republic of Congo, Ivory Coast, People's Republic of the Congo, Uganda and Zimbabwe, who have lived in Glasgow for a number of years from 2000 to the present day. In a further departure from the largely interview-based approach of most studies into migrant associations in the post-dispersal context (for example, Zetter and Pearl, 2000; Griffiths et al, 2005), I have adopted an ethnographic approach. I was an involved volunteer and sympathiser member (albeit to varying degrees) in each of the associations for four years (2007-11), and have maintained contact since this period. I attended monthly meetings, drop-in sessions, family events and social gatherings, demonstrations and public events, and participated in online fora. Each of the associations considered me as a member with different levels of involvement and roles: serving on the committee of two, providing ad-hoc translation and interpreting services and facilitating training workshops. I also carried out a total of 46 in-depth qualitative interviews with a sample of members of each association. This involvement provided me with invaluable insights into associations and the effects of diversity within diversity on association life. My approach was also heavily shaped by my experience of working as a community interpreter for ten years in and around Glasgow. And so it is through an analysis of ethnographic and qualitative data that this chapter first focuses its attention inwards, on the informal, non-regulated work of migrant associations, and second, considers for the first time the effects of diversity within diversity on association life.

Theoretical discussion

This emergence of informal and non-regulated migrant associations has been well documented in a number of academic and policy-related accounts of the collective practices of asylum seekers and refugees, where they are generally categorised as refugee community organisations (RCOs) (*inter alia* Zetter and Pearl, 2000; Griffiths et al, 2005; Home Office, 2004; Zetter et al, 2005; Amas and Price, 2008;

Home Office/UK Border Agency, 2009; Lukes, 2009; Jones, 2010; Phillimore and Goodson, 2010). Most RCO research has emerged from the post-dispersal context (from 2000 onwards) and very effectively recognises the specific circumstances relating to asylum seekers and refugees, the way in which community is conceptualised and RCOs' complex asymmetrical relations with the state in relation to integration and capacity building. These studies offer significant insights into how associations and social networks may function as a source of social capital and as a critical mechanism for coping and surviving the asylum system in the UK. While helping us to understand many aspects of association experiences in the more commonly researched dispersal regions of England, these studies tend to focus on the emergence of such groups, generating 'empirical snapshots' of associations at the early stages of their development. As a result, there is little sense of what happens to groups over time and how association life is affected by wider structural contexts. Relatedly, there is limited attention paid to the effects of internal processes and structures on associational life or to micro-level interactions between members, which are shaped by a range of variables including immigration status. The main focus tends to be on the impact of legislative change on individuals, not on associations themselves, with the RCO used as a dominant category of both practice and analysis, as a narrative of unity while, temporarily at least, ignoring a *de facto* diversity and division (Werbner, 1991b).

As a result, the majority of RCO research fails to capture the life of groups as they evolve over time or different internal and external constraints and opportunities affecting their continuity. Subsequently, they tell us very little about the effects of internal diversity on association life, about processes of change within associations over time and how changes affect association life, relationships, activities and practices. This contributes to a problem of 'refugeeness' that often comes to characterise any or all activities of migrant associations – including people claiming asylum refugees and general migrants – that have emerged from the post-dispersal context in the UK. Moreover, the categorisation and subsequent collection and distribution of information on RCOs from both governmental and non-governmental actors, such as non-governmental organisations (NGOs) and researchers, may be viewed as governmentality in practice: doing the work of rendering migrants visible (Griffiths et al, 2005), defining them by policy-relevant categories (Bakewell, 2008) and turning them into targets for specific policies (Rainbird, 2011), thus courting and co-opting them into institutional arrangements that produce effects of responsibilisation for the welfare of their so-called 'communities' (Kunz, 2010).

One alternative framework that offers one way to engage with the gaps, silences and limitations of much RCO research is Pnina Werbner's work on leadership within black and minority ethnic (BME) associations (1991a, 1991b). Werbner offers a framework that explores the stages of association lifecycle, from emergence to mobilisation, which is helpful in refocusing *away* from a top-down focus on social capital, towards a bottom-up analysis of the inner workings of associations, which arguably provides space for better understanding the nature and role of associations for their members. This framework does bring its own assumptions, namely taking for granted the very existence of stable 'co-ethnic' or 'co-national' foundations on which migrants build new lives. The extent to which this represents the experience of all migrants is questionable. Equally, in Werbner's approach (1991a, 1991b), immigration status is presented as generally undifferentiated, arguably imposing homogeneity on a highly diverse population for whom the very notion of stability in relation to the immigration status cannot be taken as a given.

Drawing from both the knowledge that has emerged from the RCO research highlighted briefly here *and* Werbner's focus on the association lifecycle and internal dynamics offers, I suggest an instructive way forward. This approach helps us to challenge the silencing of difference within refugee and migrant associations, and break away from the homogenising effects of fixed categories that take for granted a singular and undifferentiated 'refugee identity' , 'refugee experience', and, as an extension of this, a 'refugee community organisation'. To bring this theoretical framing to the focus of this book, this chapter poses two key questions: How does changing and differentiated immigration status affect association life? When the group is so internally diverse, what might this mean for how associations address concerns with group welfare?

Understanding community groups and activities

This section considers these questions in light of the research and discusses the problem with the bureaucratic category of refugee community organisation presenting the 'from below' perspective; changing immigration status: good news, bad news and effects on association life; and, finally, some strategies for coping with welfare concerns within a highly diverse group.

The problem with the bureaucratic category of RCO: the 'from-below' perspective

Although associations may have emerged from the dispersal context, whereby members would have originally been people seeking asylum, over time many members have become refugees with different types of immigration status and concomitant rights and entitlements. Moreover, each association would have had members who were general migrants – students, workers, spouses, tourists. The point is this: within migrant associations there is a highly complex internal heterogeneity relating to immigration status alone. Despite this, migrant associations are typically defined by a 'refugeeness' by third sector actors, local authorities, public sector and NGO support agencies through the bureaucratic category of the RCO. And members themselves rarely make claim to this specific identity:

> "That's where this is a bit of a problem.... From the beginning, when we set the group up, RCO was perhaps more a reality for the Scottish than for us. When the Cameroonians met up it wasn't as a refugee group ... it was more the Cameroonian way. And there were students, workers, resident and asylum seekers and refugees.... Over time these asylum seekers became refugees ... so, to place CAMASS [a Cameroonian group] as an RCO that was never what it was about for us. More a reality existing in Scotland, a reality that says everything that is new, that is different.... Because over the years there was a wave of foreigners who arrived. They said all of them who formed groups are refugee groups." (Guy, Cameroonian man, migrant)

> "When they speak of RCO, maybe they see it as them that give.... Like they need us so they exist.... RCO is like a category that is imposed ... it's fixed. We would define ourselves as a space where there is exchange and interaction that is about integration, where life is changing for all our members, asylum, refugee, students ... all of us." (Heloise, Congolese woman, refugee)

These comments reveal an important problem: top-down categories do not always fit with bottom-up identifications, revealing the tensions between categorisations and self-identifications. Rejecting the label as non-representative is an interesting strategy. As an act of agency, it can be conceptualised as a way of taking back control of the definition of the group from external actors (for example, statutory and non-statutory agencies). It has been argued that such actors have powers of categorisation (Kunz, 2010) and use this to advance their own position as experts vis-à-vis the groups' predicaments to provide a rationale for their own existence (Rainbird, 2011), and in imposing this definition, to use the RCO construct to its own ends. Associations in fact understand this situation, as the quotes indicate; namely, that certain actors 'need' RCOs to justify their own existence and position of expertise.

Changes in relation to members' immigration status reveal a complex relationship between association emergence as a response to one thing (such as dispersal) and continuity as something else (such as social, cultural or political space). Understanding this complexity requires careful attention to a number of competing external and internal factors. These may relate to the detention and deportation of members, as well as the destitute circumstances some find themselves in. While such circumstances have been central in compelling individuals to come together as a collective, to provide support in the face of such injustice, the situation is not this simple. Interviews and observation revealed that such factors also inhibited members' ability to fully and regularly participate in meetings, rendering some members less visible or more peripheral and with a weaker voice in association life. Precarity in relation to one's immigration status of course was not a universal state for all and some members spoke about their initial reluctance to be part of something that was about 'asylum' or 'refugee issues' when it did not reflect their experience as a migrant. Thus, the imposition of this bureaucratic category by well-intentioned third and public sector was in fact one factor that kept some people away from the association. At the same time, internal diversity also directly affected how associations developed over time. Across associations, general migrant members often demonstrated greater confidence in their expectations of their associations, their personal motivations for being involved and their ability to commit themselves to the future of the group. They pushed for wider, non-asylum focused, agendas relating to longer-term integration that again were not always representative of other members' needs, unintentionally excluding others from the development of the association. Nonetheless there was enormous solidarity for each other within associations, as discussed later in the chapter.

Changing immigration status: good news, bad news and effects on association life

While the impact of dispersal and the experience of *non-settlement* it produces on associations' capacities to meet members' needs has been documented in the literature on asylum and dispersal (Griffiths et al, 2005; Piacentini, 2008), there are parallel effects of positive and negative decisions on association life. First, rather than strengthening the position and resources of an organisation, increased positive decisions appeared to have a detrimental effect on association continuity. During fieldwork, members would often state that the new pressures they faced as refugees (getting a job, finding new housing, concentrating on family reunification) meant they had less time to give to the group. Such pressures relating to the 28-day 'moving-on' period – which refers to the transition period imposed on refugees to access mainstream services including securing appropriate housing, benefits and other relevant services – have gained increasing attention in academic and policy research (Carter and El-Hassam, 2003; Lindsay et al, 2010). They have also produced specific responses from associations in helping members cope during this time, which are outlined later in this chapter. Positive decisions have directly affected the foci of associations, broadening their activities to include wider 'settlement' issues, suggestive of an aspiration to longevity as an association that can evolve over time, rather than it being a question of associations having simply served their purpose (Werbner, 1991a). However, internal capabilities to deliver this agenda were invariably hindered by lack of resources and capital for associations to be effective actors in wider 'non-asylum specific' social fields. Associations were ill equipped in this sense directly because of the constraints of bureaucratic categorisation as an RCO, including lack of local authority support, human resource limitations related to staffing and limited familiarity with UK bureaucracy (Lukes, 2009).

Immigration status decisions also exposed internal tensions. Estelle, an Ivorian woman seeking asylum, described what 'waiting for a decision' meant for her:

> "We are like a scab … you pick at it and you are reminded of the pain. They [other members] don't want to be reminded of us. They don't want to be reminded of being asylum seekers. When everyone didn't have their papers we were all the same. Then some start to get their papers. They want to celebrate but they don't tell you. They don't want you to feel bad, so they go off into small groups. But then you

find out they are meeting up and you are not invited. So
it gets like a club ... I am not jealous, but I am different
now." (Estelle, Ivorian woman, asylum seeker)

In two of the groups involved in the Glasgow research, members who
remained long-term asylum seekers described a developing a sense
of 'outsiderness'. They felt they were becoming a minority within
a minority. Although a number of factors might affect decisions to
participate, such claims were suggestive of a more subtle, and rarely
discussed, hierarchy of immigration status emerging within groups.
Again, this appears to be an important feature of group life largely
overlooked in RCO and migrant association research. What was
becoming increasingly apparent was that, as more and more members
received positive decisions, those who remained asylum seekers were
rendered both more visible and invisible within the group. Difference
within was producing different effects. In some instances, members
spoke about how, as asylum seekers, they lived with a social stigma
as 'second-class human beings', but that they had now started to feel
this within their groups. Other 'general migrant' members looking
on also sensed this:

> "It's about a status, you know ... about what status you
> have. So somebody who came here maybe with a two- or
> three-year visa to study and then you have somebody who
> has been going through the asylum system ... and you
> don't feel like you are a brother or sister or friend to that
> person because they have a different status. You don't listen
> to them like you do to others. What you have done is you
> have basically created, you know, another social class for
> yourself and you think you are better than everybody else."
> (Gilles, Cameroonian man, migrant)

Through observing associations, I witnessed first-hand ebbs and flows
in participation and these were very often linked directly to changes in
immigration status, or key political moments, either in UK immigration
legalisation or to political events 'at home'. What was interesting here
was that in contrast to the fixedness of an 'RCO' label on the group
or on the supposed refugeeness of members, in reality their individual
and collective identities were most often fluid, situational, contingent
and relational and this was very much connected to the association life
cycle: it evolved in response to changing needs of members (Werbner,
1991a). While changing immigration status may have resulted in some

members feeling too different from the majority, it also resulted in different association responses to the welfare needs of all members.

Responding to poverty, destitution and financial exclusion

Austerity, combined with regressive and restrictive immigration policy is hitting hard. In the current challenging economic climate, each of the associations faces difficulties in supporting its members emotionally, socially and financially. Migrants have limited knowledge not only about available services but also about their rights and entitlements to access services, depending on immigration status (Dwyer et al, 2012). Many members spoke of struggling to make ends meet or facing obstacles in accessing financial institutions. One UK-wide report by the British Red Cross (2010) sheds light on the daily life experiences of destitute asylum seekers and refugees. It found that 69% of respondents who were destitute were staying with friends, and 28% reported sleeping rough at some stage. Many depend on 'goodwill' from family and friends, which can lead to strained relationships. Eighty-seven percent of respondents often survived on only one meal a day. Looking at the bigger picture, according to Netto and colleagues (2011), experiences of and responses to poverty among BME groups are vastly under-researched. While routes out of poverty for refugees may in many ways be similar to those for non-refugee populations, the avenues available to refugees are less open (Lindsay et al, 2010; Piacentini, 2015). Moreover, not all groups are equally disadvantaged, and, as we have seen, there is considerable diversity between groups (Netto et al, 2011). Given this complexity and diversity within such associations, how might members survive austerity? In what follows, I identify some coping strategies that have developed 'from below' precisely to address the welfare concerns of members (see also Piacentini, 2015).

Needs-driven ad-hoc support

Regardless of immigration status, in each of the associations the majority of members experienced one-off life events that brought their socioeconomic position into sharp relief:

> "My father passed away, I wanted to have a '*deuil*' [wake] for him ... I didn't have the money to pay for food, so the other members brought me this gift [money] and said use this. You must do this like we do back home, this is

your tradition. This is your duty. I accepted." (Virginie, Cameroonian woman, asylum seeker)

Such one-off events might relate to 'wake' arrangements in the event of death of a family member back home, as described here, or to births and christenings. This emphasises the ways in which association life is as much about marking life events in a way that is culturally respectful and appropriate, reflecting life 'before'. Solidarity and togetherness would be performed and experienced through speech, music and song, feasting and dancing. Co-shopping activities with members swapping cash for more restrictive welfare support (in the form of vouchers and later the pre-paid cashless Azure card) has also facilitated this and means that even those members who are struggling in the asylum system can find ways to be socially and culturally present in association life (Singh, 2010; Piacentini, 2015).

Beyond life events, welfare assistance would also extend to members who had been deported, with funds collected and sent to them (whenever practical) as a form of remittance. When a member was detained, ad-hoc funds were collected to purchase a cheap mobile phone or phone card to maintain contact. In cases of destitution, a small payment would be made to help stretch already tight funds to buy staple goods, or to offer support in kind, for example rice, milk, bread and other foodstuffs. In effect, these were a sort of impromptu destitution fund, and members often spoke about feeling empowered through both providing and receiving support in this manner. The practical aspects of concerns with group welfare are reliant on effective management committees. On occasions when more funds were needed, monthly subscriptions would be increased to help with costs, and members who could not afford this offered help in kind, either cooking or helping with preparations, with such tasks allocated during the monthly association meeting. For those associations without a monthly subscription, members would be asked to make a one-off financial donation or contribute their time mainly through assisting with preparations and cooking. Within the context of asylum and immigration policy and legislation, with its regulations and restrictions on movement and consumption, these activities are important demonstrations of solidarity and belonging, but also of a mobilisation around a wider set of political concerns, illustrative of what Werbner (1991b) would describe as extending beyond cultural goals to concerns with members' welfare, and the enactment of a social and cultural identity beyond any externally imposed 'migrant' identity.

Micro-credit

Micro-credit offers an important tool for poverty alleviation in groups where experience and collective activity are important social organisers, and where alternative sources of identity or mobility are absent or constrained (Biggart, 2001). It is particularly helpful for populations considered 'non-bankable' and who are financially excluded – as are people claiming asylum – allowing individuals to both save and borrow money at very low interest rates at different times. In the one association that had developed a micro-credit system, the scheme was initiated by the association's president, who had previous experience of micro-finance. The micro-scheme was adopted at an annual general meeting and the loan process monitored by the management committee, with loan repayments agreed over a number of months. There was no regulation by, or link to, any external organisations. Small cash amounts were borrowed by a handful of members to purchase equipment for clothes making and hairdressing. Even though the willingness was there to make it a success, the scheme unfortunately ran into problems. These included late repayments, disagreement over penalties, and blurring of roles of the management committee around administering the loan and the repayment system. More fundamentally, a combination of poor understanding among members that money borrowed had to be repaid with interest, a lack of business acumen (partly attributed to years of worklessness as people sought leave to remain) and changes in immigration status adversely affected the sustainability of projects. Although the micro-credit scheme was eventually abandoned, the activities were absorbed into a broader social enterprise model.

Social enterprise

As one association leader explained, "We don't want to become a generation on benefits", and this impetus led two associations to develop social enterprise opportunities that not only helped members back into work but also focused on the specific needs of their communities in Scottish society. Broadly defined, social enterprise concerns the local community acting together to provide services needed by the local population, particularly where the service cannot be provided through the market economy. But it also has broader social, political and cultural goals (Werbner, 1991a; Somerville and McElwee, 2011). The social enterprise schemes set up aimed to build on existing skills, train members, share learning and promote the associations. Such schemes included mobile hairdressing, selling beauty products and providing beauty treatments, and the provision of a mobile PA system for hire for events, and sewing machines and materials for clothes making. Profits made from the ventures have been reinvested in the businesses, with one association managing to secure funds for two paid part-time workers. In Glasgow, the social enterprise model has been relatively successful for a number of reasons. It has provided opportunities for associations to identify and work out solutions to problems they face. Activities provide culturally sensitive services direct to the association's communities, and reskill members and increase employability in the process. They also fill an important gap in 'local' services and are developed from jobs and activities many members were already performing in the informal economy. These business ideas were understood as 'practising belonging' to a wider African and Scottish community, but were also a marker and statement of belonging. At association meetings and drop-in sessions, I would often hear comments such as "We are here to stay", and that like other minority ethnic populations "We need 'our' businesses." Such comments would often be made with reference to established BME populations in Glasgow.

These different strategies embody the idea of an emerging associative network that meets both social and cultural objectives and is concerned with group welfare, as well as the notion of ideological convergence in their focus on the contemporary condition of their members within wider society – one that is shared by many others beyond the boundary of the association (Werbner, 1991a, pp 15-16). Such activities are not unique to the UK context. Evidence of informal non-regulated activities among associations has been identified in important work in France and Canada. This is particularly focused on the role and nature of Malian and Senegalese associations in providing informal activities for their members while also identifying similarities with other populations facing social inequalities (see, for example, Daum, 1998; Quiminal, 2000; Freedman and Tarr, 2000; Sargent and Larchanché-Kim, 2006). The emphasis on the associations in Glasgow (but also further afield in France and Canada) is on the coexistence of similarity and difference and the challenges such organisations face in relation to sustainability. Of note is their focus beyond immigration status, which aligns with the arguments in this chapter and is in keeping with the shift of focus advocated here away from bonds to a closer analysis of internal relations to an understanding of the emergence and sustainability of associations.

Conclusion

This chapter has sought to do two things. First, it advocates an alternative approach to analysing association life, by exploring some of the internal and external factors and processes that affect group emergence and sustainability. Second, it has located internal diversity within a wider analysis of how such associations respond to the very different and changing welfare needs of members, with some responses more successful than others. To achieve this broadened perspective, I have argued for a need to draw from conceptual frameworks that recognise the specificity of refugee organising (in the work of *inter alia* Zetter and Pearl, 2000; Griffiths et al, 2005; Phillimore and Goodson, 2010), and theoretical work that combines a top-down and bottom-up framework to look at effects of internal diversity and changes to immigration status on migrant associations (Werbner, 1991a, 1991b). The chapter has illustrated some of the ways in which a lifecycle approach to associations helps us to move beyond the fixedness of the 'refugee category' and recognise the incredible internal diversity contained within such associations as they evolve over time.

All of this is happening against an immigration policy context that is constantly moving. In light of changing policies, as they relate to people seeking asylum, refugees and migrants, it is difficult to know what lies ahead for these groups. For example, how are they to position themselves in a new policy characterised by funding cuts? Will this shrinking funding environment push groups to retreat back to ring-fenced 'refugee money' arguably used to 'court' migrant associations (Kunz, 2010) so as to harness their potential in filling welfare gaps left by state withdrawal of support? Can such migrant associations with mixed membership effectively compete in the wider BME sector? Will, or can, they have longevity in competing sectors? How might this move beyond 'refugeeness' contribute to broader debates of integration and 'settlement'?

These questions suggest areas for further research into association life and sustainability. The associations studied in Glasgow each negotiated the tension between particularistic identities and claims to universalistic goals. However, they are also facing tough decisions about their respective futures. For people seeking asylum, austerity means reduced access to justice through the legal system through legal cuts; reduced expert support through lack of funding to refugee agencies, charities and community groups; and potential increased pressures on wider public services in the areas of housing, health, employment, education, detention and criminal justice. For migrants generally it means unprecedented cuts to state welfare services and funding for third sector organisations, alongside high unemployment and reductions in public and private sector pay, pensions and conditions. Taken together, austerity places huge pressures on the informal activities of migrant associations to support their members. Moreover, the increasingly shrinking funding pot they can access is further undermining their work and possibilities to continue, should that be their goal. The 'impasse' of refugeeness has tended to translate into limiting such associations to 'asylum seeker funds' and refugee networks and excluding them from funds ring-fenced for BME populations. As a result, longevity for some will mean evolving into a primarily social and cultural group. For others, it may mean developing as a proactive BME organisation providing services to a wider population. These are only two of many other possible outcomes, and for associations this will mean finding a place that not only permits them to position themselves on their own terms, but also recognises this as a valid and visible position and acknowledges migrants as valued members of wider society. Either way, what Crowley (2012) calls a survival agenda may prevail: protest against the political and socioeconomic positioning of certain migrants remains unvoiced in the public arena, dissent is diminished and advocacy is limited to being practised within careful boundaries.

Key learning

There is a pressing need for critical engagement with the dominance of bureaucratic categories as developed by academic, policy and practitioner researchers. This is particularly important given the complicated ways in which differences in the immigration status of migrants directly affect the possibilities, opportunities, quality and nature of social relations between migrants within such associations, as much as between migrants and non-migrants beyond associations. Failure to see beyond labels means that the opportunity for learning across populations, based on similarity and difference, is lost.

The key learning points that emerge from this study are as follows:

- Categories are fluid, so when understanding migrant associations we need to be careful not to make assumptions about shared identities or reinforce the representation of certain populations as 'vulnerable'.
- Attention to internal diversity and dynamics provides important insights into the ways in which structural factors directly affect members' experiences of associations as they evolve over time.

- A focus on difference obscures important overlaps and interconnectedness with and across different segments within a broader population, creating further distinctions between populations.
- Research into migrant associations cannot simply be reduced to interviews or surveys but needs to be extended to close involvement in everyday existence.
- In work that seeks to fight social inequalities more needs to be done to make migrant associations' active partners, and not simply informants.

The advantages and limitations of informal migrant organisations, and the challenges of co-working, are summarised below.

Advantages

- The below the radar activities of informal and non-regulated associations tell us much more about the complexities of belonging and settlement facing migrants.
- Revealing internal tensions and the effects of internal diversity is essential to move away from homogenising these forms of collective practice.
- Studying the nature and quality of associations from below forces researchers to rethink the analytical and political fit and identify tensions between top-down categories and bottom-up experiences.

Limitations

- The wider structural context means that sustainability continues to be largely influenced by immigration legislation and policies, as well as the wider socioeconomic context.
- Despite skills development in members, human resource limitations present a very real threat to continued sustainability and opportunities for developing informal activities.
- Time and resources required for building relationships with migrant associations are necessary to better understand informal activities, but are hugely demanding.

Reflective exercises

- What are the key factors to consider when categorising migrant populations?
- How might practitioners and researchers engage with migrant associations in order to account for 'diversity within diversity'?
- What might be the ethical and political considerations in keeping certain below the radar activities of migrant associations below the radar?
- What effects might current austerity measures have on the long-term sustainability of migrant associations?

References

Ager, A. and Strang, A. (2008) 'Understanding integration: a conceptual framework', *Journal of Refugee Studies*, vol 21, no 2, pp 166-91.

Amas, N. and Price, J. (2008) *Strengthening the voice of refugee community organisations within London's second-tier voluntary sector: Barriers and opportunities*, London: City University/Information Centre about Asylum and Refugees.

Bakewell, O. (2008) 'Research beyond the categories: The importance of policy irrelevant research into forced migration', *Journal of Refugee Studies*, vol 21, no 4, pp 432-53.

Biggart, N.W. (2001) 'Banking on each other: the situational logic of rotating savings and credit associations', *Advances in Qualitative Organization Research*, vol 3, pp 129-53.

British Red Cross (2010) *Not gone, but forgotten. The urgent need for a more humane asylum system*, London: British Red Cross.

Cantle, T. (2004) *The end of parallel lives? The report of the community cohesion panel*, London: Home Office.

Carter, M. and El-Hassam, A.A. (2003) 'Between NASS and a hard place: refugee housing and community development in Yorkshire and Humberside. A feasibility study', Housing Associations' Charitable Trust, available at: www.icar.org.uk/3060/research-directory/between-nass-and-a-hard-place.html (accessed 11 July 2011).

Crowley, N. (2012). *Lost in austerity: Rethinking the community sector*, Discussion Paper C, Birmingham: Third Sector Research Centre.

Daum, C. (1998). *Les associations de maliens en France (migrations, développement et citoyenneté)*, Paris: Karthala.

Dwyer, P., Lewis, H., Scullion, L. and Waite, L. (2011) 'Forced labour and UK immigration policy: status matters?', JRF programme paper, available at: www.jrf.org.uk/sites/files/jrf/forced-labour-immigration-status-full.pdf (accessed 10 July 2015).

Fine, B. (2002) 'They f**k you up those social capitalists', *Antipode*, vol 34, no 4, pp 796-9.

Freedman, J. and Tarr, C. (eds) (2000) *Women, immigration and identities in France*, Oxford: Berg.

Griffiths, D., Sigona, N. and Zetter, R. (2005) *Refugee community organisations and dispersal: Networks, resources and social capital*, Bristol: Policy Press.

Home Office (2004) *Integration matters: A national strategy for refugee integration*, London: Home Office.

Home Office/UK Border Agency (2009) *Moving on together: Government's recommitment to supporting refugees*, London: Home Office.

Hynes, P. and Sales, R. (2010) 'New communities: asylum seekers and dispersal', in A. Bloch and J. Solomos (eds) *Race and ethnicity in the 21st century*, Basingstoke: Palgrave Macmillan.

Jones, P. (2010) 'Refugee community organisations working in partnership: the quest for recognition', Unpublished PhD thesis, University of Birmingham.

Kunz, R. (2010) *Mobilising diasporas: A governmentality analysis of the case of Mexico*, Glocal Governance and Democracy Series Working Paper 3, Lucerne: University of Lucerne.

Lindsay, K., Gillespie, M. and Dobbie, L. (2010) 'Refugees' experiences and views of poverty in Scotland', Scottish Poverty Information Unit, available at: www.vhscotland.org.uk/library/misc/refugees_experience_poverty_in_scotland.pdf (accessed 11 July 2011).

Lukes, S. (2009) *The potential of migrant and refugee community organisations to influence policy*, York: Joseph Rowntree Foundation.

Netto, G., Sosenko, F. and Bramely, G. (2011) *Poverty and ethnicity in Scotland: A review of the literature*, York: Joseph Rowntree Foundation, available at: www.jrf.org.uk/sites/files/jrf/poverty-ethnicity-Scotland-full.pdf (accessed 13 July 2015).

Phillimore, J. and Goodson, L. (2010) 'Failing to adapt: institutional barriers to RCOs engagement in transformation of social welfare', *Social Policy and Society*, vol 9, no 1, pp 181-92.

Piacentini, T. (2008) 'Contesting identities in exile: an exploration of collective self-understanding and solidarity in refugee community organisations in Glasgow', *eSharp*, no 11, Spring: Social Engagement, Empowerment and Change, available at: www.gla.ac.uk/departments/esharp/issues/11 (accessed 20 February 2011).

Piacentini, T. (2012) *Moving beyond 'refugeeness': Problematising the 'refugee community organisation'*, Working Paper 85, Birmingham: Third Sector Research Centre.

Piacentini, T. (2015) 'Missing from the picture? Migrant and refugee community organizations' responses to poverty and destitution in Glasgow', *Community Development Journal*, vol 50, no 3, pp 433-47 (doi: 10.1093/cdj/bsu047).

Putnam, R.D. (1995) 'Bowling alone: America's declining social capital', *The Journal of Democracy*, vol 6, no 1, pp 65-78.

Putnam, R.D. (ed) (2002) *Democracies in flux: The evolution of social capital in contemporary society*, New York, NY: Oxford University Press.

Quiminal, C. (2000) 'Construction des identités en situation migratoire : territoire des hommes, territoire des femmes', *Autrepart*, no 14, pp 107-20.

Rainbird, S. (2011) 'Asylum seeker "vulnerability": the official explanation of service providers and the emotive responses of asylum seekers', *Community Development Journal* (first published online 28 June 2011, doi: 10.1093/cdj/bsr044).

Sargent, C. and Larchanché-Kim, S. (2006) 'Liminal lives: immigration status, gender, and the construction of identities among Malian migrants in Paris', *American Behavioral Scientist*, vol 50, no 1, pp 9-26.

Scottish Government (2013) *New Scots: Integrating refugees in Scotland's communities*, Edinburgh: Scottish Government, available at: www.gov. scot/Resource/0043/00439604.pdf (accessed 16 July 2015).

Singh, A. (2010) 'A cashless society, the other side of the coin', Institute of Race Relations, www.irr.org.uk/news/a-cashless-society-the-other-side-of-the-coin (accessed 8 April 2014).

Somerville P., and McElwee G. (2011) 'Situating community enterprise: a theoretical exploration', *Entrepreneurship & Regional Development*, vol 23, no 5-6, pp 317-30.

Werbner, P. (1991a) 'Introduction II', in P. Werbner and M. Anwar (eds) *Black and ethnic Leaderships: The cultural dimensions of political action*, London: Routledge, pp 15-37.

Werbner, P. (1991b) 'The fiction of unity in ethnic politics: aspects of representation and the state among British Pakistanis', in P. Werbner and M. Anwar (eds) *Black and ethnic leaderships: The cultural dimensions of political action*, London: Routledge, pp 113-45.

Zetter, R. and Pearl, M. (2000) 'The minority within the minority: refugee community based organisations in the UK and the impact of restrictionism', *Journal of Ethnic and Migration Studies*, vol 26, no 4, pp 675-98.

Zetter, R., Griffiths, D. and Sigona, N. (2005) 'Social capital or social exclusion? The impact of asylum seeker dispersal on UK refugee community organisations', *Community Development Journal*, vol 40, no 2, pp 169-81.

PART FOUR

Thinking about voice, learning and emotion below the radar

ELEVEN

'Almost a whisper': black and minority ethnic community groups' voice and influence

Phil Ware

Chapter aims

Despite the increase in black and minority ethnic (BME) communities in urban, and more recently, rural England, little has been written about the voice and influence of these communities in terms of policy. This applies particularly to groups in rural areas. This chapter therefore aims to:

- explore the strategies adopted by BME community groups in terms of achieving influence;
- compare the experiences of urban and rural community groups – their similarities and differences;
- analyse the extent to which these communities are able to affect policy outcomes in relation to issues that are important to them.

Background: why understanding BME voice is important

Understanding the voice and influence of BME is important for a number of reasons. First, there has been a growth in the number of BME communities in England and Wales over the past five decades. The BME population in England and Wales rose from 74,500 in 1951 to 7.9 million by 2011, representing 14% of the total population. Further 'over the past two decades England and Wales has become more ethnically diverse' (ONS, 2012, p 4). Migrants have come not only from New Commonwealth countries but also from Africa and the Middle East (most recently Syria), as a result of war, and from Eastern Europe since EU accession. Overall, the BME population was

22.8% in urban areas and 5% in rural areas at the 2011 census (ONS, 2013, p 22).

However, the distribution of BME populations in both rural and urban areas is uneven. For example, Birmingham and Leicester are predicted to become majority BME cities in the near future. While the North East has the fifth highest number (out of 10 regions) of people living in urban settlements, it has the least diverse population of any English region other than the South West, with 'over 95% identified as White in these areas' (ONS, 2013, p 8). While rural BME populations are generally smaller than those in urban areas, the 2011 census indicated that the average BME population of rural areas comprised between 3% and 5% of the total population (ONS, 2012) an increase of 14.8% since the 2001 census. Further, the profile of rural BME communities has become increasingly diverse since 2001. For example, once 'other white/not born in the UK' data is included, the figures for minority communities in Cumbria rise from 3.5% to an average of over 7% across the county (Cumbria County Council, 2015) and in rural Norfolk from 3.8% in 2001 to 9.4% in 2011 (Norfolk Community Foundation, 2013). It is also noticeable that BME populations are increasing more rapidly (relative to overall population) in some rural areas (for example, by 143% over a decade in parts of Cumbria) and that the majority of the BME population is located in the larger settlements of predominantly rural counties. Despite these increases, there is a lack of literature on rural BME community groups, the assumption being that BME issues are an urban phenomenon (Craig, 2011). This 'superdiversity' (Phillimore, 2011) has implications for the ways in which groups organise, and for the complexity and potential fragmentation of the BME voluntary 'sector'. During the late 1960s and early 1970s, the BME population reached between 7.9% (London) and 6.8% (Metropolitan West Midland) in some urban areas. This resulted in a number of targeted policy and government funding initiatives, including the Urban Programme and (in education) Section 11 monies. In rural areas, despite growing and increasingly diverse BME populations, there have been no comparable recent policy developments.

Second, since the 2008 global financial crisis and the austerity measures introduced by successive UK governments since 2010, it has been argued that cuts have had a disproportionate impact on BME groups and organisations (Yeung, 2010; Stokes, 2011; Lachman and Malik, 2012), despite the growth of diversity in communities. This applies in particular to those rural and urban BME groups that had been supported through various Area Based Initiatives since the 1970s.

Mohan (2011) has disputed arguments that cuts have been targeted at BME organisations, arguing that they have fallen disproportionately on all poor communities, where BME groups happen to be over-represented. There has also been an impact for BME organisations at regional and national levels. Organisations such as Voice for Change, the Council for Ethnic Minority Sector Organisations and Race Equality Councils (RECs) have attempted to develop a BME voice. However, the reduction of funding and the closure of many projects, particularly RECs, and loss of other infrastructure, has limited the capacity of these organisations to provide 'voice' at a national or regional level.

In addition to population increases and the impact of austerity, there have been key shifts in policy. The 2010 Equality Act resulted in an increased focus on a range of equalities, including gender and sexuality, resulting in race/ethnicity blindness in policy through unified equalities legislation (brap, 2015).

All of these policy changes have taken place within the context of debates, often toxic, on the economic and social 'disbenefits' of migration, particularly in relation to the current Syria/refugee crisis (Dustmann and Frattini, 2014) and an increase in hate crime from 2013/14 to 2014/15 of 18%, of which 82% has been recorded specifically as race hate crime (Corcoran et al, 2015). In the post-Brexit climate, there has been a further significant increase in race hate crime, with police reporting a 57% increase after the UK voted to withdraw from membership of the European Union (*The Guardian*, 2016).

Finally, there is the status of the BME voluntary and community sector (VCS) itself. While its existence as a discreet sector is contested (see Chapter Nine of this volume, and Mayblin and Soteri-Proctor, 2011), Afridi and Warmington (2009, p 18) identified the rise of the BME VCS as a response to two main factors: first, 'the lack of appropriate provision of services by the state and mainstream voluntary organisations', and second, 'the ... tide of British racism, oppressive policing and fascist politics'. There is, however, a shared view that: 'Its development has lagged behind that of the third sector more generally, partly because of relatively recent arrival ... and partly because of racism both in state policy and within the third sector' (Craig, 2011, p 367).

Research methods

This research is a response to the lack of recent academic literature on rural BME groups, despite the rapid changes detailed earlier. While there was a flurry of practice-based materials in the early 2000s (Henderson and Kaur, 2000; de Lima, 2001), the most recent research

(Chakraborti and Garland, 2012) has not been significantly updated since its original publication in 2003.

The findings used in this chapter are based on:

- a literature review drawing on academic publications, legislation and policy documents, as well as materials produced by BME organisations themselves;
- Qualitative research consisting of 47 individual interviews carried out with a total of 51 participants from local BME groups and strategic partners;
- a further two focus groups with regional/sub-regional networks in the North West and West Midland, involving a further 35 participants.

The interviews were undertaken in an urban area in the West Midlands, the North West and London (see Table 11.1). Subsequent rural interviews were conducted in settlements in the North West, the West Midlands and the South West (see Table 11.2). Research sites and interviewees have been anonymised to copy with research ethics approval requirements.

While, given resource constraints, the research sample does not fully represent the diversity of urban and rural BME communities, identifying interviewees using snowballing techniques facilitated access to as wide a range of groups as possible in terms of diversity, size, focus and faith.

Table 11.1: Urban interview summary profile

Locality	Interviews with BME community groups		Interviews with strategic organisations		Total
	Local established BME groups	Refugee and new migrant groups	Regional policy networks	Statutory organisations	
Birmingham/West Midlands	6	1	1	1	9
London		1		2	3
Greater Manchester	5	1	1		7
Total	11	3	2	3	19
Interviewees					
Female	7	1		2	10
Male	6	2	2	1	11

Table 11.2: Rural interview summary profile

Locality	Interviews with BME community groups		Interviews with strategic organisations		Total
	Local established BME groups	Refugee and new migrant groups	Regional policy networks	Statutory organisations	
A rural area in the North West	3	3	1	1	8
A West Midlands rural area	3	2		2	7
Rural areas in the South West	5	2	4		11
Total	11	7	5	3	26
Interviewees					
Female	7	5	3		15
Male	5	4	4	2	15

Strategies for voice and influence

This section examines the strategies adopted by the groups interviewed in the urban and rural research interviews. These fell into five broad categories:

- demonstrating community needs and delivering services;
- capacity building and education;
- social and cultural activities;
- politicisation;
- partnerships.

Activities undertaken by groups included advocacy and advice with individuals on domestic violence, hate crime, mental health and addiction issues; education, recreation and integration with young and elderly people, including sport, trips and annual events; protecting culture and traditions; anti-poverty work, particularly advice work and individual advocacy; and practical voluntary help for elderly people and voluntary organisations. It was noticeable that individual advocacy, particularly on hate crime, was seen as more important in rural areas and was identified as a factor preventing development work on broader policy issues.

In terms of **demonstrating community needs**, two strategies were adopted: using data to establish BME-specific voluntary sector services and influencing mainstream statutory provision (for example, culturally appropriate foods in acute hospital services). Participants felt that the former approach had been more successful in urban areas with a critical mass of population. However, it was a 'historical' model: since the 2008 recession and the introduction the Equality Act in 2010, funding has not been available to establish (or indeed maintain) culturally specific voluntary sector services. Further, in practice, service delivery groups reported they had been 'diverted from their mission' of advocating on behalf of their community to delivering services based on outcomes decided by the funder, rather than influencing policy.

Capacity building is defined as a process by which organisations address their development needs from a self-defined starting point (CCWA, 2011), and was identified as an important strand of work for two urban groups. One said that it needed 'support to be sustainable and resilient year after year', implying that the group would collapse without capacity building support. Five urban groups said they used **formal education** as a strategy both to promote members of their own community's understanding of 'the system' in the UK and educate host communities on culturally specific needs and practices.

Politicisation, the process of seeking to exert an influence on social policy at a local, regional or national level, was seen as important by some urban groups (for example, Operation Black Vote). However, there were a number of barriers to the development of this approach, ranging from the diversity of communities within the sector, the lack of leadership of organisations and the closure of many sub-regional, regional and national infrastructure organisations in the period from 2008. Rather than acting in politically strategic ways, rural BME groups tended to be drawn into intensive individual advocacy cases where they had the resource to do so.

Partnerships were in evidence in urban areas, although they appeared to be more effective at sub-regional than regional level, and, in the view of research participants 'not at national level.' In urban areas, partnerships were seen as a way of accessing funding and resources as well as improving coordination and leadership within the BME third sector.

Not all of these strategies were readily available for rural BME community groups. Sparsity of population restricted the capacity to mobilise politically and influence decision-making processes (de Lima, 2001). Respondents variously argued that 'issues of rural areas are getting lost', and there was a difficulty in developing funding applications due to low numbers in any one community: "We don't have the numbers but the issues are real ... to those who are affected."

While urban BME groups offered **social and cultural activities** as part of a wider portfolio of work, this tended to be the main focus in rural communities. Further, in urban areas such activity was often culturally specific to one grouping; in rural areas, where the BME population was small in numbers, this involved bringing different ethnic groups together and was often organised on an inter-faith basis. One of the main reasons for undertaking these activities was that funders, especially statutory bodies, were seen as more likely offer small grants to fund them; respondents also stated that social groups made it easier to talk about issues.

However, six rural groups offered **educational opportunities** such as language classes. One refugee project in the South West undertook practical work on a voluntary basis, generally for elderly white residents, using the project "to [educate people] about why we are here and what we can add to this community". The project sought to achieve this by demonstrating a positive aspect of the presence of a refugee community. In addition, rural respondents argued that there was scope, often unrealised, to form **partnerships** with other community and/or strategic organisations. Often groups depended on a champion within the statutory sector in order to access resources, or even to be heard, rather than on formal equality structures. This type of arrangement would be through an individual who had the ability to influence policy and resources, but who would also be willing to support the aspirations of the BME third sector. This could, however, disadvantage newer arrivals in rural areas: "What little money there is tends to go to the people they [the council] know."

Overall, a minority of organisations aimed to be outward looking in that they attempted to work with others to influence policy as it affected their community. For a majority, however, in both urban and rural areas, limited and diminishing resources meant that survival dictated a more inward-looking approach than many would have chosen had more resources, and therefore time, been available. The lack of resources and the difficulty of achieving strategic impact meant that activists chose to focus on advocacy on behalf of individuals (particularly in rural areas), and recreational and educational activities, rather than attempting to exert influence on policies that affected their communities.

Challenges to developing and sustaining voice and influence

Common barriers to the implementation of successful strategies for voice and influence were outlined by the respondents in both urban and rural areas, and comprised:

- lack of funding/resources;
- the effects of the 2010 Equality Act;
- lack of recognition;
- the established voluntary sector 'taking the credit';
- the emergence of superdiversity;
- racism.

In rural areas, additional barriers included:

- sparsity of population and lack of critical mass;
- geographically dispersed communities and lack of transport;
- lack of flexibility imposed by employment patterns.

The lack of **funding and/or other resources** was the most frequently mentioned issue. Urban community groups said loss of funding resulted in a reduction of the impact that groups could have on the improvement of services and policy affecting their communities. In rural areas that had only recently experienced diversification, groups had received little funding prior to the recession in 2008, and some groups had never received statutory funds. There was little history of community or organisational development and a lack of infrastructure. Lack of support for organisations was exacerbated by the reduction in the number of RECs from nine to three in, for example, the South West. Even where groups were heavily dependent on volunteers, they could still experience difficulties covering expenses. Organisations recognised that those that generated their own funding, or survived on little income, were less affected by the recession but still lacked capacity to influence.

The **Equality Act 2010** was perceived to have diluted the resources, and impact, of BME organisations. Although respondents saw some benefit in connecting different dimensions of inequality, recognising that individuals may be discriminated against in an intersectional way, the majority of respondents felt that the Act had watered down previous legislation and led to a reduction in finance for race equality programmes, and that local authorities were less likely to undertake rigorous equality impact assessments that addressed issues of culture and ethnicity. Additionally, interviewees said that funding was more likely to be accessed by 'mainstream' umbrella VCS organisations to deliver outcomes across all equalities, further reducing income for the BME sector and adversely affecting services they provided for BME groups and communities.

Craig (2011) and Afridi and Warmington (2009) have argued that there is a **lack of recognition** of the BME VCS. Craig (2011, pp 381-2), states that 'some local authorities are now also dismantling their equalities structures' and 'the BME VCS will lose what coherent voice it has developed over the past 20 years'. The majority of participants in the research agreed there was a lack of recognition by the mainstream VCS, both of work being carried out by, and representation through, BME third sector organisations. One argued that "the issue of institutional discrimination within our society, and the ongoing issues, prevents organisations from often showing impact and success". Respondents also highlighted that "Britishness does not include black communities." An interviewee from a BME national organisation said: "The voluntary sector is not immune from racism, so has ways of marginalising certain voices and being afraid of certain voices because they are perceived to be too challenging."

In rural areas, the lack of recognition of BME communities, and their needs, by policymakers was more extreme. Where the voice of urban BME groups was seen by one interviewee to be 'almost a whisper', rural respondents felt their presence was almost non-existent, so there was no acknowledgement of BME groups' existence, let alone in policymaking.

Established/mainstream organisations at the local level were said to claim credit for meeting the needs of BME communities, suggesting that they were able to deliver appropriate services and speak on behalf of BME organisations and should therefore receive funding. Respondents from BME community-based organisations felt that such claims reinforced power imbalances between BME organisations and the mainstream VCS, with one respondent stating, "... because the infrastructure organisations are mainly run by the non-BME group, I'm not saying they're discriminating, but they don't understand the black ethnic minority needs ...".

Further, respondents expressed concern that national umbrella organisations were speaking for BME groups. A representative from a national strategic BME organisation stated: "Certainly the bigger players in the voluntary sector are very close to government and delivering government contracts, so space to critique isn't as large as it might have been in the past." However, there was also evidence that the voluntary sector was itself being squeezed by the private sector, which was selecting the most profitable work and 'parking' the rest (the more difficult, less profitable work), a situation observed in terms of the Work Programme and community justice by Rees and colleagues (2013).

Established organisations taking credit was argued to apply equally in rural areas, where one respondents stated that BME groups "were being side-lined by people in the [established] voluntary sector". While there was recognition that these medium-sized and large organisations were facing difficulties of their own, there was also a strong feeling that they were taking contracts for services to BME communities and then failing to deliver to an appropriate, culturally sensitive, standard.

The **emergence of superdiversity** was seen to affect rural and urban groups differently. In urban areas respondents claimed that established and newly arrived communities had different priorities. Members of more recently arrived communities argued that established BME organisations failed to understand their problems. As one respondent put it:

> "I think they understand a few of the problems because they are immigrants. But the difference is that maybe if

you came here with a visa ... it's a different background to how you came here as an asylum seeker or as a refugee."

Members of these newly arrived communities argued that those who had arrived in the 1960s and 1970s were more established in the wider community and that their issues were different as they experienced far less security in terms of residence, employment and access to services.

In rural areas, superdiversity had increased the number of different BME communities and meant that it was more difficult to achieve the 'critical mass' required to organise and potentially to influence policy around a specific community's needs. People and groups of different backgrounds felt that they were being 'lumped together' and their specific culture and needs were not recognised. Variously interviewees stated that "people think that East Europeans are one homogenous community" and referred to "the artificial creation of a Muslim community". Class was also seen to be an important factor in the rural West Midlands and the South West, as more affluent middle-class BME community members moved to more rural or traditionally white areas but were 'disconnected' from poorer minority communities in the area (McCabe et al, 2013).

In rural and more recently BME settled areas, racism was perceived to be problematic at an individual level, with hate crime referred to by respondents as an issue that needed confronting on a regular basis. In Cumbria, reports of race hate crime had doubled and were now affecting 6% of the local BME population. Rayner (2005) reports a similar picture in West Mercia, Cleveland, Hampshire and Staffordshire, 'all police areas with relatively small minority populations'. By contrast London had seen a decrease in the number of racist incidents reported, from 23,000 in 2000 to 9,453 in 2012/13. Interviewees referred to extreme incidents in North West and South West rural communities in particular.

Despite the fact that there was no specific question or prompt about racism in the research schedule (deliberately to avoid leading interviewees), experiences of racism were referred to by 19 of the rural interviewees and was argued to be the most pressing issue for most respondents, whether they worked at a strategic level or were members of small rural BME community groups.

While hate crime was the most overt manifestation of racism in rural areas, interviewees also referred to the ways in which they had been isolated and excluded. One woman described being the only visibly black person in her village and being excluded by local people: "I feel the odd one out because I'm not white." Another woman described how the dynamic of the room changed: "You go to a tea room, I'm sure they think black people don't drink tea."

Institutional racism was also said to be a concern for respondents, who argued that stereotyping and 'patting on the head' enabled mainstream officers to describe BME communities as vulnerable, claim money for them and deliver services on their behalf. BME communities were treated as homogeneous while their differences, strengths and individuality did not appear to be acknowledged. It was also said that racism had supposedly been solved. Organisations said they were encouraged by funders not to raise concerns about racism and that talking about it may affect funding.

In their report of *Racism in rural areas*, Blaschke and Torres (2002, p 272) argue that racism in British rural areas is related 'to the isolation of members of ethnic minorities and to the lack of structure for their integration' and that this is an issue for BME persons who may wish to visit the countryside. They also argue that BME communities are the victims of statistics and that if the statistics are low it is said that there is not much of an issue. Dhalech (2012, p 72), for example, found that the predominant approach to the issue of BME communities in rural areas was 'no problem here'. Indeed, for a number of rural respondents, passive collusion with overt racism was a survival strategy: "If you're the only black person in the village … it's like you may have to laugh at the racist jokes."

Losing voice: discussion

Research undertaken in urban areas of England into the voice and influence of BME communities (Ware, 2013) revealed that while these communities in some urban areas had a 'critical mass' of population to enable the development of groups and structures to support and represent them, their influence was weak. It was therefore expected that research undertaken in rural areas of England would reveal that BME communities have even less voice and influence. In the absence of recent literature in this field, this discussion will focus on the experience of rural BME community groups in this context.

While low population densities cause problems for rural communities generally, for BME communities these difficulties are exacerbated by the very small number of minorities living in rural areas. Even in the larger rural centres there were barely sufficient numbers to bring people together in groups, but in the deep rural areas this was extremely difficult if not impossible. Lack of transport was identified as a further barrier to bringing people together or sustaining services, both for rural communities generally but also specifically for very dispersed BME groups (Khan, 2012). Strategic organisations pointed to the issue of the time required, logistics and travel costs involved in working with geographically dispersed communities. Services were not 'rural-proofed' (fully costed into contracts) and outputs expected were seen as excessive, being designed around the greater densities of urban populations.

Additionally the diversity within these small populations meant that there were deemed to be insufficient numbers to be represented and their profile was so low that they were more likely to be overlooked in the development of rural strategies than rural communities more generally. Rural issues generally were seen as low on policy agendas and this presented a 'double whammy' for rural BME communities. As noted, it was also argued that local policymakers had a tendency to treat all BME communities "as one homogenous mass, failing to recognise differences and how these played out in terms of need".

There were also specific working patterns in rural communities, in agribusiness and the tourism trade, for example, that constituted a further impediment to people's ability to organise. In some cases people, often men, worked long hours. They were also isolated from the wider community, particularly when working on farms: "Immigrants are here for work, and they work really unsociable hours" and "don't have much time to engage with activities". The exploitation of migrant workers was seen as a particular concern by respondents and some farms were seen as unwelcoming to anyone who wanted to help workers organise on social issues let alone employment matters.

One theme referred to by writers is that of an 'invisible line' around rural England that minority communities are not expected to cross, as evidenced by the 'black people don't drink tea' quote gathered in this research. This is a perception that may be held by BME or white writers. Hannah Pool, interviewing the poet Benjamin Zephaniah in 2009, said: 'I'm always confused by black people who choose to live in the countryside. Why do it to yourself?", to which Zephaniah replied: "Because it's great... This is our country and if we keep living in inner cities people will stereotype us as inner-city people.... Don't think you can't live in the countryside because you're black" (cited in Craig, 2012, p iii).

Moss (2004) writing about birdwatching, primarily a 'countryside pursuit', investigated the reasons why so few of Britain's five million BME population took part in the hobby. Raekha Prasad, a journalist for *The Guardian*, said: 'As an Indian, the English countryside is a foreign land' (cited in Moss, 2004, p 327). The actor and playwright

Kwame Kwei-Armah said: 'I don't associate the countryside with me or anyone from an ethnic background' (cited in Moss, 2004, p 327).

This sense of a lack of a feeling of belonging is a theme that ran through the rural BME research and was not present significantly in the urban areas studied. It remains a feature of rural experiences of racism almost two decades after the work of de Lima (2001) and Henderson and Kaur (2000).

As noted, for many rural community groups, where BME communities lacked a critical, defensive, mass, overt racism was a far more significant factor than in urban areas. However, understanding the impact of racism was limited by its apparent invisibility. Despite the fact that the figures for race hate crime had increased in both the rural South West and rural North West, interviewees said that it was under-reported. This view was also supported by the Plymouth Fairness Commission (2014). Schools were found to be culpable for ignoring racism (Gill and Talbot, 2010). In this context, and alongside funding cuts, it was unsurprising that the priority for rural BME groups was to focus on supporting individuals, particularly those facing race attacks, at the expense of developing voice and influence.

Dhalech (2012, pp 74-5) found that 'the lack of consideration of racial equality in the rural agenda' had a number of consequences including 'the lack of representation and voice for BME communities' and 'a lack of support to empower BME communities to participate at all levels of society'. The findings of the research into rural BME groups supported this view and comments regarding voice and influence echoed those involved in the urban research, with participants variously responding "I don't think there's a big voice at all" and "We don't have a voice." Community group activists focused on work with individuals, often to combat racism, and on bringing people together to retain a social and cultural identity.

Voice as a whisper: conclusion

While participants in the research were able to identify some impact at individual and community level, the opportunity to be heard by policymakers was found to be extremely limited, particularly at a strategic level (Ware, 2013, 2015). One person, from a BME urban community group, summed up the predominant view by saying that they felt that the voice was lacking overall, that it was very tokenistic and that it was "very small, very quiet, a whisper". Individuals of BME background in rural settlements felt obliged to develop strategies for coping with, rather than being collectively able to challenge, racism.

The level of voice and influence for urban BME community groups has been reduced as a result of the impact of recession and the perceived shift in policies towards BME communities. This was seen to be partially the result of the Equality Act 2010 and the focus of Prevention of Violent Extremism agendas. However, respondents also argued that racism was no longer seen as an important issue. Further, with the reported 'watering down' of, for example, Equality Impact Assessments and the reluctance of local authorities to engage in single-cause funding, BME groups were suffering from reduced resources and were not a priority in terms of policy development. In all areas, there was concern that unelected leaders could be used by statutory bodies to represent their communities, variously purporting to represent communities over a region or to speak for people of similar background without a mandate from, or reference back to, those communities.

In rural settlements, voice and influence had not had the opportunity to develop to any great extent prior to the recession and therefore, while in some areas population figures were increasing, there was no commensurate increase in resources. Consequently, what little infrastructure had existed previously had been diminished and new communities had little opportunity to access resources to develop new groups to represent them and articulate their needs.

While the majority of BME communities are in urban areas, the rate of population growth in rural areas has increased, particularly since the 2001 census. The contrast between urban and rural areas, the invisible barrier, was considerable, particularly in relation to hate crime, which was far higher in rural areas relative to population size. It was also clear that the development of BME community groups was constrained by a number of factors that had less impact in urban areas. These included geographically dispersed communities and lack of transport, rigid patterns of employment and the increasing levels of, often unrecognised, diversity within small populations.

Rural groups especially found that they were unable to evidence sufficient numbers for funding, although activists argued that their needs were still significant. In all areas studied, participants said that their voice was not heard and their influence was very limited. In rural settlements (where race equality structures are largely absent), it was notable that the need to have a champion within a statutory body was seen to be crucial to the health and development of community groups.

In all areas researched, there is a need for policymakers to engage with BME community groups. Equally, the 'mainstream' VCS needs to develop, or extend, relationships with BME community groups and provide opportunities for dialogue and partnership. In particular, it needs to recognise the role that BME groups can and should play in delivering contracts, particularly in areas where members have more experience. BME groups themselves could look to identify new or alternative resources, such as sponsorship, crowd funding or community shares, to develop this work and to seek alliances within the voluntary and statutory sectors. However, there are also challenges to the practices of existing funders. For example, Taylor and Wilson's research for the Baring Foundation (2015) highlighted the need for funders to respond to the diversity of new populations and recognise that traditional forms of organisation and community representation may not be relevant to people from newer, and changing, communities.

Finally, policymakers need to learn lessons from earlier migrations in terms of understanding patterns and change within and between BME communities. They ignore 'at their peril' the evidence of increasingly diverse urban and, particularly, rural BME communities and the level of racism experienced by those communities living through current social, economic and political changes.

Key learning

- There is a substantial literature on race equality and voluntary organisations in the UK. This has largely focused on larger urban conurbations. Despite the growth in black and minority ethnic (BME) communities in rural areas, and their increasing diversity, this aspect of the equalities agenda, and research, has been largely ignored.
- BME groups have adopted a number of strategies to enhance voice and influence such as mobilising the black vote. This is more problematic in rural communities where BME communities may be dispersed, small in numbers and experience particular difficulties in organising because of patterns of employment, access to transport and venues.
- The voice and influence of the BME voluntary and community sector has reduced in recent years in the face of cuts to race equality umbrella organisations, the emergence of a single equalities agenda and, in the face of austerity measures, the move back to 'race blind' service provision. In some instances the mainstream voluntary sector has 'taken credit' for speaking on behalf of BME communities.
- BME community groups face a 'double whammy' in terms of voice and influence: the lack of specific UK policy towards rural communities in general and rural BME groups in particular.

Reflective exercises

- What should the role of the 'mainstream' voluntary and community sector be in relation to BME community groups?
- Is there an 'invisible barrier' between urban and rural settlements in relation to race?
- Do BME groups have influence on policy issues? If so, is there a difference between rural and urban community groups? How can this influence be increased?

References

Afridi, A. and Warmington, J. (2009) *The pied piper*, Birmingham: brap.

Blaschke, J. and Torres, G.R. (2002) *Racism in rural areas: Final report*, Berlin: European Monitoring Centre on Racism and Xenophobia.

brap (2015) *From benign neglect to citizen Khan: 30 years of equalities practice in Birmingham*, Birmingham: brap.

CCWA (Churches Community Work Alliance) (2011) *What is community capacity building?*, London: CCWA.

Chakraborti, N. and Garland, J. (2012) *Rural racism*, London: Routledge.

Corcoran, H., Lader, D. and Smith, K. (2015) *Hate crime, England and Wales, 2014/15*, London: Home Office.

Craig, G. (2011) 'Forward to the past: van the UK black and minority ethnic third sector survive?', *Voluntary Sector Review*, vol 2, no 3, pp 367-89.

Craig, G. (2012) *A place called Townsville. Rural racism in a North East context*, Durham: Durham University School of Applied Social Studies.

Cumbria County Council (2015) *Joint strategic needs assessment*, Kendal: Cumbria County Council.

de Lima, P. (2001) *Needs not numbers: An exploration of ethnic minority communities in Scotland*, London: Community Development Foundation.

Dhalech, M. (2012) 'Rurality, Big Society and BME communities', in M.-S. Abbas and R. Lachman *The Big Society: The Big Divide?*, Bradford: JUST West Yorkshire.

Dustmann, C. and Frattini, T. (2014) 'The fiscal effects of immigration to the UK', *The Economic Journal,* vol 124, no 680, pp 593–643.

Gill, O. and Talbot, A. (2010) *'Most of the time people don't like my colour'*, Ilford: Barnardo's South West.

Henderson, P. and Kaur, R. (eds) (2000) *Rural racism in the UK: Examples of community-based responses*, London: Community Development Foundation.

Khan, O. (2012) *A sense of place: Retirement decisions among older black and minority ethnic people*, London: Runnymede Trust.

Lachman, R. and Malik, F. (2012) *West Yorkshire public sector cuts: The impact on the BME voluntary and community sector*, Leeds/Bradford: University of Leeds/JUST West Yorkshire.

Mayblin, L. and Soteri-Proctor, A. (2011) *The black minority ethnic third sector: A resource paper'*, Working Paper 58, Birmingham: Third Sector Research Centre.

McCabe, A., Gilchrist, A., Harris, K., Afridi, A. and Kyprianou, P. (2013) *Making the links: Poverty, ethnicity and social networks*, York: Joseph Rowntree Foundation.

Mohan, J. (2011) *Mapping the Big Society: Perspectives from the Third Sector Research Centre,* Working Paper 62, Birmingham: Third Sector Research Centre.

Moss, S. (2004) *A bird in the bush: A social history of birdwatching*, London: Aurum.

Norfolk Community Foundation (2013) *Norfolk strategic needs report*, Norwich: Norfolk Community Foundation.

ONS (Office for National Statistics) (2012) *Ethnicity and national identity in England and Wales 2011*, London: ONS.

ONS (2013) *2011 Census analysis: Comparing rural and urban areas of England and Wales*, London: ONS.

Phillimore, J. (2011) 'Approaches to health provision in the age of super-diversity: accessing the NHS in Britain's most diverse city', *Critical Social Policy*, vol 31, no 1, pp 5-29.

Plymouth Fairness Commission (2014) *Creating the conditions for fairness*, Plymouth: Plymouth Fairness Commission.

Rayner, J. (2005) 'Racist attacks on the rise in rural Britain', *The Observer*, 27 March.

Rees, J., Taylor, R. and Damm, C. (2013) *Does sector matter? The experiences of providers in the Work Programme,* Working Paper 92, Birmingham: Third Sector Research Centre.

Stokes, E. (2011) *The impact of the economic downturn on BME education services*, London: Race on the Agenda.

Taylor, M. and Wilson, M. (2015) *Changing communities: Supporting voluntary and community organisations to adapt to local demographic and cultural change*, London: Baring Foundation.

The Guardian (2016) 'Cameron condemns xenophobic and racist abuse after Brexit vote', 27 June.

Ware, P. (2013) *'Very small, very quiet, a whisper.' Black and minority ethnic groups: Voice and influence*, Working Paper 103, Birmingham: Third Sector Research Centre.

Ware, P. (2015) *'Black people don't drink tea.' The experience of rural black and minority ethnic community groups in England*, Working Paper 130, Birmingham: Third Sector Research Centre.

Yeung, W. (2010) *Report on the impact of the economic downturn on black and minority third dector organisations*, London: Council of Ethnic Minority Organisations.

TWELVE

Learning to sustain social action

Jenny Phillimore and Angus McCabe

Chapter aims

This chapter aims to explore:

- how people learn for, and through, community activism;
- the role of social networks and capacity building in community learning;
- changing learning needs in evolving community groups and how those needs are met.

Context: from social capital to capacity building

Over past decades, the concept of social capital (Coleman, 1988; Putnam, 2000) has been influential in the development of policy around communities of place, interest and identity. More recently, research into social networks, and how these operate at local level, has also become important in terms of informing approaches to neighbourhood change, behavioural 'nudge' and community resilience (Edwards, 2009; Rowson et al, 2010; Cabinet Office, 2011). These concepts have been linked with the idea of capacity building to develop community groups 'capitals' (social, economic and in terms of knowledge) to meet local needs. The notion of building capacity within organisations has somewhat fallen from grace and been replaced by terminology such as 'developing skills and confidence' (IVAR, 2010) or 'capabilities' (Big Lottery Fund, 2011).

Under New Labour administrations, there was significant investment into a range of capacity-building and community engagement initiatives: from ChangeUp, Capacity Builders, Community Empowerment Networks and Take Part to the coalition's Community Organisers Programme and Big Local scheme after the 2010 election. These initiatives coincided with a growing trend towards often rather mechanistic needs analysis toolkits for voluntary and community groups (NCVO, undated), 'Kitemarks' and other quality standards, such as Community Matters, Visible Communities, Birmingham Voluntary Service Council's Quality First, and the Charities Evaluation Service's PQASSO Quality Standard. As a result, learning as a political process (Mayo and Thompson, 1995) has, in the voluntary sector, been overtaken by concepts of competencies and vocationalism (Foley, 1999).

A series of reports have highlighted some of the difficulties of, and tensions within, these capacity-building initiatives. For example, programmes lacked base-lines against which to measure 'built capacity' (NAO, 2009; TSRC, 2009). The focus of evaluations has tended to be the perceived quality of delivery (of training, advice etc.) rather than impact and outcomes in the longer term (Sender et al, 2011; Take Part Network, 2011). Where good practice and related guidance has been produced, it has tended to define community organisations as smaller, formal, voluntary groups with paid staff (Kail et al, 2011) or multi-purpose community anchors (IVAR, 2011) with incomes of up to £1 million per year and a (hierarchical) management structure. Community groups and activities that are below the radar have largely been omitted from consideration.

Further, with cuts to sector infrastructure nationally and locally, 'physical' training events have been increasingly replaced by online learning materials. This disadvantages rural groups with poor access to super-fast broadband and assumes high levels of computer literacy – which is not always the case. (Fishbourne and Derounian, 2009; Harris and McCabe, 2016).

Similarly, research into social networks and social capital has tended to assume they have intrinsic, and predominantly beneficial value and use (Putnam, 2000). Academics have tended not to explore the complex relationship and interaction between social and other forms of capital such as human, economic and cultural capital (Bourdieu, 1986; Savage et al, 2005), or the relationship between face-to-face networks and widespread access to social technologies (Harris and McCabe, 2016). Indeed, critical commentaries about social capital, even when refined into the different forms of bonding, bridging and linking capital (Somerville, 2011), note that it has a 'dark side', 'helps re-inforce inequality' (Field, 2003, p71), is unevenly distributed throughout society (Fukuyama, 2001) and does not, in itself, necessarily lead to positive outcomes, either for individuals or communities (Fukuyama, 1995).

As a result, little is known about skill and resource acquisition processes in below the radar community groups and activities that are generally dependent on voluntary labour (McCabe et al, 2009). This chapter aims to examine the role of social networks within below the radar community groups, identify how they shape the emergence and ongoing evolution of community action and explore the ways in which social networks may facilitate access to skills, knowledge and resources.

Looking at learning in community action: research aims and methods

The starting point for the research reported in this chapter was a Third Sector Research Centre review of the literature on social network theories and methods for mapping networks (Burnage, 2010). Four main approaches to mapping social networks were identified: whole-network design (Wesserman and Faust, 1994), egocentric design (Marsden, 2006), cognitive social structure (CSS) design (Krackhardt, 1987) and retrospective design – for example, the life history calendar (LHC) (Axinn et al, 1999).

While useful in thinking, at a theoretical level, around social networks and community action, each framework had its limitations. In particular, none of these approaches had the potential to illustrate 'how resources within a network (including people, skills, knowledge, finance etc.) alter over time' each presenting a snapshot of networks at a particular point in time or providing a temporal perspective for a single individual or group (Burnage, 2010, p 5).

Stage two of the research therefore involved using ideas gathered during the review to develop interview schedules that enabled participants to reflect on how their group had changed over time and to:

- identify the social networks involved in establishing/delivering the group's actions;
- outline the knowledge, skills and resources they used and their source;
- consider gaps in skills, resources and knowledge and the impacts of their absence.

Respondents were encouraged to reflect, in a narrative fashion, over the lifecycle of their group and covered a wide range of issues such as how and why they came together, how and what they had learned over time, the relative importance of different types of skills and knowledge and how skills and knowledge were shared within the group and with others.

Interviews were conducted at 11 venues (including community hubs) with 16 representatives from small, volunteer-based, community organisations. These were supplemented by three focus groups exploring the use of skills, knowledge and resources in small community groups involving 45 activists, practitioners and academics.

The sample was selected by drawing on a range of local, regional and national community networks to reflect the diversity of below the radar activities – from campaigning to mutual support, from small-scale, community-owned businesses to a group tackling domestic violence. They covered different geographical settings (rural/urban, inner city/peripheral estates), areas of relative wealth and deprivation and communities of interest or identity. Research also focused on groups that had sustained themselves over a number of years. The characteristics of the groups participating is summarised in Table 12.1. All the groups involved in the research were anonymised to comply with ethical requirements.

Despite this diversity of location, focus and activity, each of the groups in the pilot study shared certain common characteristics. All the groups were volunteer/activist led without paid/professional staff. They started below the radar as unincorporated associations, but some had moved over time to gaining some kind of legal status. All were highly visible within (though not necessarily outside) their own communities. All had a core group of six to eight activists but were able to draw on a much wider pool of volunteers. This core group tended to be stable over time despite some changes in their social networks. Crucially, none had 'failed' and there was no evidence of the intra-group conflict that has been found to characterise some community-based organisations (Taylor et al, 2006). The sample therefore consisted of community organisations that might be defined as successful in their own terms. Clearly exploring 'unsuccessful' organisations (while challenging in research terms) could have brought different perspectives and insights. However, the approach adopted enabled lessons to be learned about the factors that facilitate the growth and survival of community action.

Table 12.1: Groups participating in the research

Name	Location	Primary purpose	Activities
Brownton Village Hall Development Group	Rural	Community hub/ meeting space	Provides space for a diverse range of local groups and activities Fundraising Social events
Canute Flood Action Group (CFAG)	Rural	Campaigning	Lobbying for flood defences Fundraising Social events
Central Africa Communities Association (CACA)	Community of interest/identity	Representation/ cultural identity	Social events Representation (immigration and nationality) Social history
Cobalt Connects	Market town	Area improvements	Asset management Social events/fundraising Informal learning opportunities Promoting the local economy/ green initiatives
Faith in Volunteers England	Community of interest/identity (faith groups); inner-urban	Volunteer networking	Volunteer support Development of volunteer opportunities in faith-based organisations
Hadrian's Wall Tenants' and Residents' Association (HWTRA)	Peripheral estate	Advocacy and representation	Representing tenants Estate management Social events Community clean-ups
Heritage Hall	Peripheral estate	Community centre/hub	Preservation society Local history group Friends of the park Coffee shop/snack bar Community festival
Hopes 4 All	Peripheral estate	Multi-purpose faith-based organisation	Pre-school group Youth work Dance group Faith activities (Bible class and so on)
Noham Village Shop	Rural	Service provider: community shop	Volunteers running local community shop Fundraising Social events
Oddington Hall	Peripheral estate	Community centre/hub	Neighbourhood regeneration Room hire Social events Community development
Stop It Now (SiN)	Women's group/ interest group	Community responses to domestic violence	Support groups Advice and counselling

The learning journey

The skills, knowledge and resources developed within, and needed by, each group changed over time. Having started with generic interpersonal skills largely underpinned by shared motivations and a degree of enthusiasm, most acquired highly technical skills, ranging from shop or asset management (Heritage Hall/Noham Village Shop) through to research (CFAG) and a detailed knowledge of housing legislation (HWTRA) or safeguarding issues (Hopes 4 All). Possessing such expertise, however, was not seen as essential in the early stages of group establishment.

Starting out

When starting out, respondents identified a set of common features that had enabled the group to move from informality to some form of more structured activity. A common cause that brought people together was, in each case, the catalyst. Sometimes this was a crisis such as problems with flooding (CFAG), or the loss of local facilities (Noham Village Shop). In other instances, motivations were primarily social: a desire to overcome isolation, reduce vulnerability (SiN), offer services that mainstream agencies were not seen as providing (CACA), or offer activities for overlooked groups (Oddington Hall). Clarity of purpose and focus were also key factors:

> "I think it's important to have a common cause. If people don't have a common cause they won't come together. I think it helped that it was a short campaign not one that became long and drawn out. That helped keep energy levels high. Also we were focused.… We worked on what we could change and not on things that you cannot do." (Canute Flood Action Group)

Not all groups began with a clear idea of what they wanted to achieve – or the needs identified originally changed over time. For example, CACA started out as a social group, meeting to play football. As refugee numbers rose in the late 1990s and early 2000s, the group evolved to focus on providing immigration and citizenship advice to new arrivals because they found that members of their community were struggling to get the support they needed from mainstream agencies. CACA subsequently moved on again to become a focus for celebrating pan-African culture in England. The tenants' and residents' group was motivated by a poor housing repair service and the disruption associated with two substantial capital projects on land immediately adjoining its estate: "It is people, and quite rightly, who are concerned about where they're living" (HWTRA). This initial anger gradually transformed from an anticipated short-term campaign to HWTRA taking on an estate management role.

Similarly, the domestic violence group (SiN) was motivated by a sense of injustice. 'Raw' emotion was a key driver, in the early stages of their organising (see also Chapter Thirteen):

> "It happened ... because of something that happened to a friend of mine and I was angry and cross about it, and that's really ... you know, that was the thing, it's the passion, I suppose, and that's what we're probably trying to get through to people, what is your passion, what is the thing that will drive you forward." (Stop it Now)

Cobham Connects' starting point, however, was different: rather than responding to a crisis or adversity, the local environment was seen as excellent and needed to be preserved and developed:

> "But we are coming at it from the point of the aesthetics. 'Wouldn't it be lovely to have a green road?' We're not coming at it from the 'Oh God, we all hate ...' It's just a different way of going into the issues." (Cobham Connects)

Similarly, Heritage Hall's activity emerged from the "love of the area and the love of the building".

Some kind of common cause, coupled with interpersonal skills, was critical to initial group development. Personality characteristics of group leaders or members were frequently identified as a further important resource for groups. Leaders were frequently charismatic: full of ideas, enthusiasm and determination. Their ability to attract other activists was seen as key:

> "There's also issues as a leader, I think, in small groups that can be very good, but can also be counter-productive. It's having the skills to be a leader, but accept the fact that there are people below you that can bring something to the party and not feel threatened by it.... The controlling leader who won't let others use their skills is dangerous." (Oddington Hall)

When asked what members of social networks brought to the group, determination and perseverance were frequently identified as key assets: "Failure was not an option ... we refused to be victims" (CFAG). A further asset was the possession of strong networks between key individuals and the wider community. Often those involved in establishing groups were very well networked and able to mobilise others to work towards delivering the groups aims and objectives. Just having these kinds of people in a group enabled them to access a major resource: human capital.

> "I know a lot of people and that helps, because I've been in the village a number of years, and I've involved myself in other projects in the past, not necessarily projects but just events and happenings in the village." (Noham Village Shop)

Campaigning, especially when rapid action was needed, would have been much more difficult without these pre-existing social relationships and networks. CFAG, Browntown Village Hall and Heritage Hall used their extensive networks to identify others, often with specialist knowledge or professional skills, to address particular barriers or needs. For example, as their projects progressed, they actively sought local residents with business planning skills. While interviewees stressed the importance of personal characteristics and social networks, they also identified elements of chance and 'luck' in both coming together initially and developing as a group:

> "It was just a fluke phone call to me because I don't come to church or anything but he [the vicar] phoned me for somebody's phone number, because he'd known my husband, and he mentioned that this was going to be on the programme and he was looking for volunteers. So I rang round some friends and we all came to the meeting." (Heritage Hall)

In other cases, the patterns and levels of activity in and around these networks also changed over time. In the case of CFAG, relationships were described as 'dormant' for over two years after the success of their campaign, only to be 'revitalised' when flood defences failed in 2015. The network of tenants who took on a campaigning role with HWTRA gradually withdrew as they were not interested in estate management.

Moving on: drawing on skills, knowledge and resources

In terms of moving on from initial group formation, interviewees highlighted an important mix of 'soft' and 'hard' skills. The specific technical skills required evolved over time and included financial and buildings management, health and safety, food hygiene, marketing and communications and many more competences, depending on the nature of activities and actions. Interviewees were, however, adamant that possession of such skills alone was not enough to ensure success of their groups. Certain types of interpersonal skills that facilitated team working were critical to ensuring that heterogeneous groups of people could work together effectively. The ability to negotiate and inspire confidence were also important:

> "The confidence of the people.… The belief in themselves is far more important … because some people have come here and thought, 'Am I capable of doing it?' 'Well, yes you are. Four or five years later, look at you. Look at what you know.'" (HWTRA)

Furthermore recognising and celebrating success and acknowledging contributions was seen as a crucial, if often forgotten, aspect of community organising. CFAG, for example, regularly contacted everyone who supported the campaign (from very active members to those who had signed petitions/organised fundraising events) to thank them. For HWRTA, celebrating successes and organising social events helped 'keep the energy going'.

Generally, these skills, certainly in the early stages of development, were not seen as community or voluntary sector specific. Indeed, none of the community activists interviewed had a background in the formal voluntary sector. Rather, they talked about transferable skills, brought from their work place, their life experience, or from trade union activity: "Here I use what I have learned through my work. But this is more fun than work." (Heritage Hall)

Those involved in the community shop, Cobham Connects and Brownton Village Hall talked about being able to draw on the professional skills of active members: for example, in Cobham Connects an IT specialist designed the community website and a self-employed business woman managed the finances.

Developing skills, knowledge and resources

As groups evolved and moved towards achieving their goals, they identified a range of learning needs. These changed over time.

> "People started with nothing when they arrived. Slept in each other's flats and on each other's floors. After the football there was a lot of talk like … how do I renew my visa, how do I deal with this immigration problem? Now it has moved on. What we have identified is the barriers to employment and education. So we have been doing something about that, getting an education." (CACA)

> "I suppose the skills we needed did change a bit over time. So there was the data collection and putting the report together for the Environment Agency. After that it was more about lobbying and getting our case heard, involving the media, talking to the council and officers and that was new to me and a really steep learning curve." (CFAG)

As those involved in the community shop and village hall groups began to realise their goals, skills in fundraising coupled with the enthusiasm and motivation that had enabled initial progress needed to be augmented with other skills. Volunteers had to learn how to manage an asset. HWTRA moved from campaigning and negotiating to technical estate management skills. These skills were developed, however, not through formal training, but by 'seeing and doing', often by linking up with members of the community who had the requisite skills or by peer learning from similar groups in other locations. Village shop organisers visited other community-owned shops in the regional and noted the importance of "adapting what seemed to work. Taking the best bits from each."

CACA 'learned the ropes' through observing the practices at a well-established voluntary organisation that temporarily offered it office and meeting space. The design of Brownton Village Hall evolved from visiting other village halls, "looking at spaces that worked and those that didn't and discovering what attracted people [to a village hall] and could make it viable".

Some groups identified very specific learning, again through seeing, doing and networking:

"But within that group it's about people who may be running their own businesses, sharing skills and experiences, but it's just ... someone might say, 'Oh I've got a problem with this on my computer' and someone else can say, "Oh I can sort that out.' Or someone else might say, "Where can I ...? I really need to find a new ..." something and someone else says, 'Well I know the person you need to speak to.'" (Cobham Connects)

HWTRA found out about tenant management organisations (TMOs) by chance through an internet search. However, it only decided to change its status to a TMO after meetings with several others and through exploring alternative estate management options through site visits.

Addressing skills gaps

Surveys repeatedly highlight fundraising skills as one of the key problems in the voluntary sector (Brown et al, 2011; BVSC, 2014) alongside governance issues (IVAR, 2010). Most, as noted, focus on larger organisations with paid staff. Interestingly, none of our respondents highlighted fundraising or governance as key learning needs at any stage in their development. Funding did, as the groups evolved, become a more important issue, enabling them to do more or, in terms of capital projects, achieve their goals. However, fundraising skills were also developed by 'trial and error' (Brownton Village Hall), by learning while doing, or through identifying someone in the social network with appropriate skills, rather than attending courses.

Networks were critical in identifying expertise and addressing skills gaps. This applied both within the community, 'knowing who was around and who could do what', but also when external support was required. For example, while respondents were well networked within their area/community of interest, as they evolved and took on greater levels of responsibility, vertical as well as horizontal relationships became more important – relationships that were often absent at the outset. In terms of using those networks, the focus tended to be on the person helping them, rather than their employing organisation. Relationships were essentially 'individualised'. HWTRA, for example, experienced the local housing department as a barrier, "but Jim and Ray have been really helpful". CFAG established relationships with district and county councillors, but again referred to them in first name terms rather than their official role. The groups in Noham and Brownton developed links with national village hall and community shop network organisations, but again talked about individuals rather than organisations per se. This disassociation from organisations reflects earlier studies that indicate that community groups are 'embedded more in networks of individual agency than institutional strategy' (Edwards and Woods, 2006, p 61).

Sharing skills, knowledge and resources

There was limited evidence of extensive skills sharing within each group: "People focus on what their speciality is, if they have one" (Noham Village Shop). Activists worked to existing skills sets and at a level they were comfortable with. However, groups were keen to share their learning with others if required. Noham Community Shop adopted a 'seeing and doing' model to share its expertise:

> "We host visits at the shop from other shops. We've got one coming up, actually, next week … who haven't actually opened a shop yet, but they're hoping to open a community shop, and we're hosting a visit and usually spend three or four hours, this will be the third one that we've done.... We try and get together a cross-section of our group, perhaps four or five of us, a finance person, a buyer, someone from marketing, so that we can cover all aspects of the business." (Noham Village Shop)

Similarly, other tenants' and residents' associations considering estate management options now visit HWTRA. Skills sharing appeared more common (if less formalised) in the groups with a more fluid membership. Members of CACA used the skills gained to establish refugee and support groups in places they had moved to elsewhere in the UK. Members of CFAG were using the fundraising skills they had gained to support international projects and to form a village action group that tackled issues such as housing beyond the immediate need for a flood barrier. Cobham Connects noted:

> "We're at quite an exciting point because we're literally taking what we've learnt now and thinking about what value it has for other people." (Cobham Connects)

Gains for people, groups, and communities

Those interviewed talked about what had been gained from their own, and wider community, perspectives. Activism had involved developing or refining particular personal skills:

> "How to work with people, (elected) members, officers who are coming with a political agenda. So political skills, how to work your way round systems and understand bureaucratic systems.... More generally I think some people learned some highly technical skills like designing questionnaires and doing research." (CFAG)

A HWTRA committee member also remarked on what he had gained from his involvement in the group:

> "I personally can take an awful lot away from what I've been doing in the voluntary capacity, it's added a hell of a lot to my CV and you couldn't pay for it in all honesty. So as much as I sometimes moan that I'm £3,500 down [in expenses], I couldn't have bought that." (HWTRA)

CACA members were highly educated and in professional employment in their countries of origin. However, this education and employment history was not recognised in the UK and they knew little about UK systems and institutional culture (Phillimore and Goodson, 2010). Involvement in the group offered members the opportunity to familiarise themselves with the way things worked in the UK and to develop skills and experience that helped them get a job or a better job:

> "She started working in a restaurant. But with us she was doing advice and went and got her NVQ in Advice Guidance and Counselling and now she is an adviser with the council." (CACA)

Further, interviewees highlighted broader social and economic benefits for the wider community associated with the development of their community organisation:

> "It's all linked to the shop, but it brings in other people as well, like, for instance, local tradespeople who've done work for us in the building, particularly when we were

developing the coffee shop area. What a value it's been to them, not just directly with what we've paid them, but with other work they've picked up because other people have seen them working in the shop and asked them to do jobs for them." (Noham Village Shop)

CFAG and Noham Community Shop felt that their actions had contributed to building new networks and relationships within the locality, bringing together people across class or other divides. Participating in community activities was also said to be a good way of helping newcomers to fit into the local community and to develop social networks of their own. CACA believed that its experience of running the group had enabled it to develop networks and projects across African communities in the UK. This was a move from its early work, which that focused more on a single country of origin or region of residence.

Informality and friendliness were key characteristics of the way groups operated, even when fully constituted and involved in highly structured/managerial activities such as running an estate or village hall (Gilchrist, 2016). For Noham Village Shop, establishing a community-owned business was not only about "providing somewhere for convenient shopping" but also creating "a social meeting place", a sentiment that was repeated elsewhere:

> "I really enjoy coming up here. And the other big thing is … you make so many friends. I mean, you can come in here any day and you're going to meet people that you know and you're happy to see." (Heritage Hall)

As more formal structures emerged, for each group these needed to be flexible and to facilitate participation, rather than being rigid, hierarchical and alien to a particular community's way of working.

Passion – plus knowledge: how things work

Our original intention was to map, both literally and visually, relationships within and between groups and identify the level of importance of particular skills, leadership and knowledge that an individual might bring to below the radar group development. What emerged was something different; a combination of skills and knowledge of collectives:

"Everyone was equally important – whether they got names on petitions, helped with the research, organised fund raising events or did things like provide lighting at those events or get bands to perform at the 'Bund Aid' event. I would say it was not about any one person or any one set of skills being more important than others." (Canute Flood Action Group)

Technical knowledge was important, but, as noted, community connections were most important. Furthermore, knowledge without passion and a shared cause was seen as 'meaningless'. The collective abilities and capacities of all involved brought groups their strength and were critical to their success. Each member of the group could be conceived as being part of a jigsaw. If any part was missing, the group might not function effectively so the missing piece had to be sourced via social networks.

A key assumption in trying to map changing skills, knowledge and resources over time, is that community groups experience critical events in their lifetime. As external researchers, it was possible to identify such events for the groups involved: the community shop losing its premises just before its planned opening and a founder member and driver of the campaign group dying. This thinking did not, however, match the narrative of participants. For them, the life of the group was seen as a journey, rather than as a series of critical events. The stories told highlighted a perception of natural progression.

Our findings demonstrate that community groups use a wide range of resources, social networks and skills to reach their goals. Many of those resources could be described as human capital, developed from other spheres or their lives: paid work, raising children or running other voluntary groups. Emotional capital was also critical (see Chapter Thirteen) – personality traits and emotions that motivated group members to work for the good of their community.

Wide-ranging connections meant access to support, in the form of volunteer time and to the specialist skills needed to run organisations effectively. As resource needs changed over time, groups moved from what, in Putnam's (2000) terms, might be described as bonding capital, that which exists between members of the bounded community of geography or interest, to bridging and linking capital as groups sought and exchanged knowledge from and with other organisations by observing how they worked. Some, but by no means all, also developed linking capital with agencies or institutions, though typically such connections were developed via individuals' personal or professional social networks, rather than through any formal networking on the part of the organisation.

Learning to support community learning: final reflections

Much of the investment in learning for community action has, and continues to be, focused on formal training (IVAR, 2010) and the language of training needs analysis (NCVO, undated). This approach assumes that there is a set of specialist technical skills that needs to be in place for community organisations to flourish. Our participants did not talk about training as instrumental to their learning. Indeed, often training was seen as 'patronising' or 'not useful', and did not recognise the tension between communities as a space for learning at people's own pace and on their own issues, and more top-down, formalised, learning on what policymakers and others assume is needed to strengthen community organisations and activities (Johnston and Coare, 2003).

People learned by seeing and doing and connecting, through social networks and 'horizontal' peer experiences:

> "What I'm trying to encourage people to see is that a different perspective. Just 'cause Joe Bloggs says it and he's given you a lecture, it doesn't mean to say that Joe's right." (HWTRA)

Learning in below the radar community groups developed collectively and by targeting and recruiting individuals into the group, rather than being an isolated and individualised activity. Further, our analysis suggests that there is not a hierarchy of learning. The 'soft' skills of being well connected, being able to negotiate and bring emotion and passion to a cause are as important as technical knowledge and are vital ingredients in the success of below the radar community activity. As Cairns (2003) noted: 'While community activists clearly do a great deal of learning it does not necessarily come from [the] formal training' (p 121).

Final reflections: spaces for learning

Networks and networking were clearly important for the learning of research participants. However, as successful groups, other forms of capital came into play: human, financial, cultural and environmental (Bourdieu, 1986; Savage et al, 2005). Each respondent described the complex weave of skills and knowledge (from communications through to understanding health and safety legislation) required to run even a small, semi-formal, community group. Social networks by themselves were insufficient. Indeed, policy initiatives and models of working (such as asset-based community development) that focus exclusively, or predominantly, on building social capital as a means of addressing community needs while ignoring issues of access to other forms of human and economic capital are unlikely to succeed. Those active in Stop It Now withdrew not because of a lack of social networks or capital. Rather, accessing financial capital on a marginal peripheral estate proved impossible.

Research in formal voluntary organisations has tended to stress the importance of formalised, often accredited learning (Lasa, 2012) and, traditionally, capacity-building initiatives rather than peer-to-peer support have tended to finance that formalised learning (McCabe et al, 2007). Much less is known about informal, experiential, learning in community groups (Wenger, 1998). Yet informal learning is acknowledged to come from a whole range of activities related to work, family or leisure. It is often not structured and incidental (CEC, 2000). Academics writing in this field stress the communal, rather than individualised, characteristics of informal, community-based, learning and that informal learning is 'situated' in local issues, activities and cultures (Colley et al, 2002, p 5). What this literature does not address, and was beyond the scope of the current research, was both how (or whether) activists learn from the 'failure' of other groups and how they develop the skills to effectively transmit knowledge.

Learning through experience in community activity may have very practical outcomes for those involved, including access to employment. Those outcomes were not the motivation for, or purpose of, learning in community groups. Rather participants talked of the 'practical intelligence' (Oddington Hall) required to run their organisation. Learning was by 'seeing and doing' rather than training per se. Such embedded 'practical intelligence' has tended to be undervalued in a culture where formal learning and accreditation is rewarded. What it requires is spaces (both in terms of time and venues) for those active in their community to come together to share ideas and knowledge. It is those very spaces (see Chapters Four and Six) that, in times of austerity, are under threat.

Key learning

- Over the last decade there have been a plethora of capacity building programmes aimed at developing skills and knowledge in community groups. Such initiatives have, however, focused on the provision of formal learning and largely ignored the important role of peer and informal learning at the community level.
- Community action builds on the enthusiasm of individuals and groups. The motivations for organising may be various but are often rooted in emotion: anger, fear, a sense of injustice or a simple desire to enhance associational life. These emotional dimensions have largely been ignored both in the literature and the desire to 'build community capacity'.
- Capacity building has fallen out of favour. Infrastructure bodies supporting these initiatives in the past have either closed or lost the resources to offer face to face support and advice. There has been a growing emphasis on offering such support online. This further disadvantages small groups without access to information technology or the required broadband speeds (particularly in rural areas).
- Policy, and much of the academic and practice literature, continues to stress the role of developing social capital in deprived neighbourhoods as a 'buffer' against austerity. Such neighbourhoods may have an abundance of, often unrecognised, social capital: what they lack is access to other forms of capital – in particular, financial.

Reflective exercises

- Reflecting on your own experience, how did you 'learn' to be active in your own community?
- Consider the value of embedded 'practical intelligence' and informal learning for social action and building community groups.
- Policy debate has been dominated by ideas of social capital and social networks. What other forms of capital might community groups need and how are those capitals 'built'?

References

Axinn, W.G., Pearce, L.D. and Ghimire, D. (1999) 'Innovations in life history calendar applications', *Social Science Research*, vol 28, no 3, pp 243-64.

Big Lottery Fund (2011) *Building capabilities for legacy and impact: Discussion paper*, London: Big Lottery Fund.

Bourdieu, P. (1986) 'The forms of capital', in J. Richardson (ed) *Handbook of theory and research for the sociology of education*, New York, NY: Greenwood.

Brown, H., Livingstone, M., Spillane, G. and Talja, J. (2011) *UK Small Charity Sector Skills Survey 10/11*, London: FSI.

Burnage, A. (2010) *Understanding the transfer of resources within and between below the radar community groups using social network analysis – methodological issues*, Birmingham: Third Sector Research Centre.

BVSC (Birmingham Voluntary Service Council) (2014) *The state of the sector*, Birmingham: BVSC.

Cabinet Office (2011) *Strategic national framework on community resilience*, London: Cabinet Office.

Cairns, T. (2003) 'Citizenship and regeneration: participation or Incorporation?', in T. Coare and R. Johnson, *Adult learning, citizenship and community voices: Exploring community based practice*, Leicester: NIACE.

Coleman, J. (1988) 'Social capital in the creation of human capital', *American Journal of Sociology*, vol 94, Supplement: Organisations and Institutions: Sociological and Economic Approaches to the Analysis of Social Structure, pp S95-S120.

Colley, H., Hodkinson, P. and Malcolm, J. (2002) *Non-formal learning: Mapping the conceptual terrain. A Consultation Report*, Leeds: University of Leeds Lifelong Learning Institute.

CEC (Commission of the European Communities) (2000) *Making a European area of lifelong learning a reality*, CEC: Brussels.

Edwards, B. and Woods, M. (2006) 'Voluntarism and new forms of governance in rural communities', in C. Milligan and D. Conradson (eds) *Landscapes of voluntarism: New spaces of health, welfare and governance*, Bristol: Policy Press.

Edwards, C. (2009) *Resilient nation*, London: Demos.

Field, J. (2003) *Social capital*, London: Routledge.

Fishbourne, S. and Derounian, J. (2009) *Skills and knowledge needed in the near future by English rural communities*, Dunfermline: Carnegie UK Trust.

Foley, G. (1999) *Learning in social action: A contribution to understanding informal education*, London: Zed Books.

Fukuyama, F. (1995) *Trust: The social virtues and the creation of prosperity*, London: Hamish Hamilton.

Fukuyama, F. (2001) 'Social capital, civil society and development', *Third World Quarterly*, vol 21, no 1, pp 7-20.

Gilchrist, A. (2016) *Blending, braiding and balancing: Combining formal and informal modes for social action*, Birmingham: Third Sector Research Centre.

Harris, K. and McCabe, A. (2016) *Trouble in utopia? Community action and social media*, Birmingham: Third Sector Research Centre.

IVAR (Institute for Voluntary Action Research) (2010) *Big and small: Capacity building, small organisations and the Big Lottery Fund*, London: IVAR.

IVAR (2011) *Assessing the impact of multi-purpose community organisations*, London: IVAR.

Johnston, R. and Coare, P. (2003) 'Reviewing the framework', in P. Coare and R. Johnston (eds) *Adult learning, citizenship and community voices: Exploring community based practice*, Leicester: NIACE.

Kail, A., Keen, S. and Lumley, T. (2011) *Community Organisations: A Guide to Effectiveness*, London: New Philanthropy Capital.

Krackhardt, D. (1987) 'Cognitive social structures', *Social Networks*, vol 9, no 2, pp 109-34.

Lasa (2012) *Third sector learning and development survey results*, London: Lasa/London Councils.

Marsden, P.V. (2006) 'Network methods in social epidemiology', in J.M. Oakes and J.S. Kaufman (eds) *Methods in social epidemiology*, New York, NY: John Wiley and Sons.

Mayo, M. and Thompson, J. (eds) (1995) *Adult learning, critical intelligence and social change*, Leicester: NIACE.

McCabe, A., Chilton, L., Purdue, D., Evans, L., Wilson, M. and Ardron, R. (2007) *Learning to change neighbourhoods: Lessons from the Guide Neighbourhoods Programme*, London: Department for Communities and Local Government.

McCabe, A., Phillimore, P. and Mayblin, L. (2009) *Below the radar groups and activities in the third sector: A summary review of the literature*, Birmingham: Third Sector Research Centre.

NAO (National Audit Office) (2009) *Building the capacity of the third sector*, London: NAO.

National Council of Voluntary Organisations (undated) *Training needs analysis*, London: NCVO.

Phillimore, J. and Goodson, L. (2010) 'Failing to institutional barriers to RCOs engagement transformation of social welfare', *Social Policy and Society*, vol 9, no 1, pp 181-92.

Putnam, R. (2000) *Bowling alone: The collapse and revival of American community*, New York, NY: Simon & Schuster.

Rowson, J., Broome, S. and Jones, A. (2010) *Connected communities: How social networks power and sustain the Big Society*, London: RSA.

Savage, M., Wardle, A. and Devine, F. (2005) 'Capitals, assets and resources', *British Journal of Sociology*, vol 56, no 1, pp 31–47.

Sender, H., Khor, Z. and Carlisle, B. (2011) *National Empowerment Partnership: Final evaluation report*, London: CDF.

Somerville, P. (2011) *Understanding community: Politics, policy and practice*, Bristol: Policy Press.

Take Part Network (2011) *Black Country Take Part Pathfinder evaluation: February 2011*, Dudley: DOSTI.

Taylor, M., Wilson, M., Purdue, D. and Wilde, P. (2006) *Changing neighbourhoods: Lessons from the JRF Neighbourhood Programme*, York: Joseph Rowntree Foundation.

TSRC (Third Sector Research Centre) (2009) *Evaluation of ChangeUp 2004-2008*, Birmingham: Third Sector Research Centre.

Wenger, E. (1998) *Communities of practice: Learning, meaning and identity*, Cambridge: Cambridge University Press.

Wesserman, S. and Faust, K. (1994) *Social network analysis: methods and applications*, Cambridge: Cambridge University Press.

THIRTEEN

Authentic and legitimate? The emotional role of 'grassroots' community activists in policymaking

Rosie Anderson

Chapter aims

This chapter aims to:

- provide some conceptual and methodological tools for thinking about emotion in policymaking in general, and in particular the emotional aspect of 'activism' in political spaces;
- outline the findings of an ethnographic research project that looked at emotion in policymaking and the way 'grassroots' and 'activist' participants described their own relationship to emotion. The chapter then compares these understandings with others' description of emotion and activism in this context;
- suggest some ways of thinking about what kind of emotion work is being done by activists (and others) and how policy professionals and unpaid participants might acknowledge and incorporate this work into their wider roles.

Researching and understanding emotion in policymaking

This chapter draws on an ethnographic research project that formed the basis of a doctoral thesis in politics. I set out with a very broad and fundamental research problem to investigate what people who make policy are referring to when they talk about emotion in their working lives. I had been a policy officer in non-governmental organisations (NGOs) for several years prior to beginning my thesis, and this question was drawn from my own experience trying – and failing – to account for the place of the relational and the 'emotional' in making policy decisions. As this chapter will explain, understandings and practices around activism, particular claims about knowledge and moral agency and the idea of the 'emotional' were closely tied together in the context of the policy processes my research describes, at least according to the people who participated in that work.

Ethnography that takes place within a culture or sub-culture the researcher is familiar with or identifies with relies heavily on the researcher's capacity for acting as a 'professional stranger', and there have not been too many insider ethnographic accounts of policymaking and policymakers. It might be said that there is a fundamental incompatibility between ethnographic inquiry and the knowledge claims of states and their bureaucracies: 'It is a kind of cosmopolitan claim: to stand above the specifics of one's institution and social context. Ethnography erodes that claim' (Kuus, 2013, p 54). Acting as a 'professional stranger' (Agar, 1996) is not only difficult for the researcher, but is also challenging to the researcher's informants. However, this perhaps underestimates how well 'we' (modern Western policymakers) know ourselves, how much we are actually strangers to ourselves in many ways, and how willing people are to explore this.

To address this research challenge, I turned to the rich psychoanalytic and psychotherapeutic literatures addressing exactly this strangeness in an attempt to open up some critical distance from these knowledge claims from within the traditions of thought I and my informants have reference to. Psychosocial literatures attempt to work with rather than against the understandings of emotion held by the participants of research themselves, albeit with a critical stance, while still placing such understandings in a sociological context. This 'psychoanalytical sociology' (Clarke et al, 2006) seeks to explore the bridge between collective and individual emotional experience and practice. It considers that there are powerful affective forces that underlie emotional responses that interact with social and cultural 'rules' and constructions of appropriate affect, and also acknowledges what has been called the 'sociological turn in psychology' (Kirschner and Martin, 2010) – that our unique emotional histories are not just products of personal experience but also are a product of our socio-cultural histories. The link between the micro- and macro-sociology of emotion is made through the multitudes of bridgings between these shared and individual experiences, meanings and narratives.

Clarke (2006) outlines an approach for what is termed a psychosocial method that aims to integrate sociological and psychoanalytic practices coherently. This method is aimed at documenting 'where the respondent attaches meaning to life experiences' (Clarke, 2006, p 1163). Clarke suggests four principles for conducting empirical psychosocial research, with the broad aim of conceiving of both researcher and respondent as co-producers of meaning: using open-ended questions to allow participants to associate key concepts freely with their own meanings; eliciting a story, to see *how* the way a story is told implies relations to and between meanings and people; using 'how' questions rather than 'why' questions, as the latter tend to elicit technical or sociological answers rather than stories rooted in the participant's experience; and finally, using respondents' ordering and phrasing to follow up with questions, rather than our own interpretations of what they have just said (Clarke, 2006, pp 1162-4). Broadly, this orientation can be characterised as seeing not just what is said, but *how* it is said as revealing of the social context it is produced within. In my own work, it manifested as asking people to try to explain how they knew what they knew about emotion and 'being emotional' and paying close attention to the non-verbal aspects of communication.

My ethnographic fieldwork took place between January 2012 and April 2013. I worked part-time on a voluntary basis for an NGO I will refer to as 'the partnership', which was involved in a range of policy areas across the UK and Scottish governments, local government and, occasionally, Brussels departments, with the broad aim of combatting poverty. I provided unpaid policy officer-type support for the organisation, a role I had several years' professional experience in prior to starting my doctorate. The partnership and its collaborators and members gave me access to their activities to collect data. My duties consisted of supporting the organisation's activities across its programme of policy work, the majority of which related to the Scottish government. The methods used combined non-participant observation as I shadowed my new colleagues and 'learned the ropes', participant observation as I went about my work as a policy officer, and formal, recorded interviews with key participants. This has yielded a range of different types of data, specifically: extensive field notes from participant and non-participant observation; transcripts and recordings of interviews; various written documents such as briefing papers, minutes of meetings, and reports, including those I wrote myself; and the electronic communications exchanged via email or social networking sites in the course of working life.

In this chapter, I undertake a primarily descriptive task: to explain the ways in which 'the emotional' was described by different participants in policymaking; who they believed could and should be 'emotional' in that context; and the everyday practices they placed within this category of 'emotion'. As an ethnographer, I am particularly concerned with delineating the 'social knowledge' of the mind and the emotions within the context I describe, and to clearly attribute thoughts, beliefs and normative or causational models either to me or my interlocutors (Berry, 1999). However much overlap there may be between the culture, norms and practices of the academy and of policymakers in Scotland, they are not epistemologically and ontologically the same spaces. Those actors who inhabit the latter may themselves come from very different backgrounds and professional positions. There are several social phenomena that I consider to be extremely salient to this topic (gender and age being two, for example) but that my interlocutors never volunteered as relevant and often struggled to see the relevance of if I raised them. Any discussion of these matters would therefore be entirely my own speculation or analysis. Likewise, a key finding was the way 'emotion' and 'reason' were presented to me as fundamentally irreconcilable and opposite positions, although this would not necessarily be my own understanding of these concepts. In the following section, I present this 'social knowledge' of the 'split' nature of emotion; I then move on to an analysis of why this split might take the form it does.

Splitting: emotion and reason

I had expected to find that my research collaborators would identify certain behaviours as stereotypical, and that certain people would be sanctioned to behave more emotionally than others, for example, women, or the very young or very old, perhaps. What surprised me about the way emotion was articulated to me was its absolute primacy of function and occupation in determining who was considered emotional. By my informants' own insistence they and their fellow policy participants were grouped into set categories of stakeholders, each with different 'roles' that symbolised something about their relationship with emotion. One of the most direct descriptions of these roles was provided by an activist, Carla, about six months into my fieldwork. We had met through the partnership's outreach work. She was a long-standing community activist to whom the partnership staff had devoted considerable efforts to enable her to participate. I asked Carla for her practical input in spotting the emotional and she was very clear and unhesitating in her reply: I needed to watch the activists – the 'people experiencing poverty'. So the other people involved don't 'do' emotion, then, I asked? She affirmed this:

> "You'll get more truth from the community activists....
> I think they know from experience, where other people

only know from what they've read or heard, but I think
the actual person who experiences it can tell it proper."

Carla made it clear that people who worked for NGOs or in parliament or government would not be bringing any emotional content to the events I attended: "I think they just go by what they have written down," she said. She believed that this was the only way that people who worked as 'professional' policymakers had access to the 'reality' of the issues they talked about. This was in fact a hallmark of their professional status and part of what *made them what they were*. Emotion was not just a set of behaviours; it was a way of being in the world that certain embodied experiences could provide, and others by definition could not.

I observed that the civil servants involved in the partnership's policy work tended to describe the emotional dimension of their work in consistent ways. I also noted that others described their expectations of civil servants and their actual behaviour in equally consistent terms, and that these thoughts and behaviours were considered to be a key part of 'professionalism'. Specifically, public servants were not supposed to display outward signs of partiality to any one individual, and they were meant to remain as 'neutral' as possible in their physical self-presentation. One civil servant I discussed this with put these expectations in these terms:

> "It's almost like there are rules drawn up around these things, there are like patterns of behaviour, which [we] have learned, whether it be business which is you know about controlling yourself and trying to get people to listen to you or whether it be…. Yes, how to reflect that passion but also how to use it effectively and the like."

He went on to explain the double-bind of being a policy 'professional': "I can't answer those questions [about someone's personal life] because they're individual experiences. I need to respond as an individual but I'm not *there* as an individual."

This civil servant was presenting the 'personal' as being in direct opposition to everything that he must embody as a 'public' figure, at the loss of his individual presence. His bodily and vocal behaviour at the conference was in some way a performance of this absence, the reading from government documents a stratagem for faithfully suppressing any knowledge that was not rational professional knowledge; he was quite literally 'reading from a book', as Carla had put it.

The presence of two incommensurable but indispensable ways of being and knowing in the world – and more specifically in policy work – that rationality and emotion represented to my informants and I has led me to draw on the literature around the use of institutions as a defence against anxiety, and especially the psychosocial literatures that draw on Kleinian (1996) concepts of splitting as such a defence. By detaching the comforting and anxiety-provoking feelings within a subject from one another and then projecting the 'bad' outwards, splitting 'helps the ego in overcoming anxiety by ridding it of danger and badness' (Klein, 1996, p 167). While Klein herself did not focus much on applying these principles to social theory (Alford, 1989), subsequent social analysts have made extensive use of the mechanisms described by Klein, and particularly the sense of persecution that they provoke, as an explanation for the way individuals and groups identify with or persecute in turn other groups. Many researchers have observed these splits played out between individuals, and at an organisational level they are recognised as 'a collusive system of denial, splitting and projection that was culturally acceptable, indeed culturally required' (Lyth, 1990, p 449). It is not to say that this is abnormal or pathological behaviour, but it can have unintended consequences that causes widespread dissatisfaction and can limit people's options for social strategies and behaviour.

In using this language of 'splitting', I am to some degree building on and referring to the work of other policy scholars who use a psychosocial approach, for example Froggett (2002), Lewis (2004), Hoggett et al (2013) and Hunter (2009, 2012). But in examining the practical, everyday ways that people in the forums 'did' this split, I found that the split was not as straightforward as one type of knowledge being 'good' and the other being 'bad', one 'acceptable' and the other 'unacceptable'. In fact, the way participants acted out and understood their emotional selves and role necessarily worked *together* and *relied* on each other. Activists stood for emotional knowledge, symbolically representing not just the substantive contents of that knowledge, but also an entire value system that saw emotional relations as a moral necessity in good governance. By focusing on the way that knowledge contributes to power in an overtly political context, my fieldwork foregrounded the way that rationality and emotion in fact rely on each other and make use of different logics of power in the relations between participants.

I see the way emotion and rationality became split and projected into diametrically opposed categories of participant in the partnership's policy work as having its roots in quite pragmatic needs: it was to protect participants (including myself) from experiencing the clash of incommensurable beliefs and values about governance and the state. On a purely practical level, splitting knowledge and moral narratives into rationality and emotion and projecting these onto different categories of participant in the forums was an ingenious solution to an otherwise intractable problem. One story about good governance told in the forum's cultural context was that 'good' policy *never* comes from personal, somatic experience and private reasoning. The other compelling story was that moral judgement and 'the good' can *only* come from emotion and *feeling* something about the world and other people. People from all three of the self-determined categories of participant regularly professed both of these convictions. But their identity and function in the forums' policy work placed more of an emphasis on one kind of knowledge than the other. Furthermore, these two sets of beliefs made it hard to behave as an unequivocally 'good' person, and it also made it hard to relate to the idea of governance and policy decision making without experiencing some loss or conflict within one's self and about the institutions of governance. To this extent, splitting emotional knowledge and rational knowledge and making certain categories of participant stand symbolically for those knowledges at work in policy may have helped my informants and myself cope with the conflicting demands of governance and to make otherwise painful decisions or interventions.

However much splitting knowledge of the world into rational and emotional symbols was supposed to protect the participants in the partnership's policy work from experiencing anxiety, there is evidence that it generated secondary anxieties in turn. Giving this conflict between caring and dispassionate 'good' governance an objective existence in the institutions, structures and conventions of policy work limits the opportunities for a participant to 'confront the anxiety-evoking experiences and, by so doing, to develop her capacity to tolerate and deal more effectively with the anxiety' (Lyth, 1988, p 63). It is a way of evading such conflict, and because of the inherent need to do the work of policy that evasion is not likely to be able to be sustained indefinitely. At the very least, some structural limitations of policy work might expose the contradictions involved in this arrangement, and even create new anxieties for participants. At a pragmatic level, it could interfere with achieving the objectives of the partnership, namely that by bringing activists and governors together policy could integrate emotional knowledge into its rational decisions.

For this reason, I wish to be careful about being too literal about these splits. Emotion is not properly inaccessible and 'foreign' to professional categories of participants any more than rational knowledge is extrinsic to activists. Emotional and rational ways of knowing and being in the world are capacities we all have, but either knowledge may be inadmissible or unacceptable depending on the role we must play in the social context we find ourselves in. This 'split' nature of knowledge in making policy underlines the importance of the role you play in such spaces and the source of your legitimacy – what you are 'bringing to the table'. It makes it important to understand the way those roles are constructed and maintained, and the way they have become part of being a competent participant.

Emotion work

Emotional labour is 'the act of conforming (or attempting to conform) to display rules or affective requirements that prescribe on-the-job emotional expression' (Ashforth and Tomiuk, 2000, p 184). It was initially developed by Arlie Russel Hochschild to account for the interpersonal aspects of being seen to do certain jobs well. Hochschild labelled this 'emotional management', in which an individual is guided by socially sanctioned 'feeling rules', 'to govern how people try or try not to feel in ways "appropriate to the situation"', that is to say in ways consistent with the role they must play in a given context (Hochschild, 1979, p 552). Hochschild described this emotional management as a form of 'minigovernance' – a way of regulating and governing society and our relations with others at the micro-level of human interaction. Overall, it is perhaps helpful to think about emotional labour as 'people work' (Brotheridge and Grandey, 2002), that is to say that it inevitably and significantly involves an employee's relations with others and their management as a core competence or skill.

Hochschild's theory of emotional labour references labour relations and analyses of power and the means of production. Analysing the way employees labour emotionally is therefore also an analysis of material power structures; the relationship between employees and their superiors; their relationship with customers or the public more generally; the relations between men and women; and so on. From that point of view, it might be hard to see how easily a researcher could apply the concept to voluntary roles like those of the activists involved in the partnership's policy work. However, these expectations are scripted by a complex set of feeling rules that 'guide emotion by establishing the sense of entitlement or obligation that governs emotional exchanges' (Hochschild, 1983, p 56), which in turn attach to someone's wider 'feeling role' in those exchanges. Hochschild herself acknowledged that not all these emotional exchanges happen in return for payment. Some happen within the home or other private interactions, and could be thought of as unpaid 'emotion work' (Hochschild, 1979). Many of the people involved in making policy sit uneasily somewhere in-between this apparently neat distinction: they are doing unpaid emotion work – with all its connotations of voluntarism and care – but in service of the public good and in a very public forum. This was very explicitly true for those participants described as activists by the partnership's participants.

In trying to understand the way the split between emotion and rationality played out in policy participants' thoughts, beliefs and behaviours, the idea of emotion work – particularly of feeling rules – intersected with wider beliefs about who should be emotional in policymaking and how – the feeling roles of policymaking. It is with these concepts in mind that I would like to focus on the practical side of 'doing emotion' in policymaking.

Understanding activists' emotional practice

Given the perceived importance to so many academics and certain policyworkers of predictable, rational behaviour in the smooth functioning of ongoing policy formation (Hill, 2005, p 147), you might expect that such breaches of the established grammar of being professional in this context would be experienced as diminishing or as embarrassing lapses of judgement by policy participants themselves. Interestingly, this was not always the case in the context of the partnership's policy forums. Community activists spoke approvingly of their emotional behaviour.

Carla, who was living with complex health and financial problems, reflected on the way she presented herself in a video that was shown at a big poverty policy conference: "I was saying, 'This is killing me, this illness.' And my emotions, well, you don't really realise how bad it is until you start talking about it, and then when you've seen it [the video] back, I thought, 'God, I didn't realise it was that bad!'" She was frequently moved to tears during the short film, her voice trembling with what she identified as profound sadness in our discussion. She reported that the reaction from the audience was the best she could hope for: silence. She interpreted this as having had a resonance for the audience far beyond her expectations. She felt that it was actually a moment of great power for her: "I was thinking I was glad that it was having an impact and I was thinking maybe now they'll actually look at some of the written stuff and actually do something about it.

Take into account that this is reality." The silence could have had other roots – embarrassment, for example – but Carla located it within the emotional realm of policy work and interpreted it accordingly. This reflects a discourse of the power of emotion found elsewhere among my informants.

So although these outbursts of emotion were often described as disruptive and 'unprofessional' by the forum's participants of all backgrounds, a sort of tacit permission seems to have been granted by them to community activists and the grassroots to break with protocol. There is clearly more going on here than naivety. By looking beyond the sometimes rather trivialising descriptions of activism and grassroots emotionality in policy forums and focusing on their participants' practice, it emerges that their license to behave in this way serves a range of purposes for the entire policymaking community.

The physical presence of grassroots activists developed a prominent role in the way I and others discussed emotion and being emotional in the partnership's policy work. Carla was able to give me quite detailed descriptions of how people might behave if they were emotional, and also if they were not emotional, to help me understand what, in her opinion, I should be looking for in my data collection. She listed things such as animated facial expressions and hand gestures, raised and rapid speech and eye contact as being 'emotional tells'. There was also a set of behaviours she described as 'actively listening, which involved leaning forward, mirroring what other people said or did physically and holding and returning eye contact, which she believed indicated that those displaying these behaviours were emotionally present. She also told me that she knew when people were not emotionally present because she would see their attention wandering. When I asked how she could tell if someone's attention wandered, she mimed someone slumped back in their chair, eyes focused on a middle distance somewhat to the side of me, and she then shifted to doodling in an imaginary notebook. I was interested in the way Carla's description of the presentation of emotion was fundamentally about intervening in a shared physical space and moment. I was also struck by how she did not rely on describing behaviours and patterns of speech to me; she seemed to feel it was most effective to recreate the experience of that shared moment for me. In part because of Carla's directions, but also because of my own attempts to unpack how the face-to-face encounter might work on self-identifying 'professionals in ways written communication could not, I documented in some detail the way presence, representation and performance was talked about and practised in relation to activists in the partnership's policy work.

I am not going to misrepresent the stories that got told and the emotion on display from community activists in the partnership's policy events as simplistic, unrehearsed or unmediated. The partnership's staff put considerable effort into finding, nurturing and presenting individuals who have a powerfully emotional story to tell. This was very much the work that I was involved in through my engagement with the partnership as I participated in their policy events, and one way or another it occupied most of my time and that of the policy officer, Louise. For the purposes of this discussion, it is important to stress that, for the NGO informants, this first-person testimony from people directly experiencing poverty is the place where the real business of decision making starts for them as policy lobbyists and for the people they wish to influence. This was also reflected by my own experiences of observing and facilitating meetings and workshops where activists directly experiencing poverty or a related problem are encouraged to share stories and then, through various processes, reflect on what the key messages are for policymakers and how best they should present themselves.

For example, at the very start of my time with the partnership, I accompanied Louise on a trip to a community centre in North Glasgow to prepare testimony for the first annual showcase event. This testimony was always termed 'evidence' in the quasi-juridical language of the partnership's policy events. Such testimonies are often employed as the route in and through what are otherwise either inhumanly complex or boring matters and as such are considered to be the key to a productive discussion with civil servants or parliamentarians by Louise and her colleagues. The centre's users and manager were going to present to a breakout session similar in format to the one I described earlier and where I met Douglas. Louise began the preparation session by impressing on the centre's users that it was imperative that we start from personal and emotional knowledge and work outwards from there. I wrote the following: 'Louise says that she wants Linda [one of the centre users] to tell her story as a basis for putting words to needs. She reminds us that the assembly is about pinpointing what the goals are – that we need to move from vague feelings to material demands.' In practice, this process of moving from the particular and emotional to general and impersonal, so simple sounding on paper, was actually very difficult to get right in the eyes of policy practitioners such as Louise and indeed myself because of emotional knowledge's ambiguous status in policy. Because of this, great efforts were made to figure out how to 'stage' the emotional content of the testimonies. On this particular occasion, we spent over two hours returning to the same stories, working over the same ground. There were moments when I, almost instinctively, felt that I had experienced what I was looking for as the centre manager and users talked to me and Louise, but I was also aware that I was not consciously able to describe what 'it' was. On reflection, I believe these electric moments were about a particular coming together of ideas, words, physical presence and place. There is plenty of technical information about areas of deprivation and the built environment, but the problem may be better understood in some way if the centre manager, sitting a couple of feet away from you, looking directly at you, tells you: "The emotional, psychological side of watching things go to shit is devastating, particularly when those buildings were important to the community." Within this statement is not just an unsparing diagnosis of a problem, but also conveyed within the manager's personal experience of this problem is an uncompromising challenge about the injustice of things. Above all, though, there is something in the way that his body and voice changes the world around you, refocuses your attention, and retrieves your understanding of the matter from the endless deferments of abstraction. You *feel* in a visceral way, and as a result get a suggestion of where and how to act. These types of moment were what Louise was looking for and drawing attention to and what the users of that community centre were being encouraged to bring to the forum.

As my time with the partnership went on, I began to suspect that, thanks to their special license to express powerful, personal emotions and experiences, community activists also seemed to have acquired a role as emotional avatars. That is to say, they somehow expressed an emotional and personal relationship to the process and content of policy *on behalf* of those who may not because of expectations for them to behave as 'professionals'. Interestingly, this was not something that had been brought up by the community activists themselves, but had been mentioned several times by professional practitioners, in particular the NGO workers.

For example, I was asked to attend a feedback session on a consultation process for a strategic policy review, chaired by Louise and attended by civil servants from Whitehall and the Scottish government. It turned out to be a good illustration of how some professionals in this context looked to activists to provide a vicarious emotional release. In part, this meeting was called because of Louise's dissatisfaction with the way the civil servants involved had behaved; at the end of the summer recess when the strategic review came to be published, none of the partnership's input seemed to have made it into the final edit or was directly reflected in its content. This omission was described as being professionally embarrassing and a kind of failure by the policyworkers involved, but for Louise, who had coordinated the submission, it had personal significance. Not only did she look unreliable or misleading to the community activists she had persuaded to give up their time and participate in the workshops (a source of great sadness and anxiety to her), but she also felt betrayed on what can only be described as a very personal level by her civil service contacts. When I caught up with her after summer, I found her to be visibly fuming:

> "They never bloody well used any of our material. I'm telling you, it's going to be hard to keep my own emotions under control. To be honest I'm hoping that the community activists there will do the shouting for me."

Even at the time, I was struck by the implications of what Louise was telling me: that she wanted to engineer an encounter between these civil servants and activists to witness a venting of bad feeling she could not do herself, but would nevertheless provide her with some vicarious relief, or satisfaction.

Activists' feeling roles and rules

The concept of emotion work and of feeling roles and feeling rules may help to provide a framework for understanding what exactly activists' emotional practice looks like in policymaking. At a more 'meta' level, it may also help bring into focus exactly what is being invoked by the very idea of activism and of being an activist in the context of the partnership's policy forums.

In the context of the forums I have been discussing, there were arguably very specific feeling rules – in particular around the close connection between emotional management, a lack of first-person perspective and the idea of professionalism. However, these are all feeling rules that relate to NGO workers and civil servants. These were groups of people with elaborate sets of behaviours determining what kind of emotional knowledge was permissible and where, and how they should signal that they were 'doing' the work of managing their emotionality in public. Analysing the emotion rules around community activists is complicated somewhat by the fact that this emotional role revolved around their perceived *lack* of rules and ungovernability.

Arguably, such parameters still constitute rules about feeling for community activists, but not about needing to conform to a set of inner emotions that they may not be experiencing, as in the case of emotional labour as generally defined. Rather, community activists seem to be explicitly and implicitly encouraged to break the conventions of the policy world in unpredictable ways; they are there to experience and act on their first-person relationship to something that really matters to them, to act on their emotional knowledge. In the setting of these policy forums, that could be argued to be their primary feeling rule.

However, when emotion work is considered as something designed to produce a particular emotional state in others, activists' roles appear to be considerably more rule-bound. Arguably, participants identified as activists who were paid, unpaid or somewhere in between were there to perform a particular emotional role according to a set of socially sanctioned rules, and to produce a particular emotional experience in others. In the case of the civil servants and other employees of a government or parliament, this was about having a 'shot in the arm' of lived, visceral experience from people directly experiencing the things they were trying to legislate on or govern – in this case, poverty. As one civil servant put it, these encounters with 'reality' were essential for making not merely effective but also just and normatively right decisions – for acting as a moral agent – "otherwise you don't really get a sense of what you're doing, or why you're doing it". For others, like the policy officer Louise, they were avatars of her own emotional states – people who could name unnameable things and act on taboo, 'unprofessional' subjects such as rage, guilt or sorrow.

Emotional labour places its emphasis on labour relations, in which 'parts of the self are made available … to be consumed by customers' (Williams, 2003, p 517) with implied statements about alienation, domination and subordination. While some of this could be relevant to policy work – there are many paid professionals involved – it may not capture everything that goes into the practice of the work of policy. Policy work is generally normatively understood as 'more than' work – (unpaid) activists, third sector workers and professional representatives participate, often out of hours, because they *care*, but this care is also expected to be exhibited in the commitment of politicians to similarly gruelling working lives and their willingness to experience a lack of personal privacy in the course of their duties.

Fittingly, the cultural label for the complex set of beliefs and behaviours that comprise emotion share an etymological root with motivation. It is this sense that participants in public life and debate about the common good should be driven – compelled, even – to participate because it is morally necessary to do so that makes discussion of its potential personal and social cost difficult. However, it perhaps makes a good concluding point that unacknowledged emotional labour and emotion work is often discussed in organisational studies literatures as contributing to 'burn–out', or the literal or psychological withdrawal of an employee due to high levels of emotional stress.

Burn–out is often described as a 'syndrome' in the sense that it follows a defined pattern of behaviours: 'three distinct states in which employees feel emotionally "spent" (emotional exhaustion), display a detached attitude to others (depersonalisation), and experience a low sense of efficacy at work (diminished personal accomplishment)' (Brotheridge and Grandey, 2002, p 17). If participating in policymaking is fundamentally people work, and if the feeling rules and feeling roles of being an identified activist in that policymaking space is a key part of fulfilling others' emotional needs and expectations to make the whole process work, might this help practitioners and researchers understand the careers of campaigners and campaigning organisations better over their life course?

Key learning

- Introducing emotion into the analysis of policy needs to be taken far more seriously as an aspect of political studies. It opens up new fields for exploring what is at stake and who is in a position of power and authority that do not necessarily merely reproduce the potentials and inequalities of other more established forms of influence and knowledge.
- The way in which anxieties about incommensurable ideals of 'good' governance were managed by the partnership's policy participants was to split these incommensurable expectations of governance between two self-identifying groups: activists such as community organisers and professionals such as civil servants. Splitting knowledge in this way helped the wider policymaking community to maintain its own sense of legitimacy and moral integrity while making use of 'dangerous' knowledge.
- Activism was associated with an emotional stance in relation to, and knowledge of, the world, contrasted with the bureaucratic and rational stance of professionals. This was first-hand, somatic knowledge of the policy issue under discussion.
- The emotional and social wellbeing of unpaid volunteers who are recruited into participating in policy is surely as much a concern of the policymaking community as questions of access and information, and concepts of empowerment should also include having the opportunity to make choices about the emotional content of the way you present yourself.

Reflective exercises

- The findings presented here are drawn from observations of one group of people in a particular place at a particular time. To what extent do you recognise these descriptions of the feeling rules and roles of people who are involved in making policy? Is there anything that you would add or take away? Do you agree or disagree with some of the more normative statements participants made about the nature of good governance?
- Some people think that identifying the emotional work done in certain jobs is a positive thing: it acknowledges how taxing this kind of work can be and gets people talking about their working relationships more openly. Others think that it can actually help in the commodification process of people's emotional selves and make them yet another 'performance indicator'. In the context of volunteers or self-identified activists, do you think these concerns apply?
- Emotional recruitment, in which community representatives and activists are expected to express what professionals may not, presents several problems of power and status within the context of policy making forums. If a professional may not behave in certain ways because it will be regarded as socially incompetent by their peers, what are the ethics of encouraging or recruiting people who will contravene these feeling rules?

References

Agar, M. (1996) *The professional stranger: An informal introduction to ethnography*, San Diego, CA: Academic Press.

Alford, C.F. (1989) *Melanie Klein and critical social theory*, New Haven, CT and London: Yale University Press.

Ashforth, B.E. and Tomiuk, M.A. (2000) 'Emotional labour and authenticity: views from service agents' in S. Fineman (ed) *Emotion in organizations*, London: Sage Publications.

Berry, J.W. (1999) 'Emics and etics: a symbiotic conception', *Culture and Psychology*, vol 5, no 2, pp 165-71.

Brotheridge, C.M. and Grandey, A.A. (2002) 'Emotional labor and burnout: comparing two perspectives of "people work"', *Journal of Vocational Behavior*, vol 60, no 1, pp 17–39.

Clarke, S. (2006) 'Theory and practice: psychoanalytic sociology as psycho-social studies', *Sociology*, vol 40, no 6, pp 1153-69.

Clarke, S., Hoggett, P. and Thompson, S. (2006) 'Moving forward in the study of emotions: some conclusions', in S. Clarke, P. Hoggett and S. Thompson (eds) *Emotion, politics and society*, Basingstoke/New York, NY: Palgrave Macmillan.

Froggett, L. (2002) *Love, hate and welfare: Psychosocial approaches to policy and practice*, Bristol: Policy Press.

Hill, M.J. (2005) *The public policy process: A reader* (4th edn), Harlow/New York, NY: Pearson Longman.

Hochschild, A.R. (1979) 'Emotion work, feeling rules, and social structure', *American Journal of Sociology*, vol 85, no 3, pp 551-75.

Hochschild, A.R. (1983) *The managed heart: Commercialization of human feeling*, Berkeley, CA/London: University of California Press.

Hoggett, P., Wilkinson, H. and Beedell, P. (2013) 'Fairness and the politics of resentment', *Journal of Social Policy*, vol 42, no 3, pp 567-85.

Hunter, S. (2009) 'Feminist Psychosocial Approaches to Relationality, Recognition and Denial', in M.F. Ozbiligin (ed) *Equality, diversity and inclusion at work: A research companion*, Cheltenham: Edward Elgar.

Hunter, S. (2012) 'Ordering differentiation: reconfiguring governance as relational politics', *Journal of Psycho-Social Studies*, vol 6, no 1, 3-29.

Kirschner, S.R. and Martin, J. (2010) *The sociocultural turn in psychology: The contextual emergence of mind and self*, New York, NY: Columbia University Press.

Klein, M. (1996) 'Notes on some schizoid mechanisms', *Journal of Psychotherapy Practice and Research*, vol 5, no 2, pp 160-79.

Kuus, M. (2013) *Geopolitics and expertise: Knowledge and authority in European diplomacy*, Chichester: John Wiley & Sons.

Lewis, G. (2004) *Citizenship: Personal lives and social policy*, Bristol: Policy Press.

Lyth, I.M. (1988) *Containing anxiety in institutions: Selected essays*, London: Free Association Books.

Lyth, I.M. (1990) 'Social systems as a defense against anxiety: an empirical study of the nursing service of a general hospital', in, *The social engagement of social science: A Tavistock anthology*, London: Free Association.

Williams, C. (2003) 'Sky service: the demands of emotional labour in the airline industry', *Gender, Work and Organization*, vol 10, no 5, pp 513-50.

FOURTEEN

Conclusion: thinking back and looking forward

Angus McCabe and Jenny Phillimore

Thinking back over almost a decade of research with below the radar community groups, what has changed? At one level, very little. To adapt Davidson and Packham's phrase (2012), community groups continue to emerge, grow, die and, if not thrive, get by.

Yet, in other ways, plenty has changed. Much has been written on the impact of the austerity cuts on charities and smaller, formal, voluntary organisations operating at a community level (Milbourne 2013; Kenny et al, 2015). Some of the groups interviewed in our research that grew following Area Based Initiative funding have either closed, become dependent on the Big Lottery, replaced small-scale local authority grants with Awards for All money or attempted to survive (in the short term) on reserves or by returning to their roots in volunteering. Some activists have burnt out or 'retreated' from taking on the big issues that impact on their communities.

Loss of income, with less money (never mind funding) circulating around many communities, has been just one factor (see Chapters Four and Six) that has affected groups. Uncertain labour markets have also had an impact on levels of volunteer involvement and activism. The reduction in access to pro-bono advice and no-/low-cost meeting spaces has also taken its toll (see the case studies in Chapter Six). Further, partly to survive, some groups have taken on new, service delivery, roles diversifying from their original purpose of advocating on behalf of their community. The extent to which this has affected their ability to lobby and act, predominantly, as a voice for their community requires further examination, as does whether such groups are sufficiently competent to take on new service delivery roles.

With further cuts and hard times to come (Hillier, 2016), what does the future for small voluntaries and, in particular, below the radar community groups hold?

Predicting the future of the third sector, or wider civil society, is notoriously difficult. Visioning is fraught with problems. As Deakin

(1995) noted, the anticipated demise of charity in 1945, with the introduction of the welfare state, was more than slightly wide of the mark. Similarly, as noted, prophesies of a doomed voluntary and, particularly, community sector in 2010 have proved false.

A second note of caution is that, whilst this book is intended to build a wider understanding of informal community groups and actions this remains, beyond the formal charity sector (Rees and Mullins 2016), an under-explored area and further research is required. It has not, for example, explored the gendered nature of community action (Curno et al, 1982; Dominelli, 2006). It has barely touched on the assumed transformative power (for good or evil) of new social media in associational life and community mobilisation (Roberts, 2014) and has only mentioned in passing the increasing role of faith-based organisations in public life (Dinham et al, 2009). Further work is also required to understand the social value (or disvalue) of community groups. Can that value be expressed in the financialised models of social return on investment or, as Hilary Ramsden and colleagues argue in Chapter Eight, is it possible to accept that voluntary activities have an intrinsic value that cannot be monetarised?

The following predictions are therefore offered with some caution. Indeed, some are posed as questions for further research and debate.

What is evident, with continuing austerity, is that the hopes that short-term deficit reduction strategies could be ridden out and some kind of 'normal service' reinstated have faded (Parker, 2015; see also Chapter Six). Co-production has become a by-word for creative responses to managing austerity and creating a new contract between local government, statutory agencies and the communities they serve (Bovaird et al, 2015). Questions can be raised as to whether there will be enough enthusiasm, never mind capacity, for communities to 'co-produce' and what exactly they might be co-producing. Indeed, where community groups have taken on public services previously provided by local authorities (for example, in sectors such as play and youth work), the experience has often been one of feeling forced (often through pressure from within a community) into a position of doing so rather than one of genuine co-production with previous providers or funders McCabe et al, 2016a).

On the one hand, for those that have survived thus far, there are some grounds for optimism. In increasingly diverse communities, there are a growing number of vibrant new community groups (Phillimore, 2015). Faith-based actions continue to proliferate (McCabe et al, 2016b). Some of the more apocalyptic predictions about voluntary action post-austerity and the 2010 election have not happened (Abbas and Lachman, 2012). Indeed, there are those commentators who see continuing austerity as a catalyst for positive change in the relationship between communities and the state (McLean and Dellot, 2011; Parker, 2015). Further, a growing number of Community Development and Land Trusts have created innovative solutions to, for example, a lack of affordable rural housing and, particularly in Scotland, played a role in revitalising rural economies. Still others have exploited new approaches to securing funding, even for small-scale community ventures, such as crowd funding, issuing community shares (for establishing village shops, for example) and peer lending (for community-led housing initiatives). How sustainable these models are, beyond the start-up phase, remains to be seen.

On the other hand, is such innovation reserved for more affluent areas? As Chapters Six and Twelve indicate, what small community groups in poor neighbourhoods lack is not social capital (which they may have in abundance) but access to other forms of capital – financial, human, cultural and environmental. What has been played out between many communities, through localism and related agendas that were assumed to offer them new opportunities, has in many cases been the conundrum of St Matthew's Gospel: to those that have, more shall be given (Matthew 13:12).

There are more pessimistic voices too. In these scenarios, the 'new thrift' (Jensen, 2013) demonises the poor (Jones, 2011) and contributes to the breaking down of 'old' solidarities. This has certainly made life more difficult for those activists and community groups that are 'of' and 'with' the poor. New community groups may emerge, but they may be increasingly homogeneous and concerned with protecting existing positions and privileges of particular groups, rather than working towards social justice and fundamental change (Jordan, 2010). Voice and influence have waned (see Chapter Twelve) and a sense of 'third sector' strategic vision has been lost (NCIA, 2015). In part this has been due to the loss national and regional infrastructure and support agencies, from the Community Development Exchange and Urban Forum through to Community Matters. At a more profound level, it has resulted from pressure to be 'doing more and saying less' (Aiken, 2014). The UK government gives the impression that it believes it is not the role of community, faith or other groups to speak out about injustice and poverty. Instead their place seems to involve meeting increasing local needs with patience and, ideally, in silence (McCabe et al, 2016b).

Setting aside optimistic and pessimistic visions, two (perhaps worrying) trends emerged over the period of this research. One has been a rhetoric, across the voluntary and community sector groups involved in the research, of 'them' and 'us', the 'haves and the 'have nots', that has become more entrenched (see Chapter Six) There is certainly an increasing gap between the large charities and smaller organisations (NCIA, 2015; Crees et al, 2016). To assume, however, that this is simply a post-austerity trend would be mistaken. As early as 2007, the Charity Commission was warning of a growing divide between larger charities, well positioned to tender for public services, and smaller community-based voluntaries that were losing out in that process. A second trend has been the, often passive, acceptance that austerity is here to stay, at least for the foreseeable future. There is no alternative – so survival becomes a virtue in and of itself.

Accepting either of these optimistic or pessimistic scenarios without question may be dangerous. Optimism may not be grounded in the lived experiences of marginalised communities. Equally, the pessimists seem to hark back at times to some golden (recent) age of voluntary action – of an independent, vocal, voluntary sector with access to resources. It is possible to question whether that golden age ever existed, or if it did, at what cost to organisations did those accessed resources come (see Chapter Five).

Of further concern is that much of the debate on the 'third sector' has become internally, philosophically, focused. Is there a sector at all (Macmillan, 2013)? Is there, rather, a fragmented, fractious, sector that no longer has a strategic unity (Alcock, 2010)? Can core shared values be identified (see Chapters Four and Five and Kenny et al, 2015)? Does this matter or should we accept that voluntary action is 'a loose and baggy monster' (Kendall and Knapp, 1996) and acknowledge, if not celebrate, the 'diversity within diversity' that Teresa Piacentini (Chapter Ten) and Hilary Ramsden and colleagues (Chapter Eight) identify?

In addition, a number of commentators have questioned the extent to which government, and in particularly local government, remains fit for purpose (Parker, 2015). A similar, rigorous, debate has yet to be had between the third sector (however defined), the wider public and policymakers. Such discussion as has taken place has often felt like a trading of insults around ideological purity versus perceived, self-serving, pragmatism (Aiken, 2014; NCIA, 2015). It is likely that there will be ongoing and intensified debates about the appropriate respective roles of the state, private sector and voluntary action in the delivery of services to and for the public (including statutory public services). However, there needs to be a greater level of sophistication in, and a stronger evidence base to inform, those debates.

But what, specifically, might the future hold for small-scale below the radar community groups and actions? Perhaps three trends, or challenges, can be identified.

First, under austerity measures, the assumption has been, and is likely to continue to be, the pressure to do more, yet the feasibility of doing so is questionable. As noted, voluntary action is both a finite resource (see Chapters Four and Six and Mohan, 2012) and, certainly when the data on formal volunteering is explored, is unevenly distributed. What those interviewed for our research particularly valued was the hyper-local nature of small-scale community actions, their connectedness with neighbourhoods or communities of interest and expert knowledge about those communities. By their very nature, they lack the scale to address sheer levels of need in deprived communities – facing increased demands within finite resources. To assume that community groups, or more formal voluntary organisations, can effectively plug the gaps left by a retreat from collective welfare models (Alcock, 2016) in which the state is a key player, is at best wishful thinking and, at worst, disingenuous. The haves will continue to have and those who have not will struggle – more.

Second, already informal groups (without constitutions or set hierarchies) seem likely to adopt increasingly informal ways of operating. Further, some have posited the view that organisational structures no longer have primacy and organisations, as Gilchrist (2016) suggests, are no longer fit for purpose. What is needed, and will emerge, is a more relational, networked, way of working in and with communities. These ideas about the predominance of social networks rather than organisational structures as an increasingly important, if not dominant, way of organising are reinforced in the literature on Web 2.0 and social media technologies. Commentators have made substantial claims for the transformative power such technologies:

> By making it quick and easy for anyone to share information with others, modern social media gives ordinary people a collective agenda-setting power that was previously restricted to large publishers and broadcasters, and that is capable of striking fear into those in authority. (Standage, 2013, p 239)

These technologies challenge traditional, organisational and political hierarchies (Bennett and Segerberg, 2011; Castells, 2015), democratise information flows and have become a tool for mass mobilisation and protest from the Arab Spring (Alaimo, 2015) to the Maidan Square protests in Kiev (Kurkov, 2014). They offer the vision of a globally networked society in which the boundaries of the personal and political are blurred. Bodhanova (2014) argues that currently, and in the future, 'the revolution will be live-streamed, tweeted and posted on Facebook' (p 136), but then goes on to caution that 'After all, technology is only an instrument: it does not necessarily guarantee a specific type of outcome' (p 140) and remind us that the regimes overthrown by the Arab Spring have been replaced by equally repressive governments or movements.

Finally, how such macro-level claims are being played out at the micro-level of community groups, certainly in the UK, is rather more uncertain. For instance, researchers exploring the use of social media in the voluntary sector note that they are largely used as a marketing and broadcasting tool rather than a means of promoting debate and dialogue (Phethean et al, 2012). They are used primarily as a social networking tool rather than a means of mobilising (Bussu, 2016) and they do not, at a neighbourhood level, replace face-to face contacts and networks (Harris and McCabe, forthcoming). What seems certain, however, is that social media will continue to change, if not transform, the ways in which individuals, groups and communities communicate and are likely to extend informal, personalised approaches to (mass) communication – even at the micro-level of below the radar groups (Aiken, 2016).

Those arguing that informality is the way forward also point to faith-based social action and inter-faith work. The traditional forums for dialogue (with a strong emphasis on, and energy invested in, achieving representativeness) have by and large collapsed to be replaced by personal relationships between faith leaders and 'encounters' between those of different faiths (McCabe et al, 2016b). While it is unlikely that organisations will be abandoned altogether, it is probable that multiple and fluid forms of organising will evolve and co-exist. What has not been seen, however, is wholesale dismantling of corporate or governmental structures – though these too continue to evolve. As the community sector moves towards even more relational, networked, ways of working, as well as of possibly 'doing politics', there will be consequences for the ways that power relationships between the state, corporations and communities are played out. This is evidenced in the following comment from one of our research participants, representing a local development agency:

> "I don't want to predict what the future, say in five years,
> will look like for voluntary never mind community groups.

There may be a leaner but more efficient and effective
sector, a more entrepreneurial and business like sector – or
just a leaner one. *What we will see played out in some form is a
profound change in the relationships between people, government
and the sector."* (Emphasis added)

There are those that argue the third sector has, indeed, become leaner
and meaner (NCIA, 2015), more business-like and, with the ever-
increasing expansion of large charities along the lines of the retail
giants, a tendency to adopt more commercial modes of operation –
so-called 'Tescoisation' (Hind, 2014). This has played out, in terms
of the relationship between 'people and the sector', as a backlash
against, predominantly larger, charities and aggressive fundraising
strategies. In terms of the relationship between people, communities
and government, even more profound forces are evident. On the one
hand, there is growing disenchantment with political and corporate
elites (Sayer, 1015); on the other, a view that, among some politicians
and in parts of the media, politicians, *community* is the problem (Jones,
2011; McKenzie, 2015).

For all the debate, what is evident is that, regardless of political, policy
and financial changes, a constant (which will ensure the continued
emergence, survival and evolution of community organisations) is
that people will continue to crave associational life and be motivated
to come together to seek solutions to problems that matter to them
while making meaningful connections with each other that form an
important part of social life. Community groups are, and will remain,
grounded in emotional engagement (Chapter Thirteen) – emotions
that may result in conflict but also provide spaces for solidarity and
creativity (Chapters Six and Twelve). These are, and shall be, largely
impervious, or resistant, to co-option either by 'standard' managerial
ways of working or external policy agendas (Chapters Five and Six).
Perhaps the fluctuations and shifts we have outlined throughout this
book (see also Taylor, 2012) are more likely to affect the extent to
which community groups are able to be effective in grassroots-driven
change than their desire for such change. Whether those groups
become increasingly homogeneous, as Jordan (2010) has argued, or,
in an age of superdiversity, more heterogeneous, remains to be seen.

However, when thinking about below the radar community groups
now, and in the future, perhaps the last words should belong, not to
activists, practitioners or academics but to the novelist, playwright and
poet Samuel Beckett: 'Ever tried. Ever failed. Never mind. Try again.
Fail again. Fail better' (1983, p 47), or, perhaps more optimistically –

and realistically – for activists and their communities: 'I can't go on. I'll go on' (1958, p 418).

References

Abbas, M.-S. and Lachman, R. (2012) *The Big Society: The Big Divide?*, Bradford: JUST West Yorkshire.

Aiken, M. (2014) *Voluntary services and campaigning in austerity UK: Saying less and doing more*, London: NCIA.

Aiken, M. (2016) *The cyber effect*, London: John Murray.

Alcock, P. (2010) 'A strategic unity: defining the third sector in the UK', *Voluntary Sector Review*, vol 1, no 1, pp 5-24.

Alcock, P. (2016) *Why we need welfare: Collective action for the common good*, Bristol: Policy Press.

Alaimo, K. (2015) 'How the Facebook Arabic page "We are all Khaled said" helped promote the Egyptian revolution', *Social Media and Society*, vol 1, no 2, available at: http://sms.sagepub.com/content/1/2/2056305115604854.full.pdf+html

Beckett, S. (1958) *The unnamable*, London: Calder/Grove Press.

Beckett, S. (1983) *Worstward Ho*, London: Calder.

Bennett, W.L. and Segerberg, A. (2011) 'Digital media and the personalization of collective action: social technology and the organization of protests against the global economic crisis', *Information, Communication & Society*, vol 14, no 6, pp 770-99.

Bodhanova, T. (2014) 'Unexpected revolution: the role of social media in Ukraine's Euromaidan uprising', *European View*, vol 13, no 1, pp 133-42.

Bovaird, T., Stoker, J., Jones, T., Loeffer, E. and Pinilla Roncancio, M. (2015) 'Activating collective co-production of public services: influencing citizens to participate in complex governance mechanisms in the UK', *International Review of Administrative Sciences*, vol 82, no 1, pp 47-68.

Bussu, S. (2016) *Big Local online. The social media presence of Big Local: How areas are using social networks*, London: Local Trust.

Castells, M. (2015) *Networks of outrage and hope: Social movements in the internet age*, Cambridge: Polity Press.

Charity Commission (2007) *Stand and deliver: The future of charities providing public services*, London: Charity Commission.

Crees, J., Dobbs, J., James, D., Jochum, V., Kane, D., Lloyd, G. and Ockenden, N. (2016) *UK civil society almanac 2016*, London: NCVO.

Curno, P., Lamming, A., Leach, l., Stiles, J., Ward, V. and Ziff, T. (1982) *Women in collective action*, London: Association of Community Workers.

Davidson, E. and Packham, C. (2012) *Surviving, thriving or dying: Resilience in small community groups in the North West of England*, Manchester: Manchester Metropolitan University.

Deakin, N. (1995) 'The perils of partnership: the voluntary sector and the state 1945-1992', in J. Davis Smith, C. Rochester and R. Hedley (eds) *An introduction to the voluntary sector*, London: Routledge.

Dinham, A., Furbey, R. and Lowndes, V. (2009) (eds) *Faith in the public realm*, Bristol: Policy Press.

Dominelli, L. (2006) *Women in community action*, Bristol: Policy Press.

Gilchrist, A. (2016) *Blending, braiding and balancing: Combining formal and informal modes for social action*, Birmingham: Third Sector Research Centre.

Harris, K. and McCabe, A. (forthcoming) *Trouble in utopia? Community action and social media*, Birmingham: Third Sector Research Centre.

Hillier, A. (2016) 'Local action: community groups are braced for yet more cuts', *Third Sector Magazine*, 21 January, available at: www.thirdsector.co.uk/local-action-community-groups-braced-yet-cuts/local-action/article/1379733

Hind, A. (2014) '"Tescoisation" of the charity sector – take two?', civilsociety.co.uk, 1 December.

Jensen, T. (2013) 'Riots, restraint and the new cultural politics of wanting', *Sociological Research Online*, 18 (4) 7, pp 1-20, available at: www.socresonline.org.uk/18/4/7.html

Jones, O. (2011) *Chavs: The demonization of the working class*, London: Verso.

Jordan, B. (2010) *Why the Third Way failed: Economics, morality and the origins of the 'Big Society'*, Bristol: Policy Press.

Kendall, J. and Knapp, M. (1996) *The voluntary sector in the UK*, Manchester: Manchester University Press.

Kenny, S., Taylor, M., Onyx, J. and Mayo, M. (2015) *Challenging the third sector: Global prospects for active citizenship*, Bristol: Policy Press.

Kurkov, A. (2014) *Ukraine diaries: Dispatches from Kiev*, London: Penguin.

Macmillan, R. (2013) '"Distinction" in the third sector', *Voluntary Sector Review*, vol 4, no 1, pp 39-54.

McCabe, A., Wilson, M. and Macmillan, R. with Morgans, P. and Edwards, M. (2016a) *Our bigger story: The first chapter. Big Local first interim evaluation summary report*, London/Birmingham: Local Trust/Third Sector Research Centre.

McCabe, A., Buckingham, H. and Miller, S. with Musabyimana, M. (2016b) *Belief in social action: Exploring faith groups' responses to local needs*, Birmingham: Third Sector Research Centre.

McKenzie, L. (2015) *Getting by: Estates, class and culture in austerity Britain*, Bristol: Policy Press.

McLean, S. and Dellot, B. (2011) *The civic pulse: Measuring active citizenship in a cold climate*, London: RSA.

Milbourne, L. (2013) *Voluntary sector in transition: Hard times or new opportunities?*, Bristol: Policy Press.

Mohan, J. (2012) 'Geographical foundations of the Big Society', *Environment and Planning A*, vol 44, no 5, pp 1121-9.

NCIA (National Coalition for Independent Action) (2015) *Fight or fright: Voluntary services in 2015*, London: NCIA.

Parker, S. (2015) *Taking power back: Putting people in charge of politics*, Bristol: Policy Press.

Phethean, C., Tiropanis T. and Harris, L. (2015) 'Engaging with charities on social media: comparing interaction on Facebook and Twitter', *Internet Science*, vol 9089 of the series Lecture Notes in Computer Science, pp 15-29.

Phillimore, J (ed) (2015) *Migration and social policy*, Cheltenham: Edward Elgar.

Rees, J. and Mullins, D. (eds) (2016) *The third sector delivering public services. Developments, innovations and challenges*, Bristol: Policy Press.

Roberts, J. (2014) *New media and public activism: Neoliberalism, the state and radical protest in the public realm*, Bristol: Policy Press.

Rochester, C. (2013) *Rediscovering voluntary action: The beat of a different drum*, Basingstoke: Palgrave Macmillan.

Sayer, A. (2016) *Why we can't afford the rich*, Bristol: Policy Press.

Standage, T. (2013) *Writing on the wall. Social media: The first 2,000 years*, London: Bloomsbury.

Taylor, M. (2012) 'The changing fortunes of community', *Voluntary Sector Review*, vol 3, no 1, pp 15-34.

Index

lack of funding leading to lack of
  influence 229
long-term effects of 78–9, 84,
  285
as opportunity for new mutualism
  125
and the personalisation agenda
  142–3
power and community groups
  79–83
refugees and migrants' groups
  212–13
research focus on large groups 2
and sector distinctiveness 52, 66
survival during 113–28
autonomy 52–3, 106, 138, 158,
  188

B

Backus, P. 27
Bacon, N. 73, 83
Bailey, B.A. 165, 166, 167
Bakewell, O. 202
Barbetta, P. 13
Barnes, M. 15
Bazalgette, P. 161
Belfiore, E. 161, 162
belonging, sense of 163, 166, 209,
  211, 234
'below the radar'
  common challenges 17–19
  defining 8–11, 19–20, 62
  mapping 32–3
  nature of activity 13–14, 33–42
  scale of 11–13
  as a sector 14–16
  use of term in policy documents
    74
Bendle, L.J. 165
Benns, K. 16
Berger, J. 190
Big Local 8, 241
Big Lottery funding 122, 125, 241
Big Society 8, 18, 28, 71–2, 74–9,
  114–16, 121
Billis, D. 52
Birmingham Voluntary Service
  Council 242
Blackburn, S. 11, 17

Blaschke, J. 232
Bloemraad, I. 43
Blume, T. 116
BME (Black and minority ethnic)
  groups
  BME third sector in UK 177–94,
    223
  community cohesion agendas 28
  disproportionate effects of funding
    cuts 117
  motivations for starting 54
  as 'sub-sector' of below the radar
    sector 10, 15
  terminology of 'Black' and
    'minority ethnic' 178
  voice and influence 221–37
Bodhanova, T. 286
Bogdán, M. 149
bottom up working 72, 203, 204
  see also top down working
Bourdieu, P. 162–3, 242, 256
Bovaird, T. 73, 79, 80, 116, 282
Brexit 124, 148, 223
bricolage 41–2, 139, 145
bridging capital 255
Brotheridge, C.M. 270, 277
Building Britain's future (HM
  Government, 2009) 73, 81
bureaucracy 52, 58–9, 101, 136,
  204, 206
Burnage, A. 243
burnout 56, 57, 63, 126, 136, 277
Burt, E.L. 165, 166
Bussu, S. 286
Butarova, M. 32, 42
Butt, J. 178

C

Cabinet Office 28, 71–2, 81, 241
Calhoun, C. 157–8
Cameron, D. 77, 81, 115
campaigning 80, 82, 100, 136,
  144–5, 248
Cantle, T. 200
Capacity Builders 142, 241
capacity-building 10, 77–8, 138,
  226–7, 241–3
capital assets 10, 61, 118
Cardy, K. 166